Palgrave Studies in European Union Politics

Series Editors
Michelle Egan
American University
Washington, USA

Neill Nugent
Manchester Metropolitan University
Manchester, UK

William E. Paterson
Aston University
Birmingham, UK

Following on the sustained success of the acclaimed European Union Series, which essentially publishes research-based textbooks, Palgrave Studies in European Union Politics publishes cutting edge research-driven monographs. The remit of the series is broadly defined, both in terms of subject and academic discipline. All topics of significance concerning the nature and operation of the European Union potentially fall within the scope of the series. The series is multidisciplinary to reflect the growing importance of the EU as a political, economic and social phenomenon.

More information about this series at
http://www.palgrave.com/gp/series/14629

Hans Vollaard

European Disintegration

A Search for Explanations

Hans Vollaard
Utrecht University
Utrecht, The Netherlands

Palgrave Studies in European Union Politics
ISBN 978-1-137-41464-9   ISBN 978-1-137-41465-6   (eBook)
https://doi.org/10.1057/978-1-137-41465-6

Library of Congress Control Number: 2018937889

This Palgrave Macmillan imprint is published by the registered company Macmillan
Publishers Ltd. part of Springer Nature.
The registered company address is: The Campus, 4 Crinan Street, London, N1 9XW,
United Kingdom

Preface and Acknowledgements

When I both started and finished writing this book, my then home town of Leiden in the Netherlands was celebrating its relief from a Spanish-Habsburg siege in 1574. Leiden's relief constituted a significant boost for an uprising that sought to defend local privileges in the Low Countries against the influence of the centralising Habsburg Empire. Eventually, the northern part of the Low Countries left this vast, multilayered, polycentric, and multinational empire. An independent confederative republic resulted from this "Nexit", which was at that time a loosely organised, but economically competitive, actor at the global level. Not least because of the university established in Leiden in 1575 as a reward for its endurance, the Netherlands became a centre of knowledge of military engineering, growing tulips, protestant theology, and, also, political science. It is no wonder that the disintegration of a large European empire is an event that is still celebrated annually in Leiden, with two parades, *aubades*, music shows, a church service, and a large fair. With a certain fervour, Leiden's residents sing sixteenth-century hymns that refer to a glorious fight for freedom. All of this made me wonder whether or not similar festivities would one day be held to commemorate the disintegration of another vast, multilayered, polycentric, and multinational polity, the European Union. Or would the European Union be remembered with melancholy and regret, like the Austrian-Hungarian Empire that only seemed like a pretty decent place to live for a wide variety of people with the benefit of hindsight? I suppose this would depend on whether the European Union fell apart as a result of vociferous independence movements or as a result of a slow sinking into oblivion. The normative assessment of the European Union will also, undoubtedly, shape the way it would be remembered.

As a political scientist, I do not take a position in favour of or against the disintegration of the European Union. Nevertheless, I am quite happy to see that public attention to the subject has increased over the past several years. I devoted one of the chapters of my PhD dissertation to the subject of European disintegration (defended in 2009), but I initially shelved the topic in favour of others. Colleagues argued that I would not be able to pursue a fundable research project on something that had not yet occurred. I have continued to hear that remark repeated when I wrote this book at the request of Palgrave Macmillan (I therefore remain grateful to Steven Kennedy for the invitation to write the book). With the looming Brexit that has changed. However, as will be explained in this book, disintegration is not just a matter of a member state leaving the European Union. It is not simply a Grexit or Brexit. Disintegration also involves the withholding of resources, pulling out from (certain) decision-making processes, and decreasing compliance with EU law, whether by member state governments or businesses, individuals, and sub-state authorities. These *partial* withdrawals have been seen before in the history of the European Union and that of its predecessors. Without developing the analytical tools to describe and explain political phenomena, such as European disintegration, their very occurrence might be missed. These tools are necessary to sharpen our focus on the crucial factors and actors at play in this kind of large-scale processes. Many have also quipped that I might be too late—finishing this book *after* the European Union had already come to an end. My standard response was that books analysing the fall and decline of the Roman Empire centuries ago are still written and sold successfully today. Seeing as the European Union is still here, I hope that the insights presented in this book may be of help in our efforts to better understand its evolution.

I would like to express my gratitude to the many people who contributed directly or indirectly to these insights. In particular, I would like to mention, in alphabetical order, Stephan Auer, Hester van de Bovenkamp, Michael Burgess, Annegret Eppler, Jan Erk, Erik Jones, Sandrino Smeets, Amy Verdun, Douglas Webber, and Jan Zielonka, as well as the publisher's anonymous reviewers for their inspiration and constructive comments. Furthermore, I am also grateful for the opportunities to present my work on various occasions, including seminars at Maastricht University, INSEAD Fontainebleau, and Leiden University, as well as on panels at the conferences of the Council of European Studies in Paris, the ECPR Standing Group on the European Union in Trento, and the NIG annual conference in Maastricht. I would also like to say special thanks to Jessica Kroezen for her editing. Finally, my gratitude goes out to those who showed patience with me in finishing this book, Imogen Gordon Clark of Palgrave Macmillan, and even more so my beloved wife, Hester van de Bovenkamp. I hope this book will contribute to a fruitful debate on European disintegration.

Utrecht, The Netherlands   Hans Vollaard

CONTENTS

Abbreviations

AfD	Alternative für Deutschland
AFSJ	Area of Freedom, Security, and Justice
CAP	Common Agricultural Policy
CEECs	Central and Eastern European Countries
CFSP	Common Foreign and Security Policy
CJEU	Court of Justice of the European Union
COREPER	*Comité des Répresentants Permanents* (Committee of Permanent Representatives)
CSCE	Conference on Security and Cooperation in Europe
CSOs	Civil Society Organisations
EC	European Communities
ECB	European Central Bank
ECHR	European Court of Human Rights
ECJ	European Court of Justice
ECSC	European Coal and Steel Community
EDC	European Defence Community
EEA	European Economic Area
EEC	European Economic Community
EEU	Eurasian Economic Union
EFTA	European Free Trade Area
EMU	Economic and Monetary Union
ENP	European Neighbourhood Policy
ESDP	European Security and Defence Policy
EU	European Union
EURATOM	European Atomic Energy Community

FDI	Foreign Direct Investment
G8	Group of Eight
G20	Group of Twenty
GATT	General Agreement on Tariffs and Trade
GNP	Gross National Product
ICT	Information and Communication Technologies
IMF	International Monetary Fund
JHA	Justice and Home Affairs
KKE	*Kommounistikó Kómma Elládas* (Communist Party of Greece)
LAOS	*Laikós Orthódoxos Synagermós* (Popular Orthodox Rally)
MNEs	Multinational Enterprises
NATO	North Atlantic Treaty Organization
NGOs	Non-governmental Organisations
OCA	Optimum Currency Area
OECD	Organisation for Economic Cooperation and Development
OEEC	Organisation for European Economic Cooperation
OSCE	Organization for Security and Cooperation in Europe
PASOK	*Panellinio Sosialistiko Kinima* (Panhellenic Socialist Movement)
R&D	Research and Development
SEA	Single European Act
SIS	Schengen Information System
SU	Soviet Union
SYRIZA	*Synaspismós Rizospastikís Aristerás* (Coalition of the Radical Left)
UK	United Kingdom
UKIP	United Kingdom Independence Party
UN	United Nations
USA	United States of America
VVD	*Volkspartij voor Vrijheid en Democratie* (People's Party for Freedom and Democracy)
WEU	Western European Union
WTO	World Trade Organization

LIST OF TABLES

CHAPTER 1

Introduction

1.1 The Need for Explanations of European Disintegration

How far in advance would you really be able to tell that the European Union (EU) is disintegrating or has disintegrated? Would you actually be aware of European disintegration if it were to occur? Is it just a matter of formally dissolving the EU or is it a process that is out of the control of decision-makers? What should you look for as an indication of the current state of European (dis)integration at this moment? And which factors do you think are fundamental to explaining the present and future course of European (dis)integration? These are crucial questions for any political observer of EU politics, whether they work as a risk manager, a journalist, a policy strategist, or a political scientist. These questions have become particularly relevant since the outbreak of the debt crises in the Eurozone and the Brexit referendum. The scenario of European disintegration has featured prominently in public debates, but confusion about the fate of the EU and the process of European integration more generally abounds. Some argued that the expulsion of Greece, for example, would have strengthened the Eurozone, as it would limit the economic disparities within the European monetary union and as such the need for financial transfers between member states reluctant to share. Others contended that a possible Grexit would precipitate the departure of other member states

© The Author(s) 2018
H. Vollaard, *European Disintegration*, Palgrave Studies in European Union Politics, https://doi.org/10.1057/978-1-137-41465-6_1

from the Eurozone due the pressure of the financial markets betting on further exits. Some perceived the rescue of the Euro as essential to maintaining the political underpinnings of the entire process of European integration. Others advocated the dissolution of the Economic and Monetary Union (EMU), as the solution required to preserve the Euro—a sizeable EU budget, EU taxes, and EU transfers—would only fuel the Eurosceptic call for the dissolution of the entire EU. Some have thought of the debt crises as just part of a series of recurring crises *in* the process of European integration, whereas others have considered it to be a fundamental crisis *of* European integration.

Contradictory analyses of the state of the EU and European integration more generally have also cropped up in other discussions. Will the end of British EU membership allow the EU to act more coherently in light of less disagreement on issues such as the Euro, social policy, Schengen, and foreign policy? Or would a Brexit cripple the EU's influence in international politics, making membership less attractive to present and future member states? And do the attempts to constrain so-called "welfare tourism" help to maintain support for the EU within the Eurosceptic parts of the population, or do they constitute a step towards the end of the free movement of persons in the internal market, a fundamental element of the European integration process thus far? Is the rise of Euroscepticism at the level of the European Parliament and some national parliaments a sign of the end of the EU or of the growing involvement of even anti-system parties and citizens in EU politics? Is a stronger EU essential to the process of European integration, or can it do without (Zielonka, 2014)? Scenarios of the EU's future range from full-scale federalisation, a stronger core Europe with some exits, muddling through with the present EU's institutions, a combination of the EU becoming paralysed, neglected, and obsolete, to its complete collapse (see, for instance, European Commission, 2017; King Baudouin Foundation et al., 2013; Krastev, 2012; Rabobank, 2017). Confusion and contradictions are thus rife in perspectives on the course of European (dis)integration.

Academic analysis can help us to move beyond the cursory reflections of the day. It enables us to make explicit the various ways of thinking about European disintegration, and it can offer us a better understanding of the definition, indicators, factors, mechanisms, outcome and likelihood of European disintegration. First and foremost, academic analysis helps us to make sense of political dynamics by being selective. Theories are an important tool in this respect. They structure our observations of phenomena like European disintegration, order existing knowledge and steer our attention, sensitise us to the structural dynamics below the surface of daily events reported in the media, raise research questions for subsequent inquiry, executed in a systematic, coherent, consistent, and thorough manner (Peters, 1998, p. 110; Rosamond, 2000, p. 4, 9). In this way, theories could help us to recognise and explain European disintegration in a more orderly fashion, showing us what choices can be made more and less easily (cf. Peters, Pierre, & Stoker, 2010). To be sure, theories may be proven wrong. It is, therefore, important to present theories in the form of testable statements to see whether they hold up to empirical evidence. This book adopts an explanatory approach, and will not discuss whether or not political developments like European disintegration are a good or a bad thing.

Given the confusion in the public debate on European disintegration, now is the right time to seek academic reflection on the subject. So, which theories are currently available to explain European disintegration? At first glance, there are next to none, even in the field of EU studies (Eppler & Scheller, 2013a; Glencross, 2009, p. 2; Jones, 2016; Webber, 2013; Zielonka, 2014). Theories of regional integration or more specifically of European integration have largely focused on just that: integration, not *dis*integration. A variety of recent challenges to European integration have certainly been studied, but they have not provided an explanation of European disintegration either. Analyses of Euroscepticism have primarily discussed its definition and origins, rather than its disintegrative potential (Brack & Startin, 2015, p. 241; Leconte, 2010). Enlargement studies have explored the relationship between widening and deepening as well as the impact of European integration on candidate and new member states. Thorough reflection on the EU's overstretched absorption capacity has been limited, however (though see Delhey, 2007; Toshkov, 2017; Vobruba, 2003). And even though enlargement has led to a profound examination of differentiated integration, it only refers to a situation in which not all member states join in in future efforts to forward the process of European integration, not how enlargement could instead lead to *less* integration (see, e.g., Leuffen, Rittberger, & Schimmelfennig, 2012). Many analyses have also been executed on the financial, legitimacy, monetary, economic, and refugee crises the EU experienced. They yet rather explored the impact of these crises on policies, policy-making process, institutional relations, citizens' opinions and identities, and divisions between and within member states than the very existence of the EU

(Falkner, 2016; Fossum & Menéndez, 2014; Rittberger & Schimmelfennig, 2015; Trenz, Ruzza, & Guiraudon, 2015).

EU studies, or the study of international relations, comparative politics, political history, and political economy more generally, may be excused for their limited attention to European disintegration given the fact that European integration has always increased in terms of institutions, competences, policy areas, and legislative output. It has also continuously widened its geographical scope, with the exception of Algerian departments of France (1962) following Algeria's independence in 1962, Greenland (1985) after it obtained home rule from Denmark, and the island of Saint Barthélemy (2012) in the aftermath of its secession from the French overseas department of Guadeloupe. Continuous integration has even been the case in the context of the Eurozone crisis: the EU has gained more say in national economic policies and Croatia joined in 2013 as the union's 28th member state. Problematic, however, is the fact that most present-day EU theories would likely fail to recognise disintegration if it were occurring because they have shifted their focus from grand-theorising the transformation of the entire EU system towards exploring bits and pieces of EU governance, and the impact of European integration on EU member states (Taylor, 2008, p. 109). Thus, students of the EU have lost sight of the big picture in the context of (dis)integration. And what cannot be properly recognised and described cannot be properly explained.

1.2   The Search for an Explanation of European Disintegration

One of the few publications with the explicit goal of conceptualising European disintegration is therefore a most welcome contribution (Eppler & Scheller, 2013b). The authors emphasise the multi-dimensional nature of European (dis)integration, from its economic, institutional, and territorial aspects, to socio-cultural and legal ones. Integration in one dimension may not be accompanied by integration in another. On the contrary, too much integration in one dimension (for instance, institutional) could provoke disintegration in another (for instance, socio-cultural). Given its multi-dimensional nature, it is necessary to clearly explain the kind of European disintegration this book seeks to explain. This book focuses on the disintegration of the EU understood as a system of interactions through which authoritative allocations of values are made and implemented (cf. Easton, 1965). As such, it takes an explicitly political understanding of

European disintegration, which involves aspects of allocation of values such as the EU's legislative output, the scope of its policies, its competences, its institutions, the involvement and sense of belonging among its members (states and citizens), and the size of its territory (cf. Lindberg, 1971). Integration concerns the making of a system of authoritative allocations from other systems of authoritative allocations, whereas disintegration is the unmaking of such a system. This book offers a search for the most fruitful explanation of the disintegration of the EU.

Notwithstanding the scholarly neglect of European disintegration, the literature on European integration and also on international cooperation and comparative politics may yet be fruitful sources to conceptualise and explain it. The classic grand theories of intergovernmentalism and neofunctionalism on the *making* of the EU can be turned "on their heads" to define and explain European disintegration, the *un*making of the Europolity (cf. Webber, 2013). These will be discussed in Chaps. 2 and 3 in combination with related theories of international cooperation such as comparative regionalism and (neo-)realism. In the subsequent chapters, European disintegration is explored from a comparative perspective. In the end, the EU may be unique with respect to its exact shape and form, but not with regard to the disintegrative mechanisms it is subject to. Explanations of the rise and fall of federal systems, empires, and states will therefore be reviewed. The book discusses each explanation of how disintegration has been understood: how should it be conceptualised, what are indicators of disintegration, and can it take place at the same time as integration? In addition, the book presents what the various accounts perceive to be the most important factors explaining disintegration.

This book does not include a comparative analysis of disintegrating currency areas. The perspective of the optimum currency area (OCA) has informed many contributions on the sustainability if not end of the EMU and the EU itself. Even before the launch of the EMU a rise of disintegrative conflicts on economic policies within the EU was foreseen (Feldstein, 1997). The OCA perspective indicates the economic preconditions under which it would be beneficial for countries to give up monetary independence and join a monetary union (Artis, 2002). It suggests that if members' economic structures do not resemble each other sufficiently, external shocks and single monetary policies will impact differently across the monetary union's area. Mobility of labour and capital, mutual budgetary support, and flexible prices and wages could absorb these asymmetric shocks. OCA-based accounts may indicate why the EMU would face more difficulties than other currency areas such as the USA, why peripheral countries such as Greece would fit less easily into the current EMU, and why diverging economic structures may aggravate the EMU's problems (Eichengreen, 2010, 2012; Sadeh, 2012). OCA-based accounts may thus point at some crucial factors that can promote the survival or (partial) dissolution of the EMU. Nevertheless, the OCA perspective cannot fully explain the process of making and unmaking of what has been foremost a political project (Eichengreen, 2012; Feldstein, 2012; McKay, 1999; Sadeh, 2012; Sadeh & Verdun, 2009). Moreover, it cannot account for instances of disintegration before the launch of the single currency, or for disintegrative moves in member states that have not been fully participating in the EMU, such as the UK. For the sake of parsimony, a more encompassing theory would therefore be preferable.

Predicting the fate of any political organisation is a daunting task, as the case of the eminent federalism expert William Riker illustrates (McKay, 2004). In the late 1980s, he predicted that Czechoslovakia, Yugoslavia, and the Soviet Union would remain stable for the foreseeable future because of their centralised nature. He was proven wrong soon after—as were many other scholars. However, the benefit of hindsight does not necessarily provide clarity either. Explanations of the inevitability and also the extent of the disintegration of the Soviet Union—assuming it does not still live on today as the Russian Federation—are still a matter of debate (Motyl, 2001). This also holds true for older instances of disintegration. Until now, at least 210 very diverse factors have been put forward to explain the decline and fall of the ancient Roman Empire (Demandt, 1984). Explaining European disintegration, the goal of this book, will be no less a subject of debate. Nevertheless, the overview provided in this book not only allows us to distinguish alternative conceptualisations and explanations of European disintegration, but also to seek the most promising one by evaluating their respective theoretical premises and empirical strength. All explanations are derived from general theories of regional integration and political systems. These theories are not EU specific. The empirical evidence offered by the single case of the EU does not necessarily invalidate these theories. Criticism is therefore first targeted at the theories' premises. For example, some suffer from a biased perspective on the outcome of disintegration. Territorial states should not be assumed to remain the predominant political format. A development towards loosely organised complex networks of overlapping jurisdictions is also a possibility (Zielonka, 2006). Other theories have too narrow an understanding of the complex processes of (dis)integration, or an incomplete view of how the manifold relevant factors interrelate in these processes. As a result, they cannot offer a proper description or an adequate explanation of how integration or disintegration has unfolded in the past or would unfold in the near future.

As it appears to be the most promising theory to analyse the multifaceted process of political disintegration, the final explanatory framework, inspired by the work by Stefano Bartolini (2005) on the formation of states and nations in European history, is discussed more extensively in Chaps. 6, 7, 8, 9, and 10 in an effort to demonstrate how it avoids the theoretical problems inherent in other explanations, how it makes political observers aware of the crucial mechanisms of European disintegration, and how it gives us an indication of where the EU is heading. A complete breakdown soon appears to be unlikely. No other member state is expected to follow the UK withdrawing from the EU. The lack of more attractive alternatives to the EU prevents member states from leaving. Nevertheless, Euroscepticism and dissatisfaction about the EU's social-economic benefits are rife. The EU's very structure is rather inhibitive to voice the dissatisfaction with proper effect. Without the option of full exit and effective voice, the EU therefore faces the disintegrative challenge of member states seeking partial withdrawals such as deteriorating compliance with EU law, renationalisation of EU competences, and limitations on EU budget contributions. This will sap the sustainability as the EU's capacity to enforce its rule and to strengthen the social-economic benefits for its member states, business, and citizens, which have been fundamental for EU support. The EU will thus be limping ahead with many rather grudgingly accepting it as the least unattractive option.

REFERENCES

Artis, M. J. (2002). Reflections on the Optimum Currency Area (OCA) criteria in the light of EMU. *International Journal of Finance and Economics, 8*, 297–307.

Bartolini, S. (2005). *Restructuring Europe: Centre formation, system building and political structuring between the nation-state and the European Union.* Oxford: Oxford University Press.

Brack, N., & Startin, N. (2015). Introduction: Euroscepticism, from the margins to the mainstream. *International Political Science Review, 36*(3), 239–249.

Delhey, J. (2007). Do enlargements make the European Union less cohesive? An analysis of trust between EU nationalities. *Journal of Common Market Studies, 45*(2), 253–279.

Demandt, A. (1984). *Der Fall Roms: Die Auflösung des Römischen Reiches in Urteil der Nachwelt*. München: C.H.Beck.

Easton, D. (1965). *A framework for analysis*. Englewood Cliffs, NJ: Prentice-Hall.

Eichengreen, B. (2010). The Breakup of the Euro Area. In A. Alesina & F. Giavazzi (Eds.), *Europe and the Euro* (pp. 11–55). Chicago: University of Chicago Press.

Eichengreen, B. (2012). European monetary integration with the benefit of hindsight. *Journal of Common Market Studies, 50*(S1), 123–136.

Eppler, A., & Scheller, H. (Eds.). (2013a). *Zur Konzeptualisierung Europäischer Desintegration*. Baden-Baden: Nomos.

Eppler, A., & Scheller, H. (2013b). Zug- und Gegenkräfte im Europäischen Integrationsprozess. In A. Eppler & H. Scheller (Eds.), *Zur Konzeptualisierung Europäischer Desintegration* (pp. 11–44). Baden-Baden: Nomos.

European Commission. (2017). *White paper on the future of Europe*. (COM(2017) 2025 final). Brussels: European Commission.

Falkner, G. (2016). The EU's current crisis and its policy effects: Research design and comparative findings. *Journal of European Integration, 38*(3), 219–235.

Feldstein, M. (1997). EMU and international conflict. *Foreign Affairs, 76*(6), 60–73.

Feldstein, M. (2012). The failure of the Euro: The little currency that couldn't. *Foreign Affairs, 91*(1), 105–116.

Fossum, J. E., & Menéndez, A. J. (Eds.). (2014). *The European Union in crises or the European Union as crises?*. (ARENA Report No 2/14). Oslo: Arena.

Glencross, A. (2009). *What makes the EU viable? European integration in the light of the antebellum US experience*. Basingstoke: Palgrave Macmillan.

Jones, E. (2016). *Why we need a theory of disintegration*. Retrieved June 14, 2017, from https://erikjones.net/2016/11/12/why-we-need-a-theory-of-disintegration/

King Baudoin Foundation, Bertelsmann Stiftung & European Policy Centre. (2013). *New pact for Europe: Strategic options for Europe's future* (1st report). Retrieved September 15, 2014, from http://www.newpactforeurope.eu/documents/1st_report_new_pact_for_europe.pdf

Krastev, I. (2012). European disintegration? A fraying Union. *Journal of Democracy, 23*(4), 23–30.

Leconte, C. (2010). *Understanding Euroscepticism*. Basingstoke: Palgrave Macmillan.

Leuffen, D., Rittberger, B., & Schimmelfennig, F. (2012). *Differentiated integration*. Basingstoke: Palgrave Macmillan.

Lindberg, L. (1971). Political integration as multidimensional phenomenon requiring multivariate measurement. In L. Lindberg & S. Scheingold (Eds.), *Regional integration: Theory and research* (pp. 45–127). Cambridge, MA: Harvard University Press.

McKay, D. (1999). *Federalism and European Union: A political economy perspective.* Oxford: Oxford University Press.

McKay, D. (2004). William Riker on federalism: Sometimes wrong but more right than anyone else? *Regional and Federal Studies, 14*(2), 167–186.

Motyl, A. (2001). *Imperial ends: The decay, collapse, and revival of empires.* New York: Columbia University Press.

Peters, B. G. (1998). *Comparative politics: Theory and methods.* Basingstoke: Palgrave Macmillan.

Peters, G., Pierre, J., & Stoker, G. (2010). The relevance of political science. In D. Marsh & G. Stoker (Eds.), *Theory and methods in political science* (3rd ed., pp. 325–342). Basingstoke: Palgrave Macmillan.

Rabobank. (2017). *Four scenarios for Europe: A struggling Europe in a changing world.* Utrecht: RaboResearch. Retrieved June 19, 2017, from https://economics.rabobank.com/Documents/2017/februari/The_uncertain_future_of_European_integration-201702-totaal.pdf

Rittberger, B., & Schimmelfennig, F. (2015). Kontinutät and Divergenz: Die Eurokrise und die Entwicklung Europäischer Integration in der Europaforschung. *Politische Vierteljahresschrift, 56*(3), 389–405.

Rosamond, B. (2000). *Theories of European integration.* Basingstoke: Palgrave Macmillan.

Sadeh, T. (2012). The end of the Euro-Mark I: A sceptical view of EMU. In H. Zimmerman & A. Dür (Eds.), *Can the European Union survive? Controversies on the future of the European integration* (pp. 112–129). Basingstoke: Palgrave Macmillan.

Sadeh, T., & Verdun, A. (2009). Explaining Europe's monetary union: A survey of the literature. *International Studies Review, 11,* 277–301.

Taylor, P. (2008). *The end of European integration: Anti-Europeanism examined.* London: Routledge.

Toshkov, D. (2017). The impact of the Eastern enlargement on the Decision-Making Capacity of the European Union. *Journal of European Public Policy, 24*(2), 177–196.

Trenz, H.-J., Ruzza, C., & Guiraudon, V. (Eds.). (2015). *Europe's prolonged crisis: The making or the unmaking of a political union.* Houndmills, Basingstoke: Palgrave Macmillan.

Vobruba, G. (2003). The enlargement crisis of the European Union: Limits of the dialectics of integration and expansion. *Journal of European Social Policy, 13*(1), 35–49.

Webber, D. (2013). How likely is it that the European Union will disintegrate? A critical analysis of competing theoretical perspectives. *European Journal of International Relations, 19*(4), 1–25.

Zielonka, J. (2006). *Europe as empire: The nature of the enlarged European Union.* Oxford: Oxford University Press.

Zielonka, J. (2014). *Is the EU doomed?* Cambridge: Polity Press.

CHAPTER 2

Neo-functionalism and European Disintegration

2.1 INTRODUCTION

Neo-functionalism is one of the classic theories of European integration. Its main proponents, Ernst Haas and Leon Lindberg, launched it in the 1950s and 1960s. Emblematic of the scientific approach and theoretical focus of the time, neo-functionalism sought to systematically explain the causes, process, and consequences of non-coercive regional integration across the entire world by formulating verifiable hypotheses. Since the mid-1970s, it has often been declared defunct, mainly because it has failed to explain the course of regional integration in Europe. Nevertheless, its key concept of "spillover" continues to pop up, also in recent analyses of the European Union in crisis (King Baudoin Foundation et al., 2013; Lefkokridi & Schmitter, 2014; Niemann & Ioannou, 2015; Schimmelfennig, 2014; Vilpišauskas, 2013). In addition, neo-functionalists have also discussed—albeit to a limited extent—European disintegration (Lindberg & Scheingold, 1970; Niemann & Bergmann, 2013; Schmitter, 1971). This provides more than sufficient reason to explore the potential of neo-functionalism to explain European disintegration. After outlining the main ideas of neo-functionalism on integration, this chapter discusses its understanding and explanation of disintegration. An evaluation of the potential of neo-functionalism to provide a framework for analysing European disintegration follows. The chapter rounds off with the lessons learned from a neo-functionalist take on European disintegration.

© The Author(s) 2018   11
H. Vollaard, *European Disintegration*, Palgrave Studies in European Union Politics, https://doi.org/10.1057/978-1-137-41465-6_2

2.2   Neo-functionalism and Integration

Neo-functionalism provides a clear contrast to realist approaches to international politics (see Chap. 3). Instead of considering states to be primary actors, as realists do, neo-functionalists adopt a pluralistic perspective in which non-state actors like interest groups may act autonomously from within states *and* across state borders. Instead of perceiving states as the only relevant actors in international politics, neo-functionalists thus expect non-state groups and supranational institutions to play an influential role too. Instead of power being the most important consideration, functional linkages and interests constitute the key drivers of international politics in neo-functionalist thought. Instead of power relations being determined exclusively by relative state capacities, power relations can change within and across states due to altering coalitions, shifting expectations, changing loyalties and learning on the part of state and non-state actors. In short, neo-functionalism is a theory in which political integration can move "beyond the nation-state" (1964), as of one of Haas' most famous books is entitled. Both as a political framework and actor, the state becomes increasingly interlocked and enmeshed in larger political schemes. From the various interpretations of regional integration neo-functionalists have provided over the past 50 years, regardless of whether they refer to the entire "grand" process of regional integration or only parts of it, "spill-over" can be distilled as its key concept.

Neo-functionalists distinguish various types of spillover that are the result of different underlying causal mechanisms. The following distinction is based on one of the latest extensive exposés of neo-functionalism (Niemann, 2006, Chap. 1). *Functional spillover* takes place when the goals of an integrated policy issue lead to further integrative steps, due to the perceived functional interconnections of policy issues. For example, the completion of an internal market also involved the free movement of persons, for which EU-level measures on the issues of visas, asylum, immigration, and police cooperation were perceived to be necessary. *Political spillover* refers to the process in which national elites, such as interest groups and political parties, learn to see European cooperation as means of serving their interests and subsequently establish transnational groups to push for European solutions. *Social spillover* is the impetus for European integration because of socialisation through increasing interactions and connections between national (state) actors and the accompanying shift in mutual expectations, norms, interpretations of reality, activities, or even loyalties towards the European centre. *Cultivated spillover* concerns supra-national actors such as the European Commission who actively engage state and non-state actors to seek the integration of a certain policy domain also to increase their own say, and as a result, integration continues beyond the initial preferences of these actors. In response to criticism of neglecting the international setting of the European integration process, recent neo-functionalist accounts also highlight *exogenous spillover*. External threats and shocks such as the end of the Cold War and economic competition from Japan, the USA, or China, regional responses to globalisation, and the requirement to take positions vis-à-vis others after a certain period of "internal" integration are assumed to generate more integration (Niemann, 2006, pp. 32–34; see also Schmitter, 1971, p. 244). Similar to functional spillover, exogenous spillover is basically a matter of decision-makers' per-ceptions (Niemann, 2006, p. 51). Neo-functionalists initially presented spillover as an almost automatic, self-reinforcing, and irreversible process, but they have since become more focused to spell out the conditions under which the various types of spillover take place (Niemann & Schmitter, 2009, p. 57ff).

Even if neo-functionalists generally explain the dynamics of integration *after* its launch, they have also discussed the conditions of a viable launch. Since neo-functionalism concerns regional integration, it presumes geo-graphical proximity of the states involved. Furthermore, the influential role attributed to non-state actors presupposes a pluralistic society, at the national and also increasingly at the regional level. In pluralistic societies, non-state actors such as interest groups and political parties can find coun-terparts in other states more easily with whom they can fight for a com-mon cause across territorial borders. A certain measure of compatibility of the participating states in terms of basic values, mutual expectations, and decision-making procedures, a shared sense of relevance reflected by pre-existing networks of transactions, and a high level of economic develop-ment have also been argued to increase the integrative potential of a region (Haas, 1968, pp. 268–287). Integration schemes that not only involve a set of mutual agreements but also involve supranational agents are expected to integrate more than those without because they can cultivate further integration (Haas & Schmitter, 1964, p. 713). Additionally, func-tional spillover is particularly likely to occur in situations in which policy issues are not easily isolated from each other. A technocratic and depoliti-cised approach in the initial phase of integration, even if it concerned potentially sensitive issues such as energy or the basic materials for arma-ments, could avoid the immediate provocation of anti-integrative forces.

A start to an integrative scheme like this would facilitate an incremental process of integration that would grant non-state and state actors the time they need to learn to focus on European solutions and to be socialised in the context of European norms and realities. It would also allow supranational institutions to gain the strength required to cultivate European integration by accumulating the power to determine the policy agenda, enhancing internal cohesion, attracting the involvement of national elites to form supportive coalitions and socialising them, and brokering integrative deals (Niemann & Schmitter, 2009, pp. 60–61). Due to the close links between policy issues in Western societies in general and the wide range of issues incorporated in the European integration process, there is a great deal of functional integrative pressure on adjacent policy issues, despite the fact that member states might not have anticipated it (cf. Pierson, 1996, pp. 137–139). Growing cross-border transactions would subsequently stimulate demand from societal actors to regulate these transactions by establishing further cross-border integrative arrangements (cf. Stone Sweet & Sandholtz, 1998). Activated by this demand, state actors could accept further integration if they perceive the benefits of integration today as being greater than the costs of anticipated functional spillover in the future (meaning an additional or greater loss of sovereignty), or if they are completely unaware of the possibility of spillover due to the often limited time horizons they face (Niemann & Schmitter, 2009, p. 58).

The description thus far may give the impression of an incremental process in which integration leads relatively smoothly to more integration. However, conflicts, controversies, and crises are not unexpected in a pluralistic approach like neo-functionalism. Even more so, crises are perceived as a means of strengthening integration, as they make clear the need to take things one step further. Ongoing spillover also involves a larger set of dramatic-political actors beyond the technocratic policy elites, who could eventually challenge the former actors to redirect their expectations, activities, or even loyalties at the European level (Schmitter, 1969). Particularly after French president Charles de Gaulle was able to stagnate European decision-making in the 1960s as a result of his sovereigntist reservations towards supranational rule, neo-functionalists have attempted to factor in countervailing forces into their accounts of regional integration (Haas, 1967, p. 316). Haas (1967, p. 328) acknowledged that in the initial phase of integration, the rather fragile technocratic spillover process is "susceptible to reversal" as pragmatic acceptance of European problem-solving schemes cannot easily withstand the resistance from "dramatic-political" actors committed to ideology or nationalism, particularly if national self-confidence in problem-solving increases (Haas, 1967, pp. 327–328; 1971, p. 31). The European integration process could bear national countervailing forces more effectively after supranational institutions were able to strengthen their cultivating powers, and learning and socialisation processes shifted at least some national elites' orientations towards European integration (cf. Niemann, 2006, p. 51).

Even if cultivating powers and processes of socialisation are consolidated, spillover will not necessarily result in progressive integration immediately, according to another neo-functionalist interpretation. Instead, integration in one policy area can evoke protective countermeasures in an adjacent policy area with stagnation in the spillover process as a result (Corbey, 1995). Only if policy rivalry between member states becomes counterproductive is pressure for further integration steps expected to follow. Additionally, the longer spillover processes have to evolve and the more policy issues that are implicated, the more complex integrative steps are because of the growing number of actors involved. If integration subsequently enters too quickly into politically sensitive policy areas, counter-factors such as nationalist resistance can arise among actors not oriented towards European integration (see also Niemann & Schmitter, 2009; Schmitter, 1971). This might be called integrative overstretch or "*Überintegration*" (Scheller & Eppler, 2013, p. 295). In addition to nationalism, spillover might also be limited by member states' diversity or a changing external environment, resulting in a dialectic process between the "logic of integration" and the "logic of disintegration" (Tranholm-Mikkelsen, 1991, p. 17).

Despite various attempts to take domestic politics into account in their explanations of integration, neo-functionalists struggle to factor in issues of identity at the mass level (Hooghe & Marks, 2008). As integration involves more than economic interest groups and has become increasingly salient to EU citizens in their daily lives since the 1990s, political entrepreneurs could mobilise tensions "between rapid jurisdictional change and relatively stable identities" (Hooghe & Marks, 2008, p. 13). A call for a "post-functionalist" approach has followed. Recent neo-functionalist accounts hypothesise that sovereignty consciousness, domestic constraints such as lack of administrative capacity or Euroscepticism, and mutual diversity among member states constrain spillover effects (Niemann, 2006, p. 47). The question is to what extent. Despite manifest reluctance at the mass level to provide loans and guarantees to debt-laden fellow member states in the context of the Eurozone crisis, functional spillover has taken place from a monetary union towards a fiscal and banking union; cultivated spillover has been exerted by supranational agencies such as the European Central Bank, while the common will among governments to solve the Euro crisis collectively point at social spillover (Schimmelfennig, 2014; Vilpišauskas, 2013). With strategies such as avoiding referenda, electing pro-Euro-parties to government, and delegating to supranational agencies, the outcomes of non-integration and integration in certain policy areas may still be explained by neo-functionalism, but not disintegration.

Neo-functionalists have increasingly detailed the conditions under which the various types of spillover occur, resulting in an increasingly hard to test set of hypotheses (Saurugger, 2014, p. 49). But what would the expected end state of integration be in the eyes of a neo-functionalist? And how could the degree of integration, the dependent variable, be measured? Haas wanted foremost to explain why and how states voluntarily cede sovereignty and set up new conflict resolution mechanisms with their neighbours (Haas, 1971, p. 6). Yet he did indicate where that might lead: "[t]he end result of a process of political integration is a new political community, superimposed over the pre-existing ones" (Haas, 1958, p. 16). Regional integration would thus not necessarily involve the complete replacement of national states, but Haas did expect national political actors to shift their expectations, activities, and also loyalties to the centre of the new community. He has been criticised for his understanding of the end goal, since by excluding any other outcome, it suffers from a teleological if not normative bias (Groom, 1978). Haas' new political community has often been understood as some sort of super state (Schmitter, 1996, p. 137). If so, neo-functionalism would not move beyond the state. However, another key neo-functionalist, Lindberg, has been more cautious and only speaks of the establishment of a new political decision-making centre towards which actors shift their activities and expectations, but not their loyalties (Lindberg, 1963). He distinguishes a multitude of dimensions of political integration—from the scope of policy areas affected, the demand flow for European regulation from relevant actors, and the resources available to regional decision-makers to comply with European legislation—which do not necessarily develop in the same direction and are not necessarily explained by the same logic (Lindberg, 1971). These dimensions indicate whether or not integration has moved on within a certain time frame without assuming a certain end goal. In principle, political integration could thus also lead to a wide variety of functional, overlapping, and competing integrative schemes at various levels, rather than one cohesive, federative system (cf. Puchala, 1971, p. 276ff; Schmitter, 1996, p. 130ff).

Despite its focus on the rational pursuit of material interests and its neglect of identity, neo-functionalism has affinities with social constructivism and sociological institutionalism (Risse, 2005; Saurugger, 2014). Indeed, preferences and interests are not necessarily fixed, as they can be modified by the mechanisms of learning and socialisation intrinsic in the process of European integration (social spillover). European integration also involves the transfer of loyalties to a new political community, at least according to the earlier writings of Ernst Haas. In neo-functionalist and related theories, there has been emphasis on the mechanism of *becoming European* by *doing European* (see also Deutsch et al., 1957; Fligstein, 2008). By working in supranational institutions or increasing cross-border contacts and interactions, foreign others might even become part of a new "us", a new European identity (Nelsen & Guth, 2015, p. 24). This identity does not necessarily conflict with the national identity. People can and do have multiple loyalties and identities, although those living in federal states more easily adopt additional identity layers than their fellow citizens in unitary and centralised states (Risse, 2005). Neo-functionalists consider disintegration to be increasingly unlikely because over time processes of socialisation and learning are expected to lead to more integration (Niemann, 2006, p. 51).

2.3   A NEO-FUNCTIONALIST EXPLANATION OF DISINTEGRATION EVALUATED

Even if neo-functionalism neglects disintegration somewhat by largely expecting integration to continue, its evaluation could still offer insight into conceptualising and explaining disintegration more fruitfully. The substantial revisions to and severe criticism of neo-functionalism offer more than sufficient material to consider. Elaborating on their attempts to include countervailing forces into their account of regional integration processes, neo-functionalists put forward the concept of "spillback", which refers to "a situation in which there is a withdrawal from a set of specific obligations. Rules are no longer regularly enforced or obeyed. The scope of Community action and its institutional capacities decrease"

(Lindberg & Scheingold, 1970, p. 137; *see also* Schmitter, 1971, p. 242). Spillback is basically understood by neo-functionalists as *reversal* of integration. In other words, national jurisdictions are restored at the expense of European competences, and expectations, activities, and loyalties shift back to national states. Disintegration is thus conceptualised as Haas' definition of integration turned upside-down: "political integration is the process whereby political actors in several distinct national settings are persuaded to shift their loyalties, expectations and political activities towards a new center, whose institutions possess or demand jurisdiction over the pre-existing national states" (Haas, 1968, p. 16).

Recent neo-functionalist accounts perceive spillback not as an outcome to be explained, but as the umbrella term for disintegrative forces in the dialectic process of integration and disintegration (Niemann, 2006, p. 47). Nevertheless, these accounts also explicitly equate disintegration with the "reversal of integration" (Idem). Since they have debated the dependent variable of integration so extensively and have suggested such a wide variety of potential political formations deviant from the nation state (Puchala, 1971; Schmitter, 1996), it is surprising that they have not been more sensitive to the differentiated outcomes that may result from the dialectic process involving both integrative and disintegrative forces. Instead, they see disintegration as the EU falling apart into its constituent national states again. But why would functional spillover not lead to integration into several global policy networks, at least with respect to some aspects of political systems outlined above, as distinguished by Lindberg? Disintegration of the EU is not necessarily a one-way, all-encompassing shift towards fully independent national states again.

Neo-functionalism also provides potential explanations of disintegration. According to neo-functionalists, spillback could result from exceptional or exogenous shocks (Schmitter, 1971, p. 243), integrative overstretch, diminishing demand flow from society for European regulation, changing interest coalitions, or declining desire for European solutions on the part of national leaders (Lindberg & Scheingold, 1970, pp. 121–122). The way in which these factors are interconnected requires further explanation, however. This also holds for the list of background conditions that are conducive to initiating regional integration (see below). At the very least, doubt is cast on the idea that the process of disintegration will simply be integration in reverse. Up until the 1980s, European integration may have been a largely behind-the-scenes, technocratic process that aimed to solve common policy problems, but countervailing forces such as the politicisation of an exclusive national identity leave a different mark on the present-day evolution of the EU (Hooghe & Marks, 2009).

One of the main criticisms of neo-functionalism concerns the neglect of external factors and actors in its accounts of European integration. The hypothesised spillover due to functional interdependencies that push supranational groups and institutions, and socialised state actors, suggests that integration originates in large part from within. The question is whether or not this spillover could have occurred if the USA had not provided security in Western Europe within the transatlantic community (cf. Hoffmann, 1966). Additionally, neo-functionalists themselves point out that most integrative impetuses between the 1980s and the Euro crisis emerged (partly) from exogenous factors such as Japanese competition, the end of the Cold War, and failing American banks (Schmitter, 2005, p. 266; Lefkokridi & Schmitter, 2014). The suggestion that exogenous factors could lead to integration (Niemann, 2006) is still wanting for an explanation of why, how, and under what circumstances this occurs beyond the simple assumption that they have some kind of a spillover effect. Furthermore, neo-functionalism should also spell out the circumstances under which and how exogenous factors might lead to spillback, instead.

The neo-functionalist failure to explain the relationship between European integration and its external setting also relates to globalisation. Growing institutionalisation in the form of the EU could facilitate European rule-making in response to globalisation. But if functional interdependencies are key to integration, why would globalisation not result in the unraveling of the EU? In the end, issues of trade, finance, aid, environment, crime, terrorism, and war could also generate a spillover effect on networks or organisations at a larger scale than the EU, such as a transatlantic economic and security partnership. Furthermore, processes of devolution and federalisation in countries like Spain, Italy, Belgium, and the UK suggest that despite intricate functional interdependencies, new centres and political communities could yet be created, also at a lower scale. The link between functional interdependencies and regional integration is therefore not straightforward. Apparently, interdependencies can coexist with both integration and disintegration. Perhaps, as later neo-functionalists have emphasised, functional linkages are primarily a matter of perception (Niemann, 2006, p. 51). For example, the monetary union has been perceived as "incomplete" and "unfinished" in the Eurozone crisis and that its effective functioning would require a banking and fiscal union (Vilpišauskas, 2013). But the incomplete nature of the monetary union could also be perceived as a reason to renationalise monetary competences because of its close interconnections with predominantly nationally organised budgetary policies and welfare states. This explanation thus remains somewhat indeterminate. It is here where more theoretical attention to the role of identity may have been fruitful. Identity can be used to form new political communities at the regional level or re-establish existing national political communities in response to growing interdependence.

Neo-functionalists point to the crucial role of supranational actors and transnational groups in cultivating perceptions focusing on the integrative potential of functional interdependence. Serious doubts exist, however, as to whether or not interest groups have played a significant role in the integration process, at least in the way the causal mechanism behind political spillover would suggest (cf. Groom, 1978). They have done so occasionally—think of the European Roundtable of Industrialists in the early 1980s, for example—but, in general, interest groups are expected to push for European integration under specific conditions only (Niemann & Schmitter, 2009, p. 59). Supranational actors such as the Court of Justice of the European Union, the European Commission, and the European Central Bank may have done more to cultivate European integration. Nevertheless, without denying the significant role of supranational actors, national governments have exerted much more influence on the course and substance of European integration, as one of the key criticisms on neo-functionalism suggests (see Chap. 3). And if unintended and unforeseen consequences are that crucial in the context of the policy complexities of European integration that national governments lose control of the integration process, this may also hold for supranational actors and interest groups. Perhaps they have already taken the path of disintegration without knowing it by overstretching integration beyond people's desire.

Neo-functionalists and their historical-institutionalist affiliates could argue that the inflexibilities of the institutional path taken by the EU would prevent national governments from seeking disintegration because of the high costs involved (Pierson, 1996). Treaty change requires unanimity. The efforts to overcome this joint-decision trap would make it a difficult enterprise for national governments not only to take further integrative steps but also disintegrative steps, such as transferring EU competences to another political entity. However, institutional inflexibilities could also result in deadlock and stalemate, leading governments and other actors to neglect EU rules rather than make efforts in vain to modify or abolish them (cf. Krastev, 2012). The growing costs of changing an expanding and enlarging EU might lower the relative price of exit. More explanation of the role of national governments in integrative and disintegrative processes is required than neo-functionalism or historical-institutionalism can offer in this respect.

According to neo-functionalist and historical-institutionalist understandings of European integration, member states cannot keep full control of the integration process, for which they become locked into it (Pierson, 1996). Supranational institutions can push for integration beyond the preferences of national governments because the latter are not always aware of where initial integrative steps will lead them due to the limited time horizons they face (focused on the next elections), a lack of information on what the supranational institutions are doing, and an incomplete understanding of the effects of spillover in light of the complex interdependencies between policy sectors (Pierson, 1996, p. 135ff). At the very moment integrative steps are laid down firmly in treaties, a reversal of integration becomes increasingly unlikely as changing treaties is a very complex enterprise, and supranational actors are there to resist disintegrative moves, while actors have increasingly adapted to the integrated institutional setting (cf. Stone Sweet & Sandholtz, 1998, p. 16, 19). Governments are thus stuck in a situation in which disintegration is unlikely and difficult to explain: "…social adaption to EC institutions and policies drastically increases the cost of exit from existing arrangements for member states" (Pierson, 1996, p. 145). Nevertheless, if the institutional path taken deviates increasingly from a member state's preferences (thus increasing the price of EU membership), the cost of changing EU policies increases, and better national or international alternatives (have) become available, it would, at some point, be rather likely that the alternative will be adopted. For instance, when free movement of labour is accepted as a way of enjoying job opportunities elsewhere in the EU, but also entails an unanticipated high number of immigrants, voters, parties, and governments may opt to reinstitute national boundary control if they see immigration in a negative light in terms of crime, availability of public services, or culture. The relative attractiveness of national or international alternatives to the EU should, therefore, be taken into account in an explanation of European disintegration.

Neo-functionalists could, however, counter that argument by postulating that after several decades of European integration, social spillover will keep EU national governments committed to integration. However, there are serious doubts as to whether contacts and interactions contribute to changes in preferences, transfer of loyalties, or construction of a European identity. Those who gained the most from European integration in its early decades—women and farmers—did not warm up to the idea of European integration very much (Risse, 2005, p. 297). The preferences of most civil servants did not change as a result of working in the European Commission (Hooghe, 2001, p. 73). At the mass level, attachment to the EU or a sense of European citizenship has not increased in a linear fashion alongside the duration of citizenship (cf. Thomassen & Bäck, 2009). The moment of entry mattered more. This suggests that member states themselves are more significant in terms of the presence of a European identity than supranational institutions or cross-border transactions. Indeed, views of European integration, be they enthusiastic, reluctant, or antagonistic, are, in large part, framed nationally (cf. Díez Medrano, 2003; Risse, 2005). They can delineate the limits of European integration. These frames can change. The Netherlands is a case in point. For a long time, a Europhile frame favouring even political integration dominated, but since the 1990s, more pragmatic, Euro-realistic, and nationalist Eurosceptic frames have come to the fore (Vollaard, 2011). Even though the Netherlands is a founding member that has close trade ties with other EU member states, its discursive frames on European integration have not become more favourable to European integration over time. Additionally, the increasing domestic impact of European integration does not automatically lead to pro-European socialisation. Instead, the more people are exposed to European integration, the more they may not only be aware of its (perceived) advantages, but also of its disadvantages, both in economic and cultural terms (cf. Kuhn, 2011). The "post-Maastricht blues" at the mass level is a clear illustration of the declining support for European integration at the very moment that it has increasingly become a part of people's daily life due to budget reforms to meet the Euro-zone criteria (Eichenberg & Dalton, 2007).

About half of the EU population would identify themselves as European today. The question is, however, whether or not they share a similar understanding of the geographical, personal, ideational, or functional scope of the term "European". A variety of European identities exist, from rather inclusive cosmopolitanism to more exclusive so-called Judeo-Christian orientations (Checkel & Katzenstein, 2009). Further European integration, be it another transfer of competences to the EU, or the accession of an Islamic nation to the union, would subsequently result in different evaluations, as opposed to widespread assent. Even if social spillover, be it through cross-border interaction and communication at the elite or at the mass levels, would take place, it would not necessarily be an exclusively *integrative* force.

In sum, learning socialisation or increasing cross-border transactions does not necessarily create support for European integration or establish a unifying European identity. Be that as it may, the hint of social-constructivist in neo-functionalist theory points to the relevance of immaterial factors like ideas, norms, identities, representation, loyalties, discourse, and culture in understanding European integration. Indeed, national political cultures set the limits of European integration. For instance, Protestant countries are more resistant to European centralisation than Catholic ones (Nelsen & Guth, 2015). At the mass level, those with an exclusive national identity are much less supportive of European integration and enlargement than fellow citizens who identify themselves as European (as well) (Hobolt, 2014; Hooghe & Marks, 2005). These findings underscore the significance of immaterial factors in explaining European (dis)integration—or disintegration—in spite of the fact that neo-functionalism does not offer a convincing explanation for how they matter.

2.4   Insights from Comparative Regionalism

Neo-functionalism initially sought to explain regional integration from a comparative perspective. For instance, Haas (1967) pointed to the crucial role of a number of background variables that might explain why European integration was much more advanced than that in Latin America, or the Arabic world. A pluralistic society would usually harbour more actors inclined to ask for increased regional cooperation to serve their interests because of growing interdependency. Additionally, symmetrical heterogeneity between the participating states would subsequently allow for the cross-border linkages between societal groups to foster further integration. With their focus on technocratic problem-solving, bureaucracies could more easily find common ground to make the rational decision to start and move integration forward. In situations in which people and leaders feel downbeat about their national situation, the option of integration could also be put forward more readily. Thus, disintegration would be a matter of the diminishing relevance of these background variables, with rising nationalist pride, growing involvement of dramatic-political elites, declining cross-border linkages, and diminishing pluralism in European societies. The question remains, however, whether or not factors explaining the initiation of integration are also relevant to explaining its continuation or decline. Neither have neo-functionalists devoted much attention how these factors are interrelated in the process of European disintegration.

Comparative analysis with the manifold other instances of regional integration in the past and present could help, however, to identify the crucial factors that explain the initiation, continuation, and decline of regional integration (Warleigh-Lack & Rosamond, 2010, p. 1006), in particular because so many integration projects have failed (Mattli, 1999). Scholars working on comparative regionalism have distinguished themselves from neo-functionalists. They considered neo-functionalism to be too rationalist, overly focused on the creation of formal institutions, biased by the instance of European integration, hindered by a teleological perspective on a regional political community as an end state, and negligent of the relationship between European regionalisation and external forces like globalisation and of the potential of national states to resist regional integration (Warleigh-Lack, 2006a, pp. 563–564, 2006b). They also rejected spillover and transfer of loyalties as necessary parts of integration processes.

In a comparative analysis of regional integration projects across the world, Walter Mattli (1999) found that the crucial demand for regional integration comes from market actors who seek to diminish the costs of international trade and investment. Integration, he argues, subsequently comes about if political leaders perceive it to be advantageous to the maintenance of their power, institutions to supervise the implementation of the international treaty exists, and a leading power is willing to assume the coordination costs. The negative effects of a regional integration project could entice other states to join or establish another integration project. An explanation of disintegration could be derived by turning this logic of regional integration on its head. Disintegration would thus be explained by the decreasing supply of commitment institutions and a regional paymaster, and the decreasing demand following from declining international economic transactions and ensuing externalities. The question is whether or not economic interdependence is sufficient in and of itself to explain the process of regional integration, however defined. In various regions across the world, the growing economic interdependence has not led to a greater political interconnectedness (Saurugger, 2014, p. 237). Apparently, other non-economic factors play a role too, which should be taken into account in any sound explanation of regional (dis)integration. Another question is whether or not the result of disintegration would be the opposite of integration, defined as "the voluntary linking in the economic domain of two or more formerly independent states to the extent that authority over key areas of domestic regulation and policy is shifted to the supranational level" (Mattli, 1999, p. 41). As emphasised above, disintegration is not necessarily a matter of the EU simply falling apart back into its constituent states.

The comparative approach propagated by Alex Warleigh-Lack may be more promising in terms of explaining disintegration, as he explicitly includes the dissolution of regional projects in his definition of regionalisation, which is "an explicit, but not necessarily formally institutionalized, process of adapting participant state norms, policy-making processes, policy-styles, policy content, political opportunity structures, economies and identity (potentially at both elite and popular level) to both align with and shape a new collective set of priorities, norms and interests at regional level, which may itself then evolve, dissolve or reach stasis" (Warleigh-Lack, 2006b, p. 758). Warleigh-Lack hypothesises that states would start and continue to cooperate regionally if they seek to manage the societal consequences of globalisation that affect them the most. And European states have more reasons to defend societal interests because of their well-developed welfare systems, to follow a Polanyian reasoning. Given ongoing globalisation, European disintegration would, therefore, be all the more unlikely. Warleigh-Lack also indicates that socialisation and the external empowerment of a regional group of states could play a role.

In addition to economic dynamics, other factors might also determine the demand and supply for regionalism, such as shared security concerns, a desire to secure the legitimacy of the participating regimes, the number and geographical proximity of the participating states, the vision of a hegemonic power, and perhaps a common sense of community (Börzel & Risse, 2016). The focus has been on explaining the emergence of regional institutions or transnational relations and interactions rather than their decline. And due to the diversity of regional projects across the world, comparative regionalism is still struggling greatly to define what can and should be compared and how (Söderbaum, 2016). For now, new regionalism offers a list of factors that (have) potentially contribute(d) to regional (dis)integration in the past and present, without specifying how these may be related. In this respect, general mechanisms indicating how context-specific factors interact in processes of regional integration can be of help (Hameiri, 2013), also in terms of exploring disintegration.

2.5   CONCLUSION

Neo-functionalism's inclination towards integration diminishes its ability to explain European disintegration. Nevertheless, lessons can be learned from the criticism and revision of neo-functionalism and related theories. First, rather than focusing exclusively on how functional interdependency and cultivating non-state actors progressively result in more European integration, national governments, domestic politics, identity issues, and external factors such as globalisation should also be included in an explanation of the rather dialectic process by which integrative and disintegrative forces work. Second, an explanation such as this would have to acknowledge that timing is of the essence (cf. Schmitter, 2005). Only if the Euro-polity has achieved sufficient resilience, can it accommodate stress from its external environment, or anti-system pressures from within (cf. Lindberg, 1971). Furthermore, an explanation of European disintegration should indicate how time or place-specific variables are interconnected; mechanisms provide a fruitful way of doing this. Lindberg's suggestion to perceive political integration, or disintegration for that matter, as a multidimensional, multidirectional process may be of help. Finally, bias in terms of the expected outcome of integration and disintegration should be avoided. No theory should make the *a priori* assumption that the disintegration of the EU implies that it will fall apart into its constituent national states. Instead, a result like this should be part of the explanation. Stating that national governments remain influential, and that European disintegration does not necessarily mean the return of national states, seems contradictory. However, we need to clearly distinguish actors—national governments—from form—states with a legitimate monopoly on taxation, legislation, and the use of violence in a clearly demarcated area (Weber, 1956, p. 27). The next chapter will show that the absence of this distinction is the reason why another classic theory of European integration, intergovernmentalism, is also a problematic starting point for explaining European disintegration.

References

Börzel, T., & Risse, T. H. (2016). Three cheers for comparative regionalism. In I. T. Börzel & T. Risse (Eds.), *Oxford handbook of comparative regionalism* (pp. 621–649). Oxford: Oxford University Press.

Checkel, J., & Katzenstein, P. (Eds.). (2009). *European identity*. Cambridge: Cambridge University Press.

Corbey, D. (1995). Dialectical functionalism: Stagnation as a booster of European integration. *International Organization, 49*(2), 253–284.

Deutsch, K. W., with Burrell, S. A., Kann, R. A., Lee Jr, M., Lichterman, M., Lindgren, R. E., Loewenheim, F. L., & Van Wagenen, R. W. (1957). *Political community and the North Atlantic area: International organization in the light of historical experience*. Princeton, NJ: Princeton University Press.

Díez Medrano, J. (2003). *Framing Europe*. Princeton: Princeton University Press.

Eichenberg, R. C., & Dalton, R. J. (2007). Post-Maastricht blues: The transformation of citizen support for European integration, 1973–2004. *Acta Politica, 42*, 128–152.

Fligstein, N. (2008). *Euroclash: The EU, European identity and the future of Europe*. Oxford: Oxford University Press.

Groom, A. J. R. (1978). Neofunctionalism: A case of mistaken identity. *Political Studies, 30*(1), 15–28.

Haas, E. B. (1958). *The uniting of Europe: Political, social and economic forces, 1950–1957*. Stanford: Stanford University Press.

Haas, E. B. (1964). *Beyond the nation-state: Functionalism and international organization*. Stanford: Stanford University Press.

Haas, E. B. (1967). *The uniting of Europe and the uniting of Latin America*. *Journal of Common Market Studies, 5*(4), 315–343.

Haas, E. B. (1968). *The collective security and the future international system*. Denver: University of Colorado.

Haas, E. B. (1971). The study of regional integration: Reflections on the joy and anguish of pretheorizing. In L. Lindberg & S. Scheingold (Eds.), *Regional integration: Theory and research* (pp. 3–44). Cambridge, MA: Harvard University Press.

Haas, E. B., & Schmitter, P. (1964). Economics and differential patterns of political integration: Projections about unity in Latin America. *International Organization, 18*(4), 705–737.

Hameiri, S. (2013). Theorising regions through changes in statehood: Rethinking the theory and method of comparative regionalism. *Review of International Studies, 39*, 313–335.

Hobolt, S. (2014). Ever closer or ever wider? Public attitudes towards further enlargement and integration in the European Union. *Journal of European Public Policy, 21*(5), 664–680.

Hoffmann, S. (1966). Obstinate or obsolete? The fate of the nation-state and the case of western Europe. *Daedalus, 95*(3), 862–915.

Hooghe, L. (2001). *The European Commission and the integration of Europe.* Cambridge: Cambridge University Press.

Hooghe, L., & Marks, G. (2005). Calculation, community, and cues: Public opinion on European integration. *European Union Politics, 6*(4), 419–443.

Hooghe, L., & Marks, G. (2008). A postfunctionalist theory of European integration: From permissive consensus to constraining dissensus. *British Journal of Political Science, 39,* 1–23.

King Baudoin Foundation, Bertelsmann Stiftung & European Policy Centre. (2013). *New pact for Europe: Strategic options for Europe's future* (1st report). Retrieved September 15, 2014, from http://www.newpactforeurope.eu/documents/1st_report_new_pact_for_europe.pdf

Krastev, I. (2012). European disintegration? A fraying Union. *Journal of Democracy, 23*(4), 23–30.

Kuhn, T. (2011). Individual transnationalism, globalisation and Euroscepticism: An empirical test of Deutsch's transactionalist theory. *European Journal of Political Research, 50,* 811–837.

Lefkokridi, Z., & Schmitter, P. (2014). Transcending or descending? European integration in times of crisis. *European Political Science Review, 7*(1), 1–20.

Lindberg, L. (1963). *The political dynamics of European economic integration.* Stanford: Stanford University Press.

Lindberg, L. (1971). Political integration as multidimensional phenomenon requiring multivariate measurement. In L. Lindberg & S. Scheingold (Eds.), *Regional integration: Theory and research* (pp. 45–127). Cambridge, MA: Harvard University Press.

Lindberg, L., & Scheingold, S. (1970). *Europe's would-be polity: Patterns of change in the European community.* Englewood Cliffs, NJ: Prentice-Hall.

Mattli, W. (1999). *The logic of regional integration: Europe and beyond.* Cambridge: Cambridge University Press.

Nelsen, B., & Guth, J. (2015). *Religion and the struggle for European Union: Confessional culture and the limits of integration.* Washington, DC: Georgetown University Press.

Niemann, A. (2006). *Explaining decisions in the European Union.* Cambridge: Cambridge University Press.

Niemann, A., & Bergmann, J. (2013). Zug- und Gegenkräfte im Spiegel der Theorien der Europäischen Integration. In A. Eppler & H. Scheller (Eds.), *Zur Konzeptualisierung Europäischer Desintegration* (pp. 45–70). Baden-Baden: Nomos.

Niemann, A., & Ioannou, D. (2015). European economic integration in times of crisis: A case of neofunctionalism? *Journal of European Public Policy, 22*(2), 196–218.

Niemann, A., & Schmitter, P. C. (2009). Neofunctionalism. In A. Wiener & T. Diez (Eds.), *European integration theory* (2nd ed., pp. 45–66). Oxford: Oxford University Press.

Pierson, P. (1996). The path to European integration: A historical institutionalist analysis. *Comparative Political Studies, 29*(2), 123–163.

Puchala, D. (1971). Of blind men, elephants and international integration. *Journal of Common Market Studies, 10*(3), 267–284.

Risse, T. (2005). Neofunctionalism, European identity, and the puzzles of European integration. *Journal of European Public Policy, 12*(2), 291–309.

Saurugger, S. (2014). *Theoretical approaches to European integration.* Basingstoke: Palgrave Macmillan.

Scheller, H., & Eppler, A. (2013). Ansätze zur theoretischen Konzeptionalisierung europäischer Desintegration. In A. Eppler & H. Scheller (Eds.), *Zur Konzeptualisierung Europäischer Desintegration* (pp. 291–344). Baden-Baden: Nomos.

Schimmelfennig, F. (2014). European integration in the Euro crisis: The limits of postfunctionalism. *Journal of European Integration, 36,* 321–337.

Schmitter, P. (1969). Three neo-functional hypotheses about international integration. *International Organization, 23*(1), 161–166.

Schmitter, P. (1971). A revised theory of regional integration. In L. Lindberg & S. Scheingold (Eds.), *Regional integration: Theory and research* (pp. 232–264). Cambridge, MA: Harvard University Press.

Schmitter, P. (1996). Imagining the future of the Euro-polity with the help of new concepts. In G. Marks et al. (Eds.), *Governance in the European Union* (pp. 121–150). London: Sage.

Schmitter, P. (2005). Ernst B. Haas and the legacy of neofunctionalism. *Journal of European Public Policy, 12*(2), 255–272.

Söderbaum, F. (2016). Old, new, and comparative regionalism: The history and scholarly development of the field. In T. Börzel & T. Risse (Eds.), *Oxford handbook of comparative regionalism* (pp. 16–37). Oxford: Oxford University Press.

Stone Sweet, A., & Sandholtz, W. (1998). Integration, supranational governance, and the institutionalization of the European polity. In W. Sandholtz & A. Stone Sweet (Eds.), *European integration and supranational governance* (pp. 1–26). Oxford: Oxford University Press.

Thomassen, J., & Bäck, H. (2009). European citizenship and identity after European enlargement. In J. Thomassen (Ed.), *The legitimacy of the European Union after enlargement* (pp. 84–207). Oxford: Oxford University Press.

Tranholm-Mikkelsen, J. (1991). Neo-functionalism: Obstinate or obsolete? A reappraisal in the light of the new dynamism of the EC. *Millennium, 20*(1), 1–22.

Vilpišauskas, R. (2013). Eurozone crisis and European integration: Functional spillover, political spillback? *Journal of European Integration, 35*(3), 361–373.

Vollaard, H. (2011). The Dutch discourses of a small nation in an inefficient Europe: Cosmopolitanism, pragmatism, and nationalism. In R. Harmsen & J. Schild (Eds.), *Debating Europe: The 2009 European Parliament elections and beyond* (pp. 85–106). Baden-Baden: Nomos.

Warleigh-Lack, A. (2006a). "The European and the universal process"? European Union studies, new regionalism and global governance. In K. E. Jørgensen, M. A. Pollack, & B. Rosamond (Eds.), *Handbook of European Union politics* (pp. 561–575). London: Sage.

Warleigh-Lack, A. (2006b). Towards a conceptual framework for regionalisation: Bridging "new regionalism" and "integration theory". *Review of International Political Economy, 13*(5), 750–771.

Warleigh-Lack, A., & Rosamond, B. (2010). Across the EU studies – New regionalism frontier: Invitation to a dialogue. *Journal of Common Market Studies, 48*(4), 993–1013.

Weber, M. (1956). *Staatssoziologie*. Berlin: Duncker and Humblot.

CHAPTER 3

Realism, Intergovernmentalism, and European Disintegration

3.1 Introduction

As explained in the previous chapter, the impetus for integration comes from *within* the integration process according to neo-functionalism. Functional spillover, socialisation, and the political entrepreneurship of supranational institutions are expected to elicit further integrative steps. Soon after the emergence of neo-functionalism in the late 1950s, opposition towards supranational integration on the part of French president Charles de Gaulle inspired rival approaches that put more weight on factors *external* to the integration process. These approaches have discussed how the international setting in Western Europe such as that produced by the Cold War, and shifting patterns in economic interdependence have influenced the path of integration. They also distinguish themselves from neo-functionalists by assuming that national states remain the main form of political organisation and the main actors in international politics. In this way, European cooperation does not go *beyond* the nation state as neo-functionalists claim. As a consequence, these approaches prefer to speak of cooperation, instead of integration, because the latter term suggests that the end state of this process would be states merging into a larger entity. After discussing how these approaches—(neo-)realism and (liberal) intergovernmentalism, respectively—explain more and also less European cooperation, the chapter outlines the theoretical and empirical problems they face. It will show that it is precisely their understanding of

© The Author(s) 2018
H. Vollaard, *European Disintegration*, Palgrave Studies in European
Union Politics, https://doi.org/10.1057/978-1-137-41465-6_3

states that constitutes a major obstacle to explaining *less* European cooperation. Nevertheless, the concluding section also indicates which valuable lessons can be learned from realism and intergovernmentalism in explaining European disintegration.

3.2   REALISM AND COOPERATION IN EUROPE

Realism is one of the most prominent approaches to the study of international relations. It encompasses a variety of theories, based on a number of core tenets (see, among others, Schweller & Priess, 1997). First, realist theories assume that states are the principal actors in international politics. Thus, interactions between people take place within and through hierarchically organised territorial states with national governments as the gatekeepers between international and national politics. States are also assumed to operate as unitary actors in international politics. Realist theories also share the notion that international politics is anarchic, which means that there is no central authority above states. Without an authority to enforce agreements or to prevent stronger states from taking advantage of weaker ones, realist theories expect conflict and competition among states to be more likely than cooperation. Since states can only fully count on themselves in an anarchic system, their key interests are security and survival. That states behave rationally is often considered a core tenet of realism too (Legro & Moravcsik, 1999), but that is contested (Taliaferro, 2000/2001, pp. 155–157).

According to realists, state power is foremost dependent upon material capabilities. Geographic features such as distance or water are great obstacles in terms of exercising military power in a conventional sense; however, long-distance nuclear missiles could compensate for this "handicap". At first sight, it seems that the greater a state's (nuclear) power, the better able a state will be to counter threats to its survival and security effectively wherever necessary. However, the state faces a so-called security dilemma as a result. If a state increases its power, other states will perceive it as becoming a greater threat to their own security, leading them to seek to increase their capabilities as well. This could precipitate an arms race, in which the state that first increases its capabilities could end up in a relatively weaker position in the long run. In realist thinking, states are therefore more concerned about their *relative* gains vis-à-vis other states rather than the absolute gains they may accrue.

States can strengthen themselves to counter a threat from another state (internal balancing), but can also form temporary alliances to deter that state from exerting its power or to defeat it in the event of war (external balancing). Counterbalancing alliances show that in realist thinking international cooperation is not impossible, it is just unlikely and relatively unstable when it does occur, as there is no central authority to enforce compliance with the alliance. But in realist thinking, cooperation may also result from a hegemonic power—a state with great capabilities—imposing its will on other states. A hegemonic power would thus function almost as an *Ersatz* central authority (cf. Gilpin, 1981). Cooperation can also emerge in a realist world when a weak state aligns itself with the greatest power in its neighbourhood in the hope that the latter will not threaten it (the so-called bandwagoning strategy). As a matter of fact, weaker states can also resort to non-cooperative strategies to ensure their survival, such as buck-passing (leaving it to other states to do the job of balancing power) or hiding (seeking isolation and neutrality to avoid threats). From the realist viewpoint, interaction and cooperation between states are thus the result of the distribution of power, expressed in terms of material capabilities, such as economic and military assets. Even if international institutions emerge from states' interactions, they reflect the distribution of power among states and have a limited impact on the relationships between states that are always ultimately seeking their own survival and security above all else. As mutual trust is not necessary to establish international institutions, they are not expected to engender mutual trust either.

The various strands of realist theorising differ on the sources of their sceptical view of the longevity of international cooperation. In classical realism, this scepticism originates in large part from a pessimistic view of human nature, according to which mankind is primarily interested in seeking power as an end in itself (Morgenthau, 1948). Specific features of an individual state, such as an aggressive inclination, are thus part of the explanation of conflict and war. But it is the anarchic system of international politics that makes it so that a struggle for power between states can go on relatively unconstrained. As opposed to emphasising the nature of man and by extension the nature of individual states, so-called structural or neo-realism emphasises the role of the anarchic structure of the international system (Waltz, 1979). Anarchy requires every individual state to engage in self-help, as there is no authority that can prevent other states from cheating, thereby reducing the costs of defection. From a neo-realist standpoint, the accumulation of power is a means of survival rather than an end in itself. Neo-realists also expect states to be functionally similar. They share uniform and fixed preferences, namely, security and survival, and imitate the most effective organisational template, often assumed to be the territorial, hierarchically organised, sovereign states.

In realist thinking, a variety of accounts exist of the conditions under which conflict and war occur. According to the hegemonic-stability theory, a preponderant great power will impose peace on weaker states because it can afford to bear the costs of maintaining mutual security in a world in which trust is exceptionally difficult to cultivate (Gilpin, 1981). Other states will simply not challenge or counterbalance a hegemonic state once it has concentrated sufficient power (Brooks & Wohlforth, 2008). If the power distribution between states were to become more equal, (violent) challenges would occur more often, according to hegemonic-stability theory. In contrast, classical realists expect that the more poles of power that emerge, the more flexible alliances will be formed to counterbalance a potential threat to peace. In yet another strand of realist thinking, states only seek internal or external balancing if some state is an actual threat (Walt, 1987). This so-called defensive realism takes not only the military and economic capabilities of states into account, but also the specific features of a state, such as its inclination to use these capabilities aggressively. In contrast, offensive realists argue that any state will maximise its power solely in an effort to pre-empt any potential (future) threat. In neo-realist thinking, anarchy implies that even great powers will have a hard time maintaining their dominant position due to the counterbalancing strategies of other states. In a situation of unipolarity, these strategies would be directed towards the single great power in the international system. If there are multiple great powers in the international arena, the threat of switching allies would render the patterns of interaction and cooperation more unstable. In contrast, a world with only two great powers will result in increased stability, at least according to neo-realist reasoning (Waltz, 1979, pp. 167–170). Such a situation of so-called bipolarity characterised the world in the Cold War period (1940s–1980s), in which the United States of America (USA) and the Soviet Union (SU) maintained a nuclear stalemate that prevented a direct, violent confrontation between them (Mearsheimer, 1990).

Whereas (neo)realists discuss the Cold War extensively, there are only a few realist accounts of European cooperation. This should not come as a surprise, since the enduring and intense nature of European cooperation is largely unexpected from a (neo)realist point of view (Grieco, 1995).

Realism would be better equipped to explain the absence and improbability of cooperation in the EU (Ojanen, 2006). However, EU member states have not only cooperated on economic and monetary issues but have also agreed in the Maastricht Treaty (in force since 1993) to launch a Common Foreign and Security Policy (CFSP) that "shall include all questions related to the security of the Union, including the eventual framing of a common defence policy, which might in time lead to a common defence" (Treaty of the European Union, art. J4.1). In the late 1990s, an institutional framework was crafted for the CFSP and a European Security and Defence Policy (ESDP) was launched. Neither CFSP nor ESDP were in response to an immediate, existential threat to the EU and its member states, but were rather focused on crisis management in the EU's "near abroad" and beyond (Howorth, 2007). European cooperation is even partly of a supranational nature, which implies that international politics between the member states are no longer fully anarchic (Collard-Wexler, 2006, p. 398). Additionally, member states have made themselves highly dependent on their neighbours and EU institutions. Increasing vulnerability as a result of interdependence and of yielding aspects of national sovereignty constitutes a paradoxical if not contradictory survival strategy (Collard-Wexler, 2006, pp. 406, 416). It has largely been neo-realist scholars who have taken up the challenge of explaining European cooperation and its decline thus far. The Cold War features prominently in their explanations.

In the eyes of the intellectual father of neo-realism, Kenneth Waltz, the balancing act between the two great powers fundamentally shaped the patterns of conflict and cooperation in Europe during the Cold War (Waltz, 1979, p. 70). The hegemonic USA was able to impose its order in Western Europe, which also fostered cooperation between the arch-enemies France and Germany, in order to counterbalance the SU (Joffe, 1984; Mearsheimer, 2001). Meanwhile, the Soviet sphere of influence in Eastern Europe limited how far Western European cooperation could extend. The USA provided protection to Western Europe with its troops, the North-Atlantic Treaty Organization (NATO), and a nuclear umbrella. It thus removed a crucial source of mutual distrust between Western European states, for which cooperation on issues not immediately relevant to survival and security could unfold, cooperation in the context of the European Economic Community, for example (Joffe, 1984; Mearsheimer, 1990, p. 47; Waltz, 1979, p. 70). According to neo-realist John Mearsheimer, European cooperation has only continued *after* the Cold

War because the USA has maintained a military presence in Europe and has kept NATO functional (Mearsheimer, 2010, p. 388).

Even though he also adopts a neo-realist understanding of international politics, Sebastian Rosato (2011b, p. 77) offers an explanation of European disintegration that differs from the one presented above. He emphasises that US protection of Western Europe during the Cold War may have created the *opportunity* for European cooperation, but not the *motive*. Instead, the "overwhelming" military and economic power of the Soviet Union compared to individual Western European states would have brought the latter together. The USA provided the necessary security within Western Europe to prevent the Soviet Union from sabotaging a European attempt at counterbalancing it (Rosato, 2011a, p. 111). However, the very fear of American abandonment constituted the major motive for Western European states to seek cooperation. As the USA protected Western Europe in the late 1940s and 1950s, Western European states were freed up to focus on strengthening their collective economic might vis-à-vis the Soviet Union, though they eventually abandoned plans to launch a European Defence Community (EDC). The exclusively European WEU (West European Union) served as the default organisation for security cooperation in the event that the USA left Europe or NATO became dysfunctional (Rosato, 2011b, p. 64).

Realists expect states to cling to their sovereignty. According to Rosato, minor powers would be willing to give up part of their sovereignty in the face of an overwhelming power if they have no viable strategic alternative (Rosato, 2011a, p. 26ff). In the economic realm, the minor powers in Western Europe could only counter the overwhelming SU effectively with the help of a central authority, as reflected by the supranational set-up of the European Coal and Steel Community (ECSC; in force since 1952), a European Economic Community (EEC; in force since 1958), and a European Atomic Energy Community (in force since 1958). In the military realm, these minor powers could resort to the intergovernmental NATO *cum* WEU instead of the supranational EDC. Partly due to its geographical position, the UK passed the buck of creating a supranational economic counterweight to the Soviet Union to France, Germany, Italy, and the Benelux countries (Rosato, 2011a, p. 83). A combination of central command and joint control in the supranational communities prevented member states from taking advantage of these communities at the expense of fellow members. In this way, Rosato offers a neo-realist explanation of the conditions under which states are willing to give up sovereignty, even on issues such as security and defence, and to establish supranational institutions.

The above explanations have in large part focused on European cooperation during the Cold War. After the Cold War, the USA did not intervene immediately in European conflicts anymore because the power balance between the USA and the SU was no longer at stake. Furthermore, in particular after 9/11, the USA has been involved in other international issues elsewhere, such as the fight against terrorism. As Western European states have been less able to rely on the unipolar USA for their security, realists have come up with explanations of the continuation of European cooperation *after* the Cold War. One explanation sees European cooperation as a product of a European counterbalancing act to offset the dominance of great powers at the international level. French initiatives to launch European foreign policy cooperation in the 1960s could have already been understood as attempts to provide a counterweight to balance both Cold War powers. Along similar lines, steps towards a single market and a shared currency in the 1980s could have resulted from an attempt to balance the economic power of Japan and the USA (Waltz, 1993, p. 70). According to the realist Seth Jones (2007), European security cooperation has developed considerably since the Cold War era in terms of collectively adopted economic sanctions, common security institutions, collective arms production, and the multilateral use of military force (see also Giegerich & Wallace, 2004). This increased cooperation can be perceived as a counterbalancing strategy wielded against the only remaining great power in the world, the USA (Andreatta, 2005, p. 26; Waltz, 2000). However, others have argued that instead of directly counterbalancing the USA, the EU only seeks to gain autonomy from the USA to protect its competitive power in the long run (Posen, 2006). As of now, the relatively weak EU member states proceed rather carefully in the area of security cooperation to avoid disturbing the powerful USA too much. This is also due to the fact that the EU is still highly dependent on it to maintain the existing economic and security order in the world (Posen, 2006). Others claim that since the USA does not constitute a threat to European sovereign states, the latter would only use a softer means of balancing to correct specific undesired American policies through ad hoc formations, diplomatic ententes or collaboration in the context of international institutions (Paul, 2005).

In outright contradiction to these explanations, there is not much—if any—evidence of increasing military investment, build-up of a European army, or alliances specifically targeted at counterbalancing the USA after the Cold War (Brooks & Wohlforth, 2005, p. 91ff; Howorth & Menon, 2009). Instead, the EU has mostly developed low-intensity security capabilities to intervene in crises in its neighbourhood, such as in the Balkans (Hyde-Price, 2006; Jones, 2007). Following the ideas presented in hegemonic-stability theory, some realists argue that the USA has simple remained too powerful to allow for any reasonable attempt at counterbalancing in Europe (Brooks & Wohlforth, 2008). Furthermore, the question remains as to whether or not European states really aim to balance the USA, even if they do seek to constrain American foreign policy (Brooks & Wohlforth, 2005; Pohl, 2013). Some realists have therefore presented European security cooperation after the Cold War as an instance of bandwagoning (Cladi & Locatelli, 2012). The EU member states have strengthened security cooperation to join the largest power in the neighbourhood, the USA, in order to prevent the USA from abandoning the weaker EU states or to gain from transatlantic cooperation. The very question remains if the EU has really acted as a collective actor vis-à-vis the USA in its bandwagoning strategy. It seems the various member states have actually adopted different strategies, ranging from bandwagoning to buck-passing, and from hiding to balancing (Hyde-Price, 2013, p. 400; Ringsmose, 2013, p. 410).

All the explanations provided above refer in one way or another to great powers at the global level. An additional neo-realist explanation points to the significance of the regional balance of power *within* Western Europe. The threat of German hegemony in Europe, it is argued, would have led France and other states to launch European cooperation or even integration including (west) Germany (Jones, 2007; Sheetz & Haine, 2012). Whenever Germany's economic or military power increased, other European states bound it more tightly in the European institutions. The launch of the European Coal and Steel Community (ECSC) and European Defence Community (EDC) could thus be seen as a response to the rearmament of West Germany (Jones, 2007, p. 35). Similarly, the initiatives to strengthen cooperation on monetary issues and foreign policy as well as enlargement with the UK in the late 1960s resulted from the growing German economic power and its more autonomous foreign policy on Eastern Europe in the face of a declining American troop presence in Europe. German unification in 1990 spurred further integration of foreign and security policies and economic and monetary policies with the Maastricht Treaty (Jones, 2007). Adopting a bandwagoning strategy,

Germany's weaker neighbours sought to have the European institutions maintain as much say as possible in the policies of a potential hegemon (cf. Grieco, 1995). Only European political unification could fully bind Germany (Waltz, 1993, p. 70), but Germany accepted the institutional bonds because it was more interested in maintaining the status quo than in changing power relationships (Jones, 2007).

Neo-realism has thus offered a variety of explanations of European cooperation and even integration, even if cooperation and integration are generally unlikely from its point of view. But whatever the exact explanation, the process of integration itself does not necessarily engender more integration as the neo-functionalist claim holds. Instead, cooperation or integration is a result of the power relationships of states in an anarchic system of international politics. The same relationships also feature in the neo-realist accounts of declining European cooperation and integration.

3.2.1   Neo-realist Accounts of Declining Cooperation and Their Evaluation

In neo-realist thinking, the changing distribution of power in the international system is the key determinant of the behaviour of states. The collapse of the Soviet Union constituted a significant alteration in the distribution of power. In Rosato's eyes, since then, European states have no longer had a reason to preserve economic integration or make any further steps towards political or military cooperation in the absence of the common, overwhelming Soviet threat (Rosato, 2011a, p. 245; 2011b, p. 83). In his view, European states have not made any meaningful steps towards economic, military, or political integration after the Cold War ended completely with the withdrawal of Soviet troops from Eastern Europe in 1994. European states may not leave European institutions immediately due to continued economic gains, but the fundamental need to stay or to foster integration has diminished.

Mearsheimer expects European cooperation to end if the USA were to cease to provide security in Europe. Assuming that the USA would withdraw its military commitment to Europe as soon as the Cold War ended, he predicted competition and conflict rather than cooperation in Europe (Mearsheimer, 1990). Without Soviet and American control, a reunified German power would be harder to contain (Mearsheimer, 1990, p. 32). As the USA would no longer suppress mutual distrust, weak states would potentially bandwagon with Germany, and larger states would seek to counterbalance the potential German hegemony. Rearmament and re-emerging nationalism would ensue. In the absence of an American nuclear umbrella, Germany would be expected to develop its own nuclear arsenal to counterbalance French, British, and Russian nuclear powers (Mearsheimer, 2001). A multipolar Europe without US involvement would be much more rife with conflict. In contrast to Mearsheimer's initial expectations, the USA continued to provide security in Western Europe through NATO, the presence of some American troops, and the nuclear umbrella. As a result, Europe has remained relatively stable and peaceful, allowing European integration to continue (Mearsheimer, 2010). American involvement in Europe is thus the crucial factor affecting European integration.

These two neo-realist explanations of European disintegration have been subject to severe criticism. In particular, Rosato has been accused of relying on a selective and inaccurate reading of European history, even by fellow realists (see, e.g., Moravcsik, 2013; Parsons, 2013). The latter argued that the French desire to contain Germany after the Second World War was of much greater significance than the Soviet threat (Sheetz & Haine, 2012). This desire could provide a possible explanation of the continuation of European integration since the end of the Cold War, despite a diminished Soviet threat (Jones, 2007; see also Krotz & Maher, 2012). The continuation of European integration after 1991, at an even faster pace, constitutes the foundation for another major empirical criticism of Rosato's as well as Mearsheimer's interpretation of European history (Ripsman, 2005, p. 682). Without a Soviet threat and with a considerable reduction in American troops in Europe, the EU member states still voluntarily agreed to foster cooperation, even on issues like security and defence (Collard-Wexler, 2006). Rosato's riposte is that changes in the distribution of power do not necessarily have an immediate impact on state behaviour (Rosato, 2011b, p. 73). That means that a neo-realist explanation is rather indeterminate on the issue of when and how the European Union might disintegrate. The very fact that neo-realists have predicted both more and less European cooperation since the Cold War, despite sharing the same theoretical tenets, casts doubt on the value of neo-realist explanations of European (dis)integration at all (Bickerton, Irondelle, & Menon, 2011, p. 9). It does not necessarily mean that neo-realism is completely defunct, but it does not appear to offer a fruitful explanation of the (exceptional?) case of European cooperation.

Neo-realism has been criticised due to the "sterility" of its explanations of European integration (Hoffmann, 1995, p. 282). Neo-realists themselves acknowledge that they cannot offer a full account of states' foreign policy behaviour, but only of the systemic and structural pressures on states in the international system (Hyde-Price, 2006; Posen, 2006, p. 160; Waltz, 1979, pp. 343–344). It is then no wonder that neo-realist accounts of European integration include a wide variety of explanatory factors in addition to anarchy and the distribution of material capabilities, such as the American intent to threaten Europe or not (Paul, 2005); whether Germany is a status quo or revisionist power (Jones, 2007); the state of the world economy, national leadership, soft power, memories, and emotions or domestic politics (Hoffmann, 1995); the significance of European institutions in terms of giving a larger say to states weaker than Germany (Grieco, 1995); and the economic gains accrued from European integration (Rosato, 2011b). Even if anarchy and shifting distributions of power are fundamental to European integration and disintegration, these additions show that a mono-causal explanation does not suffice to explain the multifaceted issue of European disintegration (Krotz & Maher, 2012, p. 179).

Neo-realism is not only blamed for missing parts of the full picture of European disintegration. Its core tenets have also been criticised in discussions of European cooperation. Stanley Hoffmann (1995, p. 281) argued that with its supranational institutions, the EU might blur the division between international anarchy and domestic hierarchy. In other words, there is no longer simply divided by anarchy and hierarchy; institutions also shape the relationships between states (Hoffmann, 1995, p. 64; Keohane, 1990). Even if realism could yet explain how European cooperation began, European institutions may be the explanation for why European states did not resort to war and conflict after the end of the Cold War. The logic would then be that institutions have diminished mutual distrust in Western Europe and have remained too beneficial to be abandoned by the participating states (Ripsman, 2005). European states might also have avoided the implications of anarchy and mutual distrust after the end of the Cold War because they have continued to accept the hierarchical, if restrained, authority of the USA in international affairs (Lake, 2009, p. 11). In other words, anarchy has, to some degree, been overcome by institutions and *international* hierarchy. Neo-realism would therefore not only be an incomplete explanation of European integration and disintegration, but also an incorrect one.

Neo-realism also faces another problem in its account of European cooperation and disintegration. Even if Rosato could provide a neo-realist explanation as to why states ceded sovereignty to a partly supranational European Union, the basic assumption is that all actors remain functionally equivalent in a competitive and conflictual world. As a result, it is assumed that disintegration involves the European Union falling apart into its constituent states again. In this way, neo-realism does not have an explanation of the transformation of political organisations in the international system (Ruggie, 1998, pp. 25–26, 131–154), and remains stuck in the so-called territorial trap (Agnew, 1998, p. 49). They can thus only imagine temporary exceptions to political organisations characterised by territorial sovereignty, a fundamental separation between the domestic realm and the foreign realm with national governments as gatekeepers in between, and the distinction of societies according to state borders. The EU would be left with two options: become a superstate or fall apart into its constituent states again (cf. Waltz, 1979, p. 182). Even if neo-realists are empirically correct that sovereign states are the dominant form of political organisation, they should not simply assume that this is the case, but explain why it is so, in particular because the EU has deviated from this template for so long.

Neo-realists argue that the state template has been widely imitated because doing so has appeared to be the most effective means of survival. The question is whether or not the territorial state has been the most effective means of remaining secure and surviving in the context of the nuclear age, which the world entered into several decades ago. Now issues of security often concern asymmetric warfare involving non-state actors and threats such as a climate change, immigration, and contagious diseases, and states have become increasingly intertwined in economic interdependence (Herz, 1957; McCormick, 2012; Van Creveld, 1990). As a result, "[s]ecurity, in different contexts, is being decoupled from statist territoriality" (McGrew, 2007, p. 27). Instead of states and military capabilities, the economic and soft power of non-state actors such as the EU could thus be more effective in terms of providing security (McCormick, 2012). The challenge to neo-realists is to clarify why a return to constituent territorial states should be the end result of European disintegration (or integration for that matter) if it is no longer the most effective manner of organising in terms of providing security. Constituent sovereign states are not necessarily the outcome of integration or disintegration. A convincing explanation of European disintegration must provide an explanation of the conditions under which political actors adopt a territorial strategy to organise security.

Somewhat confusingly, neo-realists also argue that states may not only seek territorial defence, but also universal domination (see, e.g., Waltz, 1979, p. 118). But if they expect political units to behave like empires seeking universal domination, these units do vary in form at least. Furthermore, the pursuit of universal domination clearly violates the basic logic of state rule, which is based on a geographical delineation of power (Vollaard, 2009). Furthermore, universal domination introduces an element of hierarchy in international politics, which would contradict the neo-realist take on the implications of anarchy (Lake, 2009). It underlines the need to explain why actors might be focused on defence or domination, and more specifically why they might use a (non)territorial strategy to organise security. Such an explanation should distinguish the actor from the organisational strategy adopted. To be more specific, national governments could remain significant actors in the EU even if they do not necessarily stick to the template of the territorial state in their political strategies. To avoid further confusion, the concept of the state should refer only to the organisational framework and not to actors.

In the realist school of international relations, it has largely been the neo-realists who have taken on the challenge of exploring European integration and disintegration. However, their accounts have been inaccurate, indeterminate, incomplete, incorrect, or biased. Other realist theories— offensive, defensive, classical, neo-classical, hegemonic stability—do not offer much promise either, since they also suffer from a state-centric bias. To some extent, this also holds for the related approach, (liberal) intergovernmentalism, that will be discussed below.

3.3   INTERGOVERNMENTALISM

3.3.1   From Classical Realism to Neoliberal Institutionalism

The intergovernmentalist approach to the study of European integration originated in large part from a critical response to the problems neofunctionalism faced in explaining the halting of the process of European integration in the 1960s. The criticism from its most prominent representative, Stanley Hoffmann, initially reflected affinities with classical realism (Saurugger, 2014, p. 56ff). First of all, Hoffmann pointed at the significance of international forces external to the process of European integration. For example, he argued that the USA operated both as impetus and constraint of European integration. Whereas American governments stimulated European integration as a bulwark against communism and the Soviet Union, they also tried to prevent Western Europe from becoming an entity that was fully independent of the USA (Hoffmann, 1995, p. 141). With its focus on the endogenous forces of integration, it was argued, neo-functionalism missed this part of the bigger picture. Hoffmann (1995, p. 218ff) also criticised the neo-functionalist logic of integration. Only technocratic issues dealt with by civil servants from member states could be subject to spillover. A different logic would, however, manifest itself in issues of national pride, prestige, security, independence, and survival (Hoffmann, 1995, p. 33). These high politics issues are of key significance to national states, and in the context of these issues they "prefer the self-controlled uncertainty of national self-reliance, to the uncontrolled uncertainty" of integration (Hoffmann, 1995, p. 84). According to Hoffmann, the preferences of national states differ on these issues in particular, not least because of the continuing national orientation of parties, interest groups, political leaders, and the electorate. The ensuing logic of diversity on these issues could only be overcome if the preferences of particularly larger states converge. In Hoffmann's intergovernmentalist eyes, the French-German axis—comprising the two most powerful member states in the first decades of European integration—was fundamental to any further steps made in the direction of European integration. Thus, European integration is a product of states' choices, and not of supranational or functional pressures, as neo-functionalism contends. Instead of a gradual forward-moving process, integration is marked by stops and hiccups, and is not necessarily irreversible (Hoffmann, 1995, p. 96). National states only opt for European integration when it is necessary for their own preservation (see also Milward, 1992). States thus remain the most relevant actors.

In contrast to neo-functionalism, intergovernmentalists underline the continuing significance of national states and the relevance of forces exogenous to European integration. However, Hoffmann (1995, p. 5) not only criticises neo-functionalism, but also the "impoverished realism" that exclusively focuses on the structural features of international politics, like the balance of power. Instead, national history, cultural traditions, past experiences, ideas, domestic politics, ideals, and leaders also matter in international politics. National states thus show more variety in their behaviour and nature than would be expected on the basis of the functional similarity assumed by neo-realists. As a consequence, it should not be taken for granted that security is the exclusive priority in the formulation of states' foreign policy. States' preferences are *not* fixed and uniform, according to Hoffmann's thinking. The setting of domestic priorities should therefore be examined before states enter the international arena. Yet like neo-realists, Hoffmann expects the anarchic world, without a central power, to shape and constrain state behaviour. Leaning towards liberal and institutionalist theories in International Relations, Hoffmann did not expect security and power to be the exclusive drivers of international politics (Moravcsik, 2009). Accordingly, international cooperation is not only the product of hegemonic pressure or of counterbalancing strategies. States may also seek international cooperation to serve common interests that they would not have been able to obtain individually. International cooperation is seen as instrumental for states to acquire absolute gains in a variety of policy areas; this is in contrast to the neo-realists' singular focus on relative gains in the security domain. Without a central power that can enforce international agreements, states that want to cooperate still face the problem of defection and freeriding. Neoliberal institutionalism suggests that states can still coordinate their policies with the help of international regimes. Regimes are "principles, norms, rules, and decision-making procedures around which actor expectations converge in a given issue-area" (Krasner, 1982a, p. 185). Regimes facilitate interstate "policy co-ordination" (Krasner, 1982a). They offer information about the preferences of states, which enhances the predictability of negotiations. They also provide a platform for negotiations by limiting the costs of seeking policy coordination. Regimes can also reveal and correct a lack of compliance by states, strengthening mutual commitment to international agreements. International regimes and institutions mitigate the distrust and suspicion that is inherent in an anarchic world by reducing uncertainty about the intentions of other states.

Whereas neo-realists expect regimes to be dependent on the preponderance of a hegemonic power, neoliberal-institutionalists believe that common interests of the participating states may also generate and sustain regimes. But if regimes no longer receive hegemonic support or lose their utility for the participating states, would they be abandoned as a result? Regimes can live "on their own" even if the conditions under which they were established no longer exist (Krasner, 1982b). States could fear the reputation costs associated with leaving a regime, even if continued participation no longer serves their interests. States could also forego the breakup of a regime because the costs of establishing or joining another one would be even higher. Only when changes in terms of the initial setting, common interests, hegemonic support, and the regime become too great do revolutionary shifts occur in international relations (Krasner, 1982b).

Hoffmann (1995, p. 222) casted the European Communities (ECs) as a very elaborated instance of an international regime. According to him, the many mutual linkages in the EC were made as a result of the highly interdependent nature of issues in Western Europe. However, the actual EC policy coordination on a wide range of issues primarily emerged from the convergence of state preferences on the issues at stake (Keohane & Hoffmann, 1991). The EC/EU has been rather novel compared to other regimes because the participating states have also pooled sovereignty in the Council of Ministers and have delegated sovereignty to supranational agencies such as the European Commission and the European Court of Justice (Keohane & Hoffmann, 1991). EC/EU member states no longer have complete supremacy within their territories, and are subject to outside authorities. Even if national systems remain prominent political arenas, they have become part of a densely institutionalised European coordinative network. As a consequence, in the early 1990s Hoffmann doubted that the EC/EU could still be analysed as a purely intergovernmental regime: "[t]he inappropriateness of statist, strictly intergovernmental (...) models of how European politics operates stems from the inconsistency of these images with the network metaphor (...) which serve(s) as the best approximation to the evolving reality" (Keohane & Hoffmann, 1991, p. 15). It is no wonder then that, in response to neorealism, Hoffmann and others suggested that European supranational institutions blurred the divide between anarchy and hierarchy (see above). European institutions did constrain the choices available to states, and in some cases even moulded their preferences (Keohane & Hoffmann, 1993). In the 1990s, political scientist Andrew Moravcsik elaborated upon the neoliberal institutionalist leanings in Hoffmann's thinking in his theoretical framework on liberal intergovernmentalism. Given its analytically rigorous and comprehensive nature, Moravcsik's framework is used here to explore the value of intergovernmentalism in explaining whether or not and how European disintegration might occur. The role of European institutions will be a fundamental issue in the subsequent discussion of the problems associated with the (liberal) intergovernmentalist account of European disintegration.

3.3.2   Liberal Intergovernmentalism on European Integration

In his book *Choice for Europe: Social Purpose & State Power from Messina to Maastricht* (1998), Moravcsik presented a grand theory that explains the broad patterns of regional integration (cf. Moravcsik & Schimmelfennig, 2009). It accounts for the major intergovernmental decisions resulting in European integration, and not for day-to-day EU politics (Wallace, Caporaso, Scharpf, & Moravcsik, 1999, p. 174). Moravcsik (1993, p. 479) defines integration as policy coordination in regimes. Integration can subsequently be expressed in terms of the geographical scope, the range of coordinated issues, the institutional set-up, and the impact on the participating states of a specific regime. Integration would thus not only concern the transfer of competences to a supranational community, or supranational institutions, but the intensification of intergovernmental ties as well. Moravcsik developed not only a potential interpretation of European integration, but also a clearly phrased, verifiable theoretical alternative. Hypotheses from rival theories served to put his alternative of liberal intergovernmentalism to the empirical test. For this purpose, he examined the French, German, and British positions in a series of major intergovernmental negotiations in Western Europe from the late 1950s to the early 1990s. Moravcsik's theoretical alternative is actually a synthetic framework of three theories. He perceives European integration to be too complex to be explained by a single factor, such as spillover, or the balance of power. All three theories are rationalist. The theories explain the subsequent stages in the making of major intergovernmental decisions concerning preference formation, the bargaining process between states, and the design of international institutions, respectively. Moravcsik assumes that unitarily operating states are the most important political instruments in international negotiations (Moravcsik, 1998, p. 22). In his analysis of intergovernmental bargains, states are seen as gatekeepers between domestic and anarchic international politics, playing in both arenas. The state's role as gatekeeper does not deny other actors such as international organisations a role in international politics, but other actors do operate within the policy goals set by state governments.

The first stage of intergovernmental bargaining involves the formation of state preferences. Preferences are a set of underlying objectives of a state that are more stable than a negotiating strategy or policy goal in a specific negotiation (Moravcsik, 1998, p. 20). Where do these preferences come from? Are they derived from a government's ideology or are they the product of geopolitical pressures in the international system? On the basis of his empirical analysis, Moravcsik concludes that preferences largely originate from pluralistic conflicts within national societies. Reflecting the liberal component of his framework, Moravcsik argues that individuals and groups articulate their interests, and the state aggregates them. Which interests prevail depends on the variety of interests present in a national society, and how intense, concentrated, clear, and well represented the interests of specific individuals and groups are (Moravcsik, 1998, p. 36). Collective action is more difficult if interests are weak and diffusely spread across the population, and the costs and benefits of a potential intergovernmental deal are uncertain or limited. For example, well-organised industrial sectors are better able to push their interests forward than the unwieldy group of taxpayers or consumers. In order to satisfy these powerful lobbies, governments more or less follow these interests. On issues that lack strong interest representation from society, like foreign policy, national governments have more discretion in international negotiations. Governments also have some discretion at the international level because of their informational advantage in international negotiations behind closed doors over interest groups at the domestic level. Playing the "two-level game", they can thus try to circumvent domestic pressures (Putnam, 1988). In Moravcsik's liberal view on preference formation, preferences not only differ in substance and intensity from country to country but also from policy issue to policy issue. Moravcsik has been criticised for neglecting the impact of domestic politics and institutions on shaping domestic conflicts, but the differences in political infrastructure between policy areas make preferences even more "issue-specific" (Wallace et al., 1999). States' preferences are thus not uniform and fixed as is argued in neorealism, but depend on the specific combination of domestic groups, their interest representation, and the sector-specific and state-specific institutions.

According to Moravcsik's analysis of several major decisions on European integration, preferences for integration have primarily been a response to increasing economic interdependence. Increasing flows of trade and capital have led to an increase in the mutual impact of government's policies, so-called policy externalities. A call for European integration to coordinate policies followed, particularly from countries and sectors that were highly dependent on trade and that could withstand international competition. Since all Western European countries faced increasing economic interdependence, preferences in many areas were converging towards some kind of integration. The distribution of potential winners and losers of European integration and how they could push for their interests shaped the preferences of states in subsequent European negotiations on policy coordination on market liberalisation and regulation as well as monetary stability. Up until the early 1990s, preferences for integration thus resulted from increasing economic interdependence and convergence between the negotiating states. Following the same logic, in the late 1990s, Moravcsik maintained an "optimist prognosis" with respect to economic integration: "There is an underlying functional reason for this [enlargement, monetary integration and deepening single market, HV], namely the consistent increase in social support, above all from producer interests, for the economic integration of Europe" (in Wallace et al., 1999, p. 176). And also after the Great Recession, states still had no other option than to cooperate. It would be "economic suicide" to leave the EU (Moravcsik, 2012). Integration of social policies, among others, is less likely because the associated policy externalities have remained relatively limited, and resistance to the potential redistributive consequences of integration are quite high (Moravcsik, 2005, p. 366). Given the political economy of European states, European integration may have reached its limit.

Even if prior policy convergence among states is essential, European integration also depends on the subsequent negotiations between states. What determines the substance of these negotiations? Do supranational actors have the information and skills required to craft (latent) coalitions in the domestic and European arenas to support a specific deal? In the case of the Single European Act, Moravcsik argues that they did to some extent. But in other instances, governments were sufficiently skilled and informed to completely dominate the intergovernmental negotiations. The second stage of international negotiations is thus the intergovernmentalist component of Moravcsik's theory. The intensity of states' preferences on a specific issue by and large determined the subsequent outcome of the negotiations. States that would profit from a specific agreement are more willing to make compromises than the ones facing losses or high adaptation costs. The outcome also depends on the extent to which governments are bound by domestic pressure groups, and also on the means at their disposal to facilitate an agreement, such as side payments, or linkages between various dossiers, as well as available alternatives, from non-agreement to coordination with a different group of states. If states are excluded from the benefits of a specific international agreement, or suffer as a result of it, they will be more inclined to join than if they can freely profit from them (cf. Kölliker, 2006).

The third component of liberal intergovernmentalism most clearly reflects Moravcsik's affinity with regime theory. Based on his historical analysis, he argues that European supranational institutions have been established to ensure states' compliance with the agreements based in an anarchic world without a central authority capable of enforcement, and not because of a federalist ideology or the desire to delegate authority to expert agencies that can handle complex technocratic issues without direct political influence. States also agreed to lift their vetoes in a number of areas and pool their sovereignty to facilitate efficiency of decision-making within the policy space set. Supranationalism is thus the product of a rational choice to maintain credible commitments with fellow states. In the liberal intergovernmentalist view, it would therefore be logical that supranational institutions correct individual member states to maintain the agreements made. Moravcsik insisted, however, against neo-functionalists and historical-institutionalists that institutions are instruments of states. European institutions will not socialise member states or lock them into an undesired path of development. European integration is not a self-reinforcing process and essentially depends on domestically formed preferences in response to incentives in the global economy.

3.3.3   Liberal Intergovernmentalism and European Disintegration

Liberal intergovernmentalism is a theory of regional integration. It has not given much thought, if any, to disintegration. Could it still provide some insight into the nature and causes of European disintegration by turning it on its head (cf. Webber, 2013)? As explained above, in Moravcsik's view, European integration effectively boils down to increasing policy coordination among states. European disintegration can then be expressed as a decrease in the EU's geographical scope, the range of policy issues coordinated by the EU, the institutional complexity of the EU, and the impact of policy coordination on the EU member states. The very question is, however, whether disintegration is just an issue of decreasing policy coordination among states in general or decreasing policy coordination among states within the EU. Disintegration of the EU could also be replaced by increasing policy coordination among *other* groupings of states, such as in the Council of Europe, the United Nations, or the World Trade Organization. Disintegration is therefore not simply integration in reverse. Additionally, Moravcsik developed a theory of intergovernmental decisions resulting in European integration. But would disintegration also be a matter of intergovernmental bargaining? European disintegration could also be the result of an increasing negligence of the EU's day-to-day politics by national governments and other actors. Assuming yet for the sake of argument that European disintegration is a matter of intergovernmental bargaining, what explanation can be derived from liberal intergovernmentalism?

European disintegration would be a matter of changing political economy in the first stage of preference formation. According to Moravcsik, growing economic interdependence and ensuing policy convergence between producer groups and governments in particular were fundamental to European integration, at least from the late 1950s to the early 1990s. Declining economic interdependence among EU member states might therefore be an initial cause of disintegration. The policy externalities of EU member states would concern other EU member states less, or concern only some of them, or only non-EU economies, or no other states at all. Whereas intra-EU trade rose until the early 1990s, it stagnated afterwards, with a declining trend since the Great Recession. EU countries, and EMU member states in particular, trade less with each other and export increasingly to non-EU countries like China (O'Neill & Terzi, 2014). However reliant EU member states still are on trade with other EU member states, these shifting patterns could entail a diminishing need to coordinate policies within the EU or the Eurozone. If the EU is a less appropriate platform for policy coordination to manage the mutual impact of governments' policies, support for European integration among producer groups and governments in particular would decline. The pro-integrationist call from producer groups may also weaken because the agricultural sector has declined considerably in size of labour force, while competitive producers can more easily move to other parts of the world. Furthermore, member states' economies may have become less competitive for whatever reason, leading national governments to reintroduce protectionist measures, thereby limiting European market liberalisation.

Meanwhile, the costs of European integration may become more clear, certain, and concentrated in the eyes of certain well-represented groups. Indeed, both left-wing and right-wing Eurosceptic parties have been on the rise, with their criticism of the costs of migration and the Economic and Monetary Union in terms of budget cuts in welfare states, job safety, national identity, and sovereignty. In some member states, the political salience of Eurosceptic concerns has increased (Hooghe & Marks, 2008), and Eurosceptic parties have entered parliaments and also governments (Taggart & Scszerbiak, 2013). For long, the influence of Eurosceptic parties on national governments' position on the EU has been limited, and the politicisation of the EU issue by mainstream parties has remained modest (Green-Pedersen, 2012). However, support for existing integrative deals would likely decline in response to governments demanding to (partially) disintegrate the EU on issues such as the free movement of migrants.

Another source of European disintegration from a liberal-intergovernmentalist point of view is the changing relative importance of political-economic arguments. Moravcsik based his claim of the predominance of economic interests on a series of intergovernmental decisions made between the late 1950s and the early 1990s. These decisions were made, by and large, within the same geopolitical setting of the Cold War, and well before the last SU troops left Eastern Germany at least. Geopolitical considerations of the EU's role in the world and vis-à-vis the USA in particular could have become much more prominent. The various initiatives to launch cooperation on issues of foreign and defence policy indicate as much. Additionally, the EU is said to have made a post-functional turn after the Maastricht Treaty (Hooghe & Marks, 2008). Whereas functional concerns about the efficient scale of policy coordination dominated European integration until the 1980s, issues of identity and political community have increased in prominence ever since. European integration has not entailed large-scale transfer of competences into the area of identity-sensitive issues such as social policies and education. What is more, economic integration could also increasingly be perceived in terms of identity, and identity ideologies could undermine existing deals that may still provide effective management of policy externalities. As a result, groups and individuals could now turn against the current EU, or parts of it, even though they have not done so in the past.

Disintegration could also originate from the stage of interstate bargaining. Governments may have been able to circumvent domestic Eurosceptic opposition in international negotiations because Eurosceptic individuals and groups did not have information about negotiations held behind closed doors. In member states, national parliaments, the media, and the electorate have begun to have more information about the intergovernmental deals made. As a result, they could start to demand less integration than that which they had previously accepted due to a shortage of information. Furthermore, alternative coalitions or unilateral options may have emerged that did not exist when the negotiations first took place. As a result, EU member states could start to seek cooperation in the context of other groupings, such as a northern monetary union, or bilateral agreements within and outside the EU. Additionally, the economic crisis could have limited side payments such as cohesion and structural funds to uphold deals to create a single market or a monetary union. Without sufficient funding, commitment to adhere to common agreements and standards could decline.

A proposal for disintegration could yet be met with less intense support among the member states. According to the rational, neoliberal-institutionalist underpinnings of liberal intergovernmentalism, states stick with institutions if the costs of (partial) withdrawal are perceived to be higher than those associated with maintaining the status quo. Given the EU's exceptionally wide range of coordinated issues in a densely institutionalised setting, the price of withdrawal would quickly become higher than the cost of maintaining the status quo. Maintenance of the status quo would therefore be increasingly likely, as opposed to further integration or disintegration (cf. Moravcsik, 2005). The chance of seeing converging preferences on disintegration among 28 member states is smaller than it would have been when six governments negotiated the initial European deals in the 1950s and 1960s. And if disintegration were still to take place, it is reasonable to expect that it will be decided upon more slowly than integration was. The large number of small states with limited negotiation capacities in the current EU would make it much harder to find satisfactory deals for both national and supranational actors.

3.3.4 Problems in the Intergovernmentalist Explanation of European (Dis)integration

Intergovernmentalist treatises on European (dis)integration contain several valuable lessons for those seeking to explain (dis)integration. Empirically, intergovernmentalists like Hoffmann and Moravcsik clearly showed the diversity and changeability of national preferences and the prominence of issues other than security, thereby debunking neo-realist claims about their functional similarity of states and the mono-causality of international cooperation. Additionally, European (dis)integration depends on more than one cause, such as spillover or balance of power. Furthermore, European disintegration is not necessarily European integration in reverse because the EU might be (partially) replaced by other regimes as opposed to being dissolved into its constituent national states again. The theoretical rigour of Moravcsik's comparative analysis is also exemplary. Theoretical alternatives should be put to the test by generating hypotheses that can be examined empirically. Hypotheses should be coherently derived from one and the same synthetic starting point instead of being a loose collection of statements.

Despite these lessons learned, intergovernmentalism remains a problematic source to draw on in explaining European disintegration. The fundamental problem is its state-centrism (cf. Rosamond, 2000, p. 115ff). A basic assumption of liberal intergovernmentalism is that people act through rational and unitary nation states (Moravcsik, 1998, p. 22ff). It thus assumes a divide between the international and the domestic arenas, but does not question, let alone explain, its continuation after several decades of European integration. Even if national governments remain crucial actors, European integration might change the territorial and hierarchical nature of member states to such an extent that they are no longer fully hierarchical and territorial states. Empirical research points out that even taxation and the monopoly on the legitimate use of violence have been increasingly constrained by European integration (Genschel & Jachtenfuchs, 2011; Herschinger, Jachtenfuchs, & Kraft-Kasak, 2011). Continuously increasing policy coordination could at some point lead to member states being units of a European federal system, or to an EU in which member states have become enmeshed in complex, multi-level governance networks without a clear separation of political arenas and without clear hierarchies. In such a situation, people would be less inclined to use national states as instruments to advance their preferences and to influence international negotiation. A proper explanation of integration and disintegration should denote when and how state territoriality and sovereign hierarchy are (re-)adopted. In other words, it should indicate whether or not the state is the most important actor and organisational template; that "is the *crucial* empirical question to be analyzed" (Wind, 1997, p. 17; emphasis in original) in this respect.

As a matter of fact, the recently developed approach of new intergovernmentalism considers day-to-day consensual and deliberative decision-making among representatives of national governments as part of intergovernmentalist integration in the post-Maastricht period, rather than supranational behaviour that extends beyond member states (Bickerton, Hodson, & Puetter, 2014). Regardless of whether this decision-making style can be described as intergovernmental or not

(Schimmelfennig, 2015, p. 724), the approach fails to explain why state actors would no longer seek consensus and deliberation within the EU and seek less or no integration, instead. For this reason, its explanation of European disintegration is a problematic one.

Returning to the older theory of liberal intergovernmentalism, it also falls short in its capacity to explain European disintegration for another reason. As Fritz Scharpf (in Wallace et al., 1999, p. 165) commented on Moravcsik's book, it was rather self-evident that it was in large part economic interests that determined the direction of negotiations on major decisions relating to European integration, as these decisions concerned economic issues such as the creation of an internal market and the Common Agricultural Policy. As Hoffmann argued, however, regional cooperation is also dependent on the external security situation. Even if states' governments focused on the (economic) interests of domestic interest groups in European treaty negotiations, the American security umbrella could have provided the necessary precondition required to discuss cooperation at all (cf. Waltz, 1979, pp. 70–71). An explanation of European (dis)integration should therefore neither exaggerate nor neglect security as a potential factor.

3.4   Conclusion

Theories of realism and intergovernmentalism have pointed at the significance of forces external to European integration itself, from the power of hegemonic states to economic interdependence between national societies. Intergovernmentalism has also underlined the diversity of states and the variety of factors explaining their behaviour, such as domestic politics, bargaining setting, national leadership, and the mobilisation power of producer groups. As valuable as these insights may be, they remain ill equipped to explain European disintegration because they all assume that territorial states are the key actors in international politics and the dominant political format. Instead, they should offer an explanation of the use of state territoriality. Intergovernmentalists should take their own name more literally by no longer equating states and governments. National governments might remain influential, but in a network polity rather than in anarchic Westphalian world. A good explanation of European disintegration should therefore answer the question of why political actors would (not) go beyond the organisational template of the territorial state.

REFERENCES

Agnew, J. (1998). *Geopolitics: Revisioning world politics.* London: Routledge.

Andreatta, F. (2005). Theory and the European Union's international relations. In C. Hill & M. Smith (Eds.), *International relations and the European Union* (pp. 18–38). Oxford: Oxford University Press.

Bickerton, C. J., Hodson, D., & Puetter, U. (2014). The new intergovernmentalism: European integration in the post-Maastricht era. *Journal of Common Market Studies, 53*(4), 703–722.

Bickerton, C. J., Irondelle, B., & Menon, A. (2011). Security co-operation beyond the nation-state: The EU's common security and defence policy. *Journal of Common Market Studies, 49*(1), 1–21.

Brooks, S. G., & Wohlforth, W. C. (2005). Hard times for soft balancing. *International Security, 30*(1), 72–108.

Brooks, S. G., & Wohlforth, W. C. (2008). *World out of balance: International relations and the challenge of American primacy.* Princeton: Princeton University Press.

Cladi, L., & Locatelli, A. (2012). Bandwagoning, not balancing: Why Europe confounds realism. *Contemporary Security Policy, 33*(2), 264–288.

Collard-Wexler, S. (2006). Integration under anarchy: Neorealism and the European Union. *European Journal of International Relations, 12*(3), 397–432.

Genschel, P., & Jachtenfuchs, M. (2011). How the European Union constrains the state: Multilevel governance of taxation. *European Journal of Political Research, 50*, 293–314.

Giegerich, B., & Wallace, W. (2004). Not such a soft power: The external deployment of European forces. *Survival, 46*(2), 163–182.

Gilpin, R. (1981). *War and change in world politics.* Cambridge: Cambridge University Press.

Green-Pedersen, C. (2012). A giant fast asleep? Party incentives and politicisation of European integration. *Political Studies, 60*(1), 115–130.

Grieco, J. (1995). The Maastricht Treaty, Economic and Monetary Union and the neo-realist research programme. *Review of International Studies, 21*(1), 21–40.

Herschinger, E., Jachtenfuchs, M., & Kraft-Kasak, C. (2011). Scratching the heart of the artichoke? How international institutions and the European Union constrain the state monopoly of force. *European Political Science Review, 3*(3), 445–468.

Herz, J. (1957). Rise and demise of the territorial state. *World Politics, 9*(4), 473–493.

Hoffmann, S. (1995). *The European Sisyphus: Essays on Europe, 1964–1994.* Boulder: Westview Press.

Hooghe, L., & Marks, G. (2008). A postfunctionalist theory of European integration: From permissive consensus to constraining dissensus. *British Journal of Political Science, 39*, 1–23.

Howorth, J. (2007). *Security and defence policy in the European Union*. Basingstoke: Palgrave Macmillan.

Howorth, J., & Menon, A. (2009). Still not pushing back: Why the European Union is not balancing the United States. *Journal of Conflict Resolution, 53*(5), 727–744.

Hyde-Price, A. (2006). "Normative" power Europe: A realist critique. *Journal of European Public Policy, 13*(2), 217–234.

Hyde-Price, A. (2013). Neither realism or liberalism: New directions in theorizing EU security policy. *Contemporary Security Policy, 34*(2), 397–408.

Joffe, J. (1984). Europe's American pacifier. *Foreign Policy, 54*, 64–82.

Jones, S. (2007). *The rise of European security cooperation*. Cambridge: Cambridge University Press.

Keohane, R. (1990). Correspondence: Back to the future, Part II: International Relations theory and post-Cold War Europe. *International Security, 15*(2), 192–194.

Keohane, R., & Hoffmann, S. (1991). Institutional change in Europe in the 1980s. In R. Keohane & S. Hoffmann (Eds.), *The new European Community: Decision making and institutional change* (pp. 1–39). Boulder: Westview Press.

Keohane, R., & Hoffmann, S. (1993). Conclusion: Structure, strategy, and institutional roles. In R. O. Keohane, J. S. Nye, & S. Hoffmann (Eds.), *After the Cold War: International institutions and state strategies in Europe, 1989–1991* (pp. 381–406). Cambridge: Harvard University Press.

Kölliker, A. (2006). *Flexibility and European unification: The logic of differentiated integration*. Lanham: Rowman & Littlefield.

Krasner, S. (1982a). Structural causes and regime consequences: Regimes as intervening variables. *International Organization, 36*(2), 185–205.

Krasner, S. (1982b). Regimes and the limits of realism: Regimes as autonomous variables. *International Organization, 36*(2), 497–510.

Krotz, U., & Maher, R. (2012). Correspondence: Debating the sources and prospects of European integration. *International Security, 37*(1), 178–182.

Lake, D. A. (2009). *Hierarchy in international relations*. Ithaca: Cornell University Press.

Legro, J. W., & Moravcsik, A. (1999). Is anybody still a realist? *International Security, 24*(2), 5–55.

McCormick, J. (2012). The European Union: A different kind of beast. In D. Murray & D. Brown (Eds.), *Multipolarity in the 21st Century: A new world order* (pp. 107–130). London: Routledge.

McGrew, A. (2007). Organized violence in the making (and remaking) of globalization. In D. Held & A. McGrew (Eds.), *Globalization theory: Approaches and controversies* (pp. 15–40). Cambridge: Polity Press.

Mearsheimer, J. (1990). Back to the future: Instability in Europe after the Cold War. *International Security, 15*(1), 5–56.

Mearsheimer, J. (2001). *The tragedy of great power politics.* New York: W.W. Norton.
Mearsheimer, J. (2010). Why is Europe peaceful today? *European Political Science,* 9, 387–397.
Milward, A. (1992). *The European rescue of the nation-state.* London: Routledge.
Moravcsik, A. (1993). Preferences and power in the European Community: A liberal intergovernmentalist approach. *Journal of Common Market Studies,* 31(4), 473–524.
Moravcsik, A. (1998). *The choice for Europe: Social purpose and state power from Messina to Maastricht.* Ithaca: Cornell University Press.
Moravcsik, A. (2005). The European constitutional compromise and the neofunctionalist legacy. *Journal of European Public Policy,* 12(2), 349–386.
Moravcsik, A. (2009). Europe: The quiet superpower. *French Politics,* 7(3/4), 403–422.
Moravcsik, A. (2012, April 22). Europe after the crisis. *New York Times.*
Moravcsik, A. (2013). Did balance of power politics cause European integration? Realist theory meets qualitative methods. *Security Studies,* 22(4), 773–790.
Moravcsik, A., & Schimmelfennig, F. (2009). Liberal intergovernmentalism. In A. Wiener & T. Diez (Eds.), *European integration theory* (2nd ed., pp. 67–90). Oxford: Oxford University Press.
Morgenthau, H. (1948). *Politics among nations.* New York: Knopf.
O'Neill, J., & Terzi, A. (2014). *Changing trade patterns, unchanging European and global governance* (Bruegel Working Paper 2014/02). Brussels: Bruegel.
Ojanen, H. (2006). The EU and Nato: Two competing models for a common defence policy. *Journal of Common Market Studies,* 44(1), 57–76.
Parsons, C. (2013). Power, patterns, and process in European Union history. *Security Studies,* 22(4), 791–801.
Paul, T. V. (2005). Soft balancing in the age of U.S. primacy. *International Security,* 30(1), 46–71.
Pohl, B. (2013). Neither bandwagoning nor balancing: Explaining Europe's security policy. *Contemporary Security Policy,* 34(2), 353–373.
Posen, B. (2006). European Union Security and Defense Policy: Response to unipolarity? *Security Studies,* 15(2), 149–186.
Putnam, R. (1988). Diplomacy and domestic politics: The logic of two-level games. *International Organization,* 42(3), 427–460.
Ringsmose, J. (2013). Balancing or bandwagoning? Europe's many relations with the United States. *Contemporary Security Studies,* 34(2), 409–412.
Ripsman, N. (2005). Two stages of transition from a region of war to a region of peace: Realist transition and liberal endurance. *International Studies Quarterly,* 49, 669–693.
Rosamond, B. (2000). *Theories of European integration.* Basingstoke: Palgrave Macmillan.
Rosato, S. (2011a). *Europe united: Power politics and the making of the European Community.* Ithaca: Cornell University Press.

Rosato, S. (2011b). Europe's trouble: Power politics and the state of the European project. *International Security, 35*(4), 45–86.

Ruggie, J. G. (1998). *Constructing the world polity: Essays on international institutionalization.* London: Routledge.

Saurugger, S. (2014). *Theoretical approaches to European integration.* Basingstoke: Palgrave Macmillan.

Schimmelfennig, F. (2015). What's the news in 'new intergovermentalism'? A critique of Bickerton, Hodson and Puetter. *Journal of Common Market Studies, 53*(4), 723–730.

Schweller, R. L., & Priess, D. (1997). A tale of two realisms: Expanding the institutions debate. *Mershon International Studies Review, 41*, 1–32.

Sheetz, M., & Haine, J.-Y. (2012). Correspondence: Debating the sources and prospects of European integration. *International Security, 37*(1), 189–192.

Taggart, P., & Scszerbiak, A. (2013). Coming in from the cold? Euroscepticism, government participation and party positions on Europe. *Journal of Common Market Studies, 51*(1), 17–37.

Taliaferro, J. W. (2000 [2001]). Security seeking under anarchy: Defensive realism revisited. *International Security, 25*, 128–161.

Van Creveld, M. (1990). *The transformation of war.* New York: Free Press.

Vollaard, H. (2009). The logic of political territoriality. *Geopolitics, 14*(4), 687–706.

Wallace, H., Caporaso, J. A., Scharpf, F. W., & Moravcsik, A. (1999). Review section symposium: The choice for Europe. *Journal of European Public Policy, 6*(1), 155–179.

Walt, S. (1987). *The origins of alliances.* Ithaca: Cornell University Press.

Waltz, K. N. (1979). *Theory of international politics.* Readings, MA: Addison-Wesley.

Waltz, K. N. (1993). The emerging structure of international politics. *International Security, 18*(2), 44–79.

Waltz, K. N. (2000). Structural realism after the Cold War. *International Security, 25*(1), 5–41.

Webber, D. (2013). How likely is it that the European Union will disintegrate? A critical analysis of competing theoretical perspectives. *European Journal of International Relations, 19*(4), 1–25.

Wind, M. (1997). Rediscovering institutions: A reflectivist critique of rational institutionalism. In K. E. Jørgensen (Ed.), *Reflective approaches to European governance* (pp. 15–35). London: Palgrave Macmillan.

CHAPTER 4

Federalism and European Disintegration

4.1 Introduction

At the height of the Eurozone's debt crises in the Summer of 2012, a network of European federalists presented a stark choice for the future of Europe: federal union or disintegration (Spinelli Group, 2012). The network advocated the launch of a full-fledged banking union, economic and fiscal union, and political union to effectively address the crises and restore the democratic accountability of the European Union (EU). The making of a federal union was seen as an effective path to a sustainable EU. Switzerland, Australia, India, Argentina, and also the USA, in spite of a gruesome civil war, are examples of long-standing federations. Switzerland, Australia, and the USA also emerged out of confederations, or looser unions of states. Thus, a combination of shared and self-rule (cf. Elazar, 1987) has the capacity to endure. However, many confederations, federations, and other federal systems have also broken up, including the former Yugoslavia and the Federation of the West Indies. Federal or quasi-federal entities like Canada, Belgium, Spain, Iraq, Bosnia-Herzegovina, and the UK have also been subjected to severe disintegrative stress. Comparative studies of successful and failed federal systems can be a fruitful starting point to conceptualise and explain disintegration, both with respect to the disintegration of an entire federal system (Sect. 4.3) and to the secession of a part of it (Sect. 4.4). Before these explanations of disintegration from a federal perspective are discussed, this chapter will discuss

© The Author(s) 2018
H. Vollaard, *European Disintegration*, Palgrave Studies in European
Union Politics, https://doi.org/10.1057/978-1-137-41465-6_4

definitions of federalism and related concepts in Sect. 4.2. This is not only necessary because of the wide variety of definitions and interpretations of these concepts present in the literature, but also to determine whether or not the EU sufficiently resembles a federal system to make comparison possible. As will be summed up in the concluding section, comparative federalism faces various problems with regard to conceptualising and explaining European disintegration, but it does offer some useful building blocks with which to do so.

4.2   COMPARATIVE FEDERALISM AND ITS APPLICABILITY TO THE EUROPEAN UNION

Federalism has been a widely shared source of inspiration for European integration for Christian democrats, social democrats, greens, as well as liberals. The combination of shared rule and self-rule has been seen as a means of marrying unity and diversity in the EU. An emphasis on diversity has been illustrated by calls to limit the power of EU institutions based on the principle of subsidiarity and a list of competences in the EU treaties. Conversely, federalism has also been invoked to foster public engagement with the EU through the development of extensive political infrastructure at the European level, including a government, two chambers of parliament representing citizens and member states respectively, European political parties, and autonomous tax-raising powers (Spinelli Group, 2012). Additionally, federalist proposals have often included provisions for stronger EU competences to deal more effectively with foreign or monetary crises (e.g., Fischer, 2000).

After a period of relegation to relative oblivion, the perspective of federalism has been used increasingly often to analyse the EU in a non-normative way in recent decades. Unfortunately, the study of the EU from a federalist perspective thus far has tended to neglect the issue of disintegration (for exceptions, see Kelemen, 2007; Glencross, 2009). Instead, these studies focus predominantly on the way in which federalist ideas inform the evolution of European integration (e.g., Burgess, 2000) and how comparative federalism can explain task allocation and decision-making within the EU (e.g., Benson & Jordan, 2008; Scharpf, 1988). The USA, Germany, and, more recently, Canada have been considered for comparative purposes (Nicolaidis & Howse, 2001; Scharpf, 1988; Verdun, 2015). Before discussing whether or not and how a federal perspective can be applied to the study of European disintegration, it should be made clear what federalism is all about.

Hundreds of definitions of federalism exist, and understanding of the term differs in continental Europe as compared to the Anglo-American world (Burgess, 2006, Chap. 6; Chryssochoou, 2001, p. 43). For reasons of analytical clarity, and to encompass the various manifestations of all things federal, the conceptual distinctions introduced by Ronald Watts are followed here. Federalism refers to the pragmatic or ideological advocacy of "balancing of citizen preferences for (a) joint action for certain purposes and (b) self-government of the constituent units for other purposes" (Watts, 1998, p. 120). Thus, federalism is actually a normative-philosophical concept that relates to the promotion of federal principles (Burgess, 2006, p. 2). The concept of a "federal political system" is a general, descriptive term that denotes a combination of shared rule and self-rule, by which Watts refers to the well-known, succinct definition of a federal system put forward by Daniel Elazar (1987). This concept encompasses a wide variety of species, from leagues and unions to federations and confederations, and hybrids of these species. As such, a federation can be seen as a species under the general genus of federal political system.

A federation is defined by Watts (1998, p. 121) as "a compound polity combining constituent units and a general government, each possessing powers delegated to it by the people through a constitution, each empowered to deal directly with the citizens in the exercise of a significant portion of its legislative, administrative, and taxing powers, and each directly elected by its citizens". Despite the wide variety in the way federations are formally organised and actually operate, a list can be made of characteristics that federations usually exhibit. A federation is a state (Burgess, 2000, p. 268; Forsyth, 2007, p. 150). A bicameral legislature at the federal level guarantees the representation of the single people, as well as that of the various member states. This distribution of power over the various layers of government is laid down in a constitution. Neither of the levels of government are subordinate to each other. Changes to the constitution require assent by special majorities at the various levels of government. A federal judiciary acts as an umpire vis-à-vis the distribution of power. Despite the fact that, according to this conceptualisation, federations are characterised by an internal division of sovereignty, they also have unitary features. A federation acts as one in its interactions with the rest of the world (Forsyth, 2007, p. 151). Federal governments are often, therefore, exclusively responsible for foreign policy and defence. Member states do not have the formal right of secession (although it may still be politically possible).

The EU has some features of a federation, such as direct election of the European Parliament, the supranational Court of Justice of the European Union, relative autonomy of each level of government in at least some tasks, and majority voting by governments in the Council (Börzel & Hosli, 2003, pp. 186–187; Kelemen, 2003, p. 185). Nevertheless, the EU is not a federation (Burgess, 2006; Forsyth, 2007, p. 154ff). First of all, it is not a state. It does not have the right to make war and peace, and it has no right of taxation. The EU is based on treaties, ratified by each and every member state, as opposed to a constitution that was the result of an act of a single people. The unanimous consent of all member states is still required to change the treaties, although the role of EU institutions in treaty revision procedures has increased over the years. In the European Council, where heads of states and governments are represented, decision-making pertaining to setting out the main strategies of the EU and tackling crises is still consensus based. The council, in which representatives of member state governments meet in various configurations, often makes decisions on the basis of consensus, as well. As introduced by the Lisbon Treaty, a procedure of secession specifies the right to leave of member states.

The right to secede and council governance are typical of a confederation. A confederation is a looser federal political system than a federation, and it is made up of member states and not a single people (Chryssochoou, 2001, p. 68). A confederation is based on treaties and not on a constitution. Peoples' primary loyalty is still to the member states (Burgess, 2000, pp. 266–267). Member state governments also retain the right to exercise foreign policy. In a council, governments settle conflicts peacefully and consensually. Implementation is primarily the responsibility of the member states. These characteristics of a confederation also feature more or less prominently in the EU. This is less the case with respect to other characteristics of an ideal-type confederation. Here, the general authority is subordinate to the regional governments. The general authority is not directly elected by citizens, and does not operate directly upon them. With its combination of federal and confederal elements, the EU is a hybrid (Watts, 2007), a new federal political system that lies somewhere in between federation and confederation (Burgess, 2006, p. 239).

The EU partially resembles a confederation and partially a federation. Is it, therefore, justified to draw insights from comparisons with federations and confederations? A comparison would be applicable because of partial resemblance. Also, engaging in comparison does not equate to claiming that the EU is a full-fledged federation. Additionally, the EU has already been compared to federations to examine its decision-making, task allocation, and the evolution of welfare and healthcare policies, among other things (Benson & Jordan, 2008; Obinger, Leibfried, & Castles, 2005; Scharpf, 1988; Vollaard, Van de Bovenkamp, & Martinsen, 2016). These comparative analyses are valuable in their ability to help us tease out crucial factors and mechanisms pertinent to the way the EU functions. However, the issue of disintegration is of a different nature than the day-to-day functioning of the EU. The EU's treaty-based nature seems to suggest that comparison to confederations is warranted, as it is not based on a constitution. Nevertheless, studies of the disintegration of not only confederations but federations as well will be considered in terms of their being able to explain European disintegration. First, disintegration is not just a matter of law, international or domestic, but also of politics, economics, and culture. Additionally, given the dearth of explanations of disintegration, the search for an explanation should be broad in scope. Even without arguing that the EU is a full-fledged federation, it is still possible to gain analytical insight into the process of disintegration by means of comparison.

Federations and confederations are territorial species of federal political systems. Consociations are non-territorial species of shared rule and self-rule. In them, power is divided between relatively permanent, autonomous societal segments of cultural, religious, or ethnic origin, and is shared by the segments' leaders at the central level (Elazar, 1991, p. xvi; Lijphart, 1977, p. 42). Consociations are characterised by the accommodation of societal diversity through segmental autonomy, segments' veto power, and consensus seeking in a depoliticised, diplomacy-like style of politics at the central level (Lijphart, 1977). Consociational politics have been practised or promoted in divided societies such as the Netherlands, Belgium, Austria, Lebanon, and Northern Ireland. The EU has also been examined from a consociational perspective, in particular because of the accommodative practices it employs to deal with the diversity of its segments, the member states (Chryssochoou, 2001; Costa & Magnette, 2003; Hix, 1994, p. 20; Papadopoulos & Magnette, 2010; Taylor, 1990). Nevertheless, the segments of the EU, its member states, are territorial entities. In *sensu stricto*, consociation is thus not applicable to the EU (Costa & Magnette, 2003, p. 3). But given this search for an adequate explanation of European disintegration, and for similar reasons that federations provide useful comparisons, a comparative analysis of consociations can also be taken into account. Arend Lijphart, one of the main proponents of consociationalism, identified elite prudence as the factor most crucial to sustaining an accommodative pact. Maintaining federal systems might thus be a largely voluntary matter. Studies of consociationalism also offer a list of conditions that may serve to foster accommodative behaviour, such as a political system of limited size, existing overarching loyalties, and relative economic equality (Andeweg, 2000). These studies have remained inconclusive with regard to determining the causes of consociationalism, however. Therefore, the next section discusses how disintegration can be conceptualised and explained from the perspective of comparative federalism only.

4.3   INTEGRATION AND DISINTEGRATION OF FEDERAL POLITICAL SYSTEMS

In states such as Belgium and Spain, federal arrangements were concluded to keep the state united in the face of autonomist, separatist claims. These so-called "holding-together" federations are different from "coming-together" federations, in which previously independent entities form a new overarching, federal or supranational polity (Stepan, 1999). The USA, Switzerland, and Australia exemplify this latter type of federation. Since the EU and its predecessors also originated from relatively independent entities, other examples of coming-together federations might provide useful comparative material, as an explanation of integration turned on its head might indicate why disintegration takes place.

One of the most well-known accounts of the origin of federations, specifically, is provided by William Riker. Instead of being the result of economic growth or a quest for freedom, he perceived federal bargains as "always" emerging almost entirely from rational considerations of military security (Riker, 1964). In his view, a federal bargain is offered by those who are not able or not willing to expand their power by force in order to meet a security threat. Such a pact is accepted by those who seek protection from a certain threat. Even if many consider security to be an important aspect of an explanation of the initiation of federal systems, there is a great deal of empirical evidence to fundamentally refute his claim (Burgess, 2006; McKay, 2004). Furthermore, Riker himself did not expect the European Community to become a federation because it lacked a common security threat (Riker, 1975, pp. 130–131). The Soviet Union, communism, and the prospect of another war could, however, be seen as shared security threats that led to the first steps of cooperation and integration in Western Europe, but that is not the main issue here. What is problematic in terms of Riker's explanation is that fundamental steps towards an EU federation, including the establishment of binding power on the part of a directly elected European Parliament, were made at the very moment when (these) security threats disappeared in the early 1990s (McKay, 2004). Apparently, there are factors other than military threats that matter in the making of federations.

Studies of coming-together federations show that other factors and motives matter too, like the presence of external elites, assets and will of these elites, cultural commonalities, economic insecurity, a desire for post-colonial independence, economic compatibility, institutional similarities, shared political values, social mobility, mutual predictability, and the appeal of federalism (Burgess, 2006, p. 100; Deutsch et al., 1957, p. 25ff; Etzioni, 2001; Franck, 1968). It appears that a mono-causal explanation is not sufficient to account for the initiation of a federation. How relevant the aforementioned common interests and threats are to the process differ from federation to federation. These interests and threats just constitute a list that can also be applied to the initiation of the EU (Burgess, 2006, p. 100). This list of factors is somewhat insufficient, however, because it does not provide an indication of their relative importance or account for whether or not and how they are interconnected in a dynamic process of disintegration. Moreover, some factors may no longer be relevant, as new factors have appeared in the age of globalisation and digitalisation. The usefulness of explanations of the initiation of federations is, therefore, somewhat limited.

There is another reason why explanations of the initiation of federations turned on their heads might be of limited use. Even if the presence of security threats were the only necessary and sufficient condition required to *produce* coming-together federations, Riker (1964, p. 50) argued that it is not necessarily sufficient to *maintain* a federation over time. For example, the states of the USA maintained a federal system in spite of the fact that they no longer faced major existential security threats as they did in the beginning phase. Also, other analysts of (failed) federations argue that that which is required to initiate a federation is different from what is required to maintain it (Etzioni, 2001; Franck, 1968). The question is, of course, whether or not the EU has evolved beyond its starting phase. At the very least, the EU has definitely not remained only a reality on paper. The EU does function on its own, as it no longer relies exclusively on external actors or its member states to function as a political system, even in areas in which member states prefer no or limited EU involvement, such as taxation or the financing and organising of healthcare (Genschel & Jachtenfuchs, 2011; Vollaard et al., 2016). In comparison to the first decades of US federation, the EU's rule has developed to a much greater extent in terms of breadth of policy areas and depth of interference within member states. If the EU is, therefore, no longer in its starting phase, factors other than those relevant to its initiation would have to explain its survival and its eventual demise. Additionally, if the EU can be seen as a federal system that has extended beyond its starting phase, the findings from studies of holding-together federations may also be relevant to an exploration of the EU's survival and demise.

What has been put forward, thus far, to explain the maintenance and failure of federal political systems? As said, fundamental to a federal political system is the combination of self-rule and shared rule. Given this definition, maintenance and failure of a federal system cannot automatically be equated with integration and disintegration respectively. First of all, studies of maintained and failing federal systems are often focused on the centre's limitations or encroachment upon sub-units' self-rule. A complete failure would thus be the end of self-rule, turning a federal system into a unitary one. If the full integration of sub-units into a political system is the end result of federal failure, it is clearly not an instance of disintegration. Nevertheless, the attempts of a federal centre to limit sub-units' self-rule can still provide an important explanation as to why these sub-units might seek more autonomy or secession.

The understanding of maintenance and failure of federal systems presented above has also implications for the qualification of centralisation and decentralisation as integration and disintegration, respectively. Decentralisation and centralisation are permanent features of any political system, including federal ones. Competences and budgets can shift between the various levels of government. Decentralisation is not disintegration if the granting of more competences and increased budget to the sub-units ends up sustaining the basic federal rules of the game. This also means that the basic federal rules of the game are more than just institutional arrangements. They also involve a notion of loyalty on the part of the federal centre and sub-units towards the basic federal principle (Burgess, 2012, Chap. 1). Federalism is etymologically related to the Latin words for pact, covenant (*foedus*) and trust (*fides*). Thus, without the notion of loyalty, shared and self-rule is just an institutional façade. As such, decentralisation may actually be an integrative move, if sub-units are thusly enticed to adhere more strongly to the federal system.

In this sense, asymmetric federalism (or, in EU terms, differentiated integration) is also *not* disintegration if it sustains the basic federal rules of the game that underpin the EU. Additionally, federal crises are not necessarily a question of disintegration. Federal systems are prone to political immobility and institutional sclerosis due to the near unanimity that is often required in shared decision-making (Scharpf, 1988). However, deadlock in solving certain political problems is a crisis *of* as opposed to *in* the federation if the basic federal rules of the game themselves are at stake. Conflicts on sharing and dividing rule in the present-day Iraqi federation are clear instances of the latter.

Many federal studies have focused on the secession of sub-units as the instance of disintegration (see below). Yet, disintegration can also be seen in sub-units' non-compliance with or ignorance of federal rule (Kelemen, 2007). To be sure, non-compliance is a common feature of any political system. Failing implementation of federal rule (or late and incorrect transposition of EU directives, for that matter) is, therefore, not necessarily indicative of disintegration. To qualify as disintegration, non-compliance must relate to the basic rules of the game of a federal system, that is, the combination of shared rule and self-rule (cf. Glencross, 2009). This leads to another reflection concerning the analysis of disintegration from a federal perspective. Whereas in some parts of a federal system compliance and loyalty grow, they might not do so in other parts because of secession or non-compliance. Various cases of disintegration can take place simultaneously alongside various cases of integration. Additionally, secession from a federal system by a member state does not necessarily yield the collapse of the entire system, which is another type of (federal) disintegration (Kelemen, 2007). Before discussing explanations of secession, federal studies will be analysed in search of a convincing explanation of systemic sustainability and disintegration.

In his analysis of various attempts to create federations in post-colonial Asia, Africa, and Latin America, Thomas Franck (1968, p. 177) postulated that federations might start for a variety of reasons, but if any one factor explains the maintenance of federalism, it is the long-term political-ideological commitment to the idea or the value of federal unity on the part of leaders or the population of the constituent units. This commitment can be fostered by the presence of an external threat, the sub-units' cultural commonalities or the sub-units' economic compatibility, but these factors are, in and of themselves, neither sufficient nor necessary to sustain a federation.

However, other studies of comparative federalism have identified factors other than simply a federal commitment that explain how federal systems are maintained. As a matter of fact, they offer a dishearteningly large number and variety of factors that have influenced or could potentially influence the maintenance of federalism. Maintenance might depend on the cost of dissolution or withdrawal relative to the continuation of the pact (McKay, 2004). It might also depend on the number and size of the sub-units. Dyadic federations, such as Malaysia-Singapore, Serbia-Montenegro, and Czechoslovakia, were more prone to break up because they lacked flexible coalitions of similar weight between sub-units (McGarry & O'Leary, 2009, p. 19). It might depend on the number of nations involved, as multinational federations face more existential problems than monocultural ones (Watts, 2007, p. 230). It might depend on the reluctance of richer sub-units to redistribute wealth to other sub-units in the face of economic crisis (McGarry & O'Leary, 2009, p. 9). It might depend on the location of the capital. If the capital is based in the most powerful sub-unit, as was the case in Yugoslavia, the Soviet Union, and Czechoslovakia, subsequent neglect of peripheral sub-units could elicit calls for secession (Henderson, 2002). It might depend on the centre's capacity to act decisively in quickly changing circumstances, unhampered by the requirement of consensus of the member states, as in the case of Yugoslavia (Kovačević & Samardžić, 2016). It might depend on the extent to which federal elites are able to generate legitimacy among and utility for members (Etzioni, 2001). It might depend on the presence of effective channels of communication and representation at the federal level (Etzioni, 2001). It might depend on the relative loyalty to the federal level on the part of sub-units' elites and masses. It might depend on which level has a hold on the legitimate use of violence (Etzioni, 2001). It might depend on the will and resources available to the centre (Elazar, 1987). It might depend on the presence of liberal democracy (Burgess, 2012, p. 236). It might depend on the presence or absence of a federal spirit (Burgess, 2012, p. 236). It might depend on the geographical proximity and the related opportunities for sufficient interregional communication (Hicks, 1978). It might depend on fiscal imbalances in a federal system (Hicks, 1978). It might depend on the presence of a common external threat (Hicks, 1978). It might depend on flexibility in the constitutional set-up of a federal system to meet changing demands from sub-units (Watts,

1977). It might depend on the centre's control of sub-units. In this respect, in 1987, Riker and his fellow author John Lemco expected Yugoslavia, the Soviet Union, and Czechoslovakia to be strong enough to survive for the foreseeable future (McKay, 2004). It might depend on political parties and the party system. If parties are encouraged to orient themselves both towards sub-units *and* the central level to gain influence and votes, instead of focusing exclusively on specific regions, as the Parti Québécois does in Canada, they can be an integrative force, thereby sustaining the federal system (Filippov et al., 2004; Riker, 1975). It might depend on the uniting force of shared electoral activities throughout all sub-units, like the presidential elections in the USA or referenda in Switzerland (Glencross, 2009, p. 29). Separate electoral constituencies with separate campaigns, as seen in the Belgian federal elections or the European Parliamentary elections, might be more likely to foster disintegration than unity. It might depend on the support of external facilitators, like the UK in the case of the Federation of the West Indies and the USA in the case of European integration (Etzioni, 2001; Haldén, 2009). It might depend on the presence of consociational government with accommodative decision-making involving the sub-units at the federal level (McGarry & O'Leary, 2007). It might depend on the absence of cross-cutting cleavages (Watts, 1977).

Given the variety of factors found in studies of (failing) federations, it is probably not just one single factor that explains the disintegration of a federal system (Watts, 1977, p. 53). The above-mentioned factors derived from studies of federations can, however, be used as a checklist to help determine how weak or strong the EU is relative to other (failed) federal systems. The likelihood of EU disintegration might be determined on this basis. It is also likely that certain factors that explain the maintenance of a federal system have not yet been discussed because only a certain set of (failing) federations have been studied. Nevertheless, the question remains as to whether or not it would be helpful to identify more factors. As several authors have pointed out, each individual instance of federalism features a different constellation of factors. As a result, even a complete checklist derived from previous or current instances of failed or sustained federalism might gloss over factors that are relevant to today's EU and that of tomorrow. Furthermore, some factors such as centralisation or the presence of external facilitators might have both integrative and disintegrative effects, depending on how the process of disintegration unfolds (Deutsch et al., 1957, p. 86). A simple list of one or more potentially important factors that sustain or undermine a federal system is, therefore, a somewhat insufficient starting point to explain EU disintegration. Explaining EU disintegration requires an explanation that also accounts for the way in which factors are interrelated, mutually dependent, and/or neutralising in the context of the complexities of federal systems.

According to Deutsch et al. (1957, p. 59ff), no factor or combination of factors is necessarily sufficient to explain disintegration in *all* instances. It is a matter of balancing between loads and capabilities in each and every instance of disintegration. For instance, if a federal system faces excessive military commitments, suddenly increasing political participation, economic decline, excessively delayed reforms that people are longing for, growing ethnic or linguistic differentiation, or access to elite positions is reduced, the system might not have the capacity to respond effectively to prevent disintegration. Even if this explanation somehow indicates an interrelationship between factors, it remains somewhat indeterminate what this interrelationship is. What does balance look like, here?

Some recent studies of self-reinforcing mechanisms that sustain federal systems have begun to tease out this interplay of various factors more precisely (Bednar, 2009; Kelemen, 2007). Jenna Bednar seeks to assess the robustness of federations, including the EU. In her view, a federation's robustness is a matter of compliance with the federal bargain, resilience against flaws in its design and external shocks, and the capability to adapt to changing needs. In her view, non-compliance can be a matter of the centre encroaching upon sub-units' self-rule, and sub-units breaking the rules of the federal principle or shirking their responsibilities within the federation. Correction by force is rather expensive (and impossible in the EU) and may also be counterproductive, as it has the potential to evoke anti-federalist sentiment. As such, Bednar suggests that a federation's robustness increases as its set of self-reinforcing safeguards expands, which still includes force as the ultimate means of retaliation. Structural safeguards against non-compliance relate to the fragmentation of power by means of shared competences and enshrined checks and balances. Popular safeguards function as a control on governments at both levels and can also increase the legitimacy of the federation. Parties and the party system tying the federal and sub-unit level together are the political safeguards. A constitutional court that operates as neutral umpire constitutes the judicial safeguard.

Each and every safeguard has its limitations. A structural guarantee of sub-units' veto at the federal level could lead to a deadlock, blocking the integrative or disintegrative steps necessary to allow the federation to adapt to changing needs. The electorate faces challenges of information gathering and coordination in correcting governments that violate the federal pact. A constitutional court can be considered too biased, while at the same time it may lack the capacity to enforce the implementation of its verdicts. It is, however, the full set of safeguards that guarantees a federation's robustness. For example, laying down and judicially upholding structural safeguards can engender popular support for (membership in the) federative entity. The various safeguards also provide a range of instruments from mild to severe in strength with which to respond proportionately to small and large transgressions against the federal pact. It would, thus, prevent a potential backlash against harsh enforcement by force. If a single safeguard fails to guarantee compliance due to continuous transgressions or inappropriate use, other safeguards function as a backup and correction. A variety of safeguards also allows for them to be applied rather flexibly, adjusting their use to suit new situations. Deliberation on the (flexible) use of safeguards can also generate a common federal culture underpinning the federal pact. In sum, a combination of safeguards fosters compliance, resilience, and adaptation in a federation.

This set of potentially self-reinforcing safeguards allows us to focus more clearly on the relevant factors and their mutual relationship in an effort to explore the robustness of a federation and the EU, in particular. Based on analysis such as this, in 2007, EU federalism scholar Daniel Kelemen concluded that the EU is "built to last". Bednar (2009, pp. 137–139) is more cautious in her assessment, however. Yes, structural safeguards prevent the centre's encroachment upon member states' rights. Member state governments have a substantial say in EU decision-making via the Council and the European Council. Voting by qualified majority and treaty revision by unanimity also make it more difficult for EU institutions to undermine member states' self-rule. However, the fragmentation of power at the EU level may preclude it from undertaking timely and necessary measures to adapt to the changing needs of EU institutions and member states. Additionally, EU institutions are less constrained by popular safeguards, since most of them are not directly responsible to the electorate(s). This is true for the Court of Justice of the European Union (CJEU) and the European Central Bank (ECB), in particular. These institutions have used their power to foster European integration, making the CJEU less convincing in its role as a neutral, unbiased umpire arbitrating between the EU and its member states. The lack of an umpire that is perceived to be neutral also touches upon a more problematic aspect of the EU's robustness, at least according to Bednar, regarding the limited safe-guards in place to counter rule breaking, shirking, and burden shifting by member states. The EU can only rely on the voice of law, fines, funding, and loans to prevent and/or correct transgressions by member states. It has no other coercive means of last resort. Additionally, a rather thin fed-eral culture, if it exists at all in the EU, and a stronger cultural attachment to national states prevent electorates from correcting their governments if they violate the federal principle. The option to exit that is available to EU member states also limits the effect of judicial and participatory safeguards (Bednar, 2009, p. 162).

Bednar also perceives the political safeguards in place to mediate EU-national conflicts to be "non-significant". Due to the predominantly nationally oriented campaigns for national and European elections in the member states, elites in the national governments, the Council, the European Council, and the European Parliament are encouraged to serve the interests of national electorates rather than the EU as a whole. Nevertheless, this divisive behaviour might start to be contained by European party groupings. For example, these groupings united behind their candidates for the presidency of the European Commission in the 2014 European elections. Furthermore, even Eurosceptic parties, both from economic left (including Syriza) and cultural right (including UKIP, AfD, the Danish People's Party, the Freedom Party, and Front National), have started to integrate by creating groupings at the level of the European Parliament. This integration could thus foster deliberation at the EU level, thereby enhancing the links between Eurosceptic parts of the public and the EU, as anti-system parties have done elsewhere. And however frail the party-political bonds may be in comparison to those in the USA or Germany, the entire set of safeguards might still encourage sufficient deliberation and interaction to create some sort of federal culture (Kelemen, 2007). Be that as it may, in comparison to the American and German federations, the EU's set of complementary, self-reinforcing safe-guards aimed at preventing disintegration is weaker.

The set of safeguards can, thus, be used to determine the relative robustness of the EU and to predict its chances of disintegrating, as compared to other federal systems in highlighting various interdependen-cies between the safeguards. It is also quite flexible and could be extended to include factors specific to the federation being discussed. For example, an external power could function as a sort of judicial safeguard in a federation. The federation would be more robust if the external power were accepted as a neutral umpire in conflicts over the division of power. Nevertheless, the set of safeguards still remains a sort of checklist, similar to the list of factors presented above. The mechanisms by which the process(es) of disintegration might unfold remain unclear. Additionally, the set lacks any reflection on the boundaries of a federal system, even though these have changed continuously throughout the EU's history. Even if it provides useful building blocks for understanding the (dis)integrative dynamics of federal systems, a more process-oriented and comprehensive explanation is still needed.

4.4   SECESSION AND THE EUROPEAN UNION

The previous section discussed disintegration from a systemic point of view. It discussed the features of a federal system that might explain its maintenance and disintegration. Disintegration also includes the non-compliance and secession of a member state. Many federal studies examined the latter instance of disintegration. Their starting point is John Woods' definition of the term, "formal withdrawal from a central political authority by a member unit or units on the basis of a claim to independent sovereign status" (Wood, 1981, p. 110). Wood considers secession to be the "reversal" and "antithesis" of political integration as defined by Ernst Haas (see Chap. 2). It thus involves the shift of loyalties, expectations, and activities to the subsystem of certain actors resulting in a new state. Wood's definition of secession clearly reflects a bias towards the territorial state. This also holds for other definitions, even if they vary considerably in terms of the role of the host state (is consent required or not?), the inclusion of decolonisation (are colonies member units of the host state?) and the dissolution of the Austro-Hungarian empire and Soviet Union (are these instances of secession or imperial fragmentation?) (Pavkovic, 2015). The definition selected clearly matters in terms of legal interpretation, but it also matters in terms of comparative analysis. In the search for an appropriate starting point from which to explain EU disintegration, this chapter adopts a rather inclusive definition of secession. Moreover, even if the cases involved are somewhat dissimilar, they still have in common a "process of alienation" between sub-unit and centre that provides a basis for comparative analysis (Wood, 1981, p. 110).

Given the inclusive understanding of secession adopted here, cases can be found in the time period after the right of secession was acknowledged in the context of the principle of national self-determination in the aftermath of the First World War and the collapse of the Ottoman and Austro-Hungarian empires (Horowitz, 2003). Also, later, during the process of decolonisation and in the post-communist era, secession took shape in large part as the (re-)recognition of sovereign territorial states, even if they did not contain a single nation, be it of civic or ethnic in nature. As a result, violent conflicts not only accompanied processes of secession, but also took place *within* the new states, where nationalising policies often prompted additional claims of secession (cf. McGarry & O'Leary, 2009). Both federal and unitary states in Europe have also faced the challenges of violent attempts to limit or end the centre's say in a specific geographical area, from Corsica, Abkhazia, Northern Ireland, the Basque Country, Lithuania, Croatia, Kosovo and Eastern Ukraine to Flanders, Padania, Scotland, and Catalonia. The issue of secession has also played out in other parts of the world, in the past and present, such as in Western Australia, East Timor, Aceh, East Pakistan, Tibet, the Confederate States of America, Québec, Nevis, Western Sahara, Biafra, South Sudan, and Eritrea. Secession is thus common in multinational and federal entities, like the EU.

Secession has received increasing attention in the EU after the introduction of an exit clause allowing for withdrawal of a member state in the Lisbon Treaty (2007) and the discussion of Brexit, the withdrawal of the UK from the EU. Withdrawal had been an issue prior to this, however. After the UK joined the European Economic Community (EEC) in 1973, a large segment of the British Labour Party maintained its resistance to it. When Labour entered government, it organised a referendum on the continuation of EEC membership in 1975. However, a sizeable majority of the electorate voted in favour of it. Furthermore, Algeria's independence and the introduction of home rule in Greenland resulted in a limitation of the European treaties' territorial scope in 1962 and 1985, respectively. In the various rounds of treaty making throughout EU history, the conditions and procedure of an (implicit) option of withdrawal have been discussed (Zbíral, 2007). An explicit arrangement for withdrawal came about in the deliberations on the European Constitutional Treaty, in an effort to emphasise the voluntary nature of EU membership. In the end, even the constitutions of the Soviet Union, Yugoslavia, and Ethiopia contained a right of secession. After the failed ratification of the Constitutional Treaty, its clause on the procedure to conclude an agreement on withdrawal was copied into the Lisbon Treaty with only a few technical changes. In providing for voluntary withdrawal, the clause also explicitly acknowledges the unilateral right of withdrawal of member states of the EU (Athanassiou, 2009). Forced withdrawal, or full expulsion, from the EU does not seem legally acceptable, in contrast to temporary suspension of voting rights when a member state seriously and persistently breaches EU principles. The issue of forced withdrawal gained traction during the debt crises when it was suggested that Greece be expelled from the Economic and Monetary Union (EMU).

Even if (forced) withdrawal is not *legally* possible, it is not impossible in practice. Comparative material on the subject of forced withdrawal is rather limited, with Singapore's expulsion from the Federation of Malaya in 1965 being the sole instance. This may be a reflection of the general reluctance of any type of government to give up territory. More comparative material is available on self-imposed secession, however, studied from the perspective of a variety of disciplines and approaches including constitutional and international law, history, philosophy, rational choice, economics, sociology, as well as political science. Regardless of the inclusiveness of the definition of secession, scholars still struggle to formulate a theory of secession (Dion, 1996; Hechter, 1992; Pavkovic with Radan, 2009; Wood, 1981). Scholarly analysis does, though, present a wide variety of motives, (necessary) conditions, factors, and stages of development in cases of secession.

The first category of motives, conditions, and factors is of a geographical nature and includes the geographical concentration of a certain group and pre-existing geographical distinctions (Wood, 1981, pp. 112–114). A second category concerns motives, conditions, and factors of a social nature. It includes the linguistic, religious, ethnic, or cultural basis on which the common identity of a group is fostered, for which more (territorial) autonomy is sought. An exclusive understanding of identity, a denial of the presence of other identities or groups in one and the same political entity, and a lack of interaction with other groups are believed to stimulate calls for autonomy. A psychological category of relevant motives, conditions, and factors includes the emotive sense of belonging together, among other things, both within the sub-unit and the host state, as well as the sense of alienation between sub-unit and host state. Fear around the situation of the sub-unit within the host state and confidence about its prospects outside are also of a psychological nature, although they may also reflect political, economic, and social considerations (Dion, 1996).

Another category includes economic factors, usually expressed in terms of a rational cost-benefit calculus of leaving vs. staying. Economic self-confidence has been identified as a reason why richer regions are more inclined to secede (Hale, 2000). The opposite has, however, also been argued, based on the greater desire of economically backward, peripheralised regions to leave (Hechter, 1992). Other economic factors mentioned include the geographical concentration of natural resources such as oil (in the case of Biafra and Scotland), declining willingness of rich entities to share money and work with poorer ones in the face of economic decline (in the case of Flanders and Catalonia), and closely connected welfare democracies in the present-day, globalised world (in the case of Québec). The eventual costs of exit may often be dependent upon how cooperative both the host state and the seceding region intend to be. Furthermore, it can also depend on the type of public good in question. The cost of secession is higher in the event that the new state can be excluded from the public goods produced by the host state (cf. Kölliker, 2006).

The next category consists of a variety of motives, conditions, and factors of a political nature. Major differences in political preferences (for instance, on slavery in the antebellum US, or on the economic role of state in Québec and Scotland) and the rest of the host state can stimulate secession. Systems with dominant regions are more vulnerable to secession by peripheral sub-units than ones without, as they may be better able to easily suppress smaller member states (Hale, 2004; McGarry & O'Leary, 2009). The explicit acknowledgement of a right of secession may also provide member states with the rhetorical resources required to seek secession (Anderson, 2007). The right of self-rule is also considered to increase the likelihood of secession, as it provides the institutional resources required for a member state to mobilise support for secession and lowers the costs of establishing an independent state (Anderson, 2004). However, this claim is highly contested in the federalism literature, as (more) self-rule can also have a pacifying effect (Erk & Anderson, 2009; McGarry & O'Leary, 2009). Political entrepreneurs, like regionalist parties, can play a major role in moving secession to the stage of action (Wood, 1981). They can successfully mobilise support for secession in the domestic and international arenas, even if a majority of the region's population does not favour full independence (Dion, 1996).

In the stage of action, political institutions are considered to be of importance too. In weak states, secessionists see a greater opportunity to liberate themselves from central rule. In democratic settings, willingness to address calls to do justice for a certain sub-unit and give it more autonomy is, generally speaking, more likely to be present than it would be in authoritarian systems. Additionally, democratic structures allow for a greater say on the part of sub-units, be it through the specific set-up of legislative elections, the composition of the federal government, or a constitutional court. Without institutional arrangements to allow for their voices to be heard, secessionists might turn to violence instead. External involvement would also matter in this respect in the form of trading weapons or engendering hope of international recognition as a new state, even if such geopolitical factors are usually seen as being detrimental to secession (Hechter, 1992). The use of violence also depends on the way the host state responds. A repressive response is expected to result in more violence than an accommodative one. Nevertheless, a host state might seek to discourage other sub-units from seeking secession by responding with force, since successful succession attempts can encourage others to follow suit (Hale, 2000; Walter, 2006). The developments after secessionist movements in Slovenia and Lithuania in Yugoslavia and Soviet Union, respectively, are examples of this.

This list of conditions, motives, and factors could be used to predict which geographical entity might be more prone to secession from the EU than others. These conditions can be categorised according to the following groups: (1) those related to the fear of a sub-unit of staying in a federal system and (2) those related to the confidence of a sub-unit about its survival after independence (Dion, 1996, p. 271). To be sure, this overview of conditions, motives, factors, and stages of development is not complete. Similar to the factors identified above that related to the maintenance and failure of a federal system, the question is whether or not a complete overview is of much help. Here too, several authors have pointed out that each case of secession features a different constellation of motives, conditions, factors, and stages of development. As a result, even a complete a checklist might overlook elements that are relevant to the EU today and tomorrow. Furthermore, some elements such as the extent of self-rule might have both integrative and disintegrative effects. A checklist of potential motives, conditions, and factors relating to secession is, therefore, an unsatisfying starting point from which to explain the process of EU disintegration, or more specifically, processes of secession from the EU.

Several studies of secession, however, have shown how these factors might be dynamically linked in such a process in their discussion of the connection between the extent of power-sharing at the federal level and secessionism (McGarry & O'Leary, 2009). For example, the offer of a greater voice in the federal system can effectively defuse a call for exit (Slapin, 2009). As illustrated above, these studies adopt Albert Hirschman's taxonomy of how organisations respond to internal dissatisfaction. Strangely enough, the third component of Hirschman's triad of exit, voice, and loyalty has been largely neglected.

By definition, secession studies also assume that the aim of secession is the (re)establishment of a sovereign, territorial state. However, a full account of disintegration should avoid this state-centric bias and explain *why* a system such as the EU would necessarily fall apart into its constituent states once again. First of all, secession from the EU might also mean accession to another regional organisation, rather than the full restoration of territorial sovereignty. Furthermore, a number of entities might leave the EU as a collective, for example, to establish a northern Euro-area, as was suggested during the debt crises. Additionally, why would it necessarily be the case that only geographically concentrated entities would be the ones seceding? Parallel societies of (illegal) migrants or a collective of digitally connected, foreign-held companies or banks can also effectively withdraw themselves from the system of EU rule. Even if it is somewhat hypothetical at this point to imagine this type of non-state secession, the reasons why we should *not* expect it should be explained rather than assumed.

4.5   CONCLUSION

Comparative federalism has already been the basis of a few accounts of European disintegration, and of accounts of disintegrative tendencies in other multinational, federal systems, such as the Federation of the West Indies and Canada. Comparisons of the EU to these systems could help to tease out the crucial factors relating to and the dynamics of the process of disintegration. Based on analysis of the maintenance and failure of federal systems, it is likely that a host of factors affect disintegration of the EU and secession from the EU. Certain factors can be both conducive to integration and disintegration, depending on the specific context of the (failing) federal system. The challenge remains to specify how these factors are mutually dependent on one another in the processes of EU disintegration, while avoiding a state-centric bias. To address this challenge, comparative federalism offers a few useful building blocks. First, it clearly separates explanations of disintegration of the system as a whole and by an individual member state. Additionally, it provides for a broader and subtler understanding of disintegration that extends beyond territorial secession, with its focus on non-compliance with the basic rules of the game that underpin a federal system. As said, studies of comparative federalism have generally taken the framework of the territorial state for granted. However, the EU has experienced continuing geographical expansion, which may have made its integration and disintegration follow a logic that is distinct from that of a federation, and more similar to that of an empire. The following chapter will, therefore, discuss disintegration from an "imperial" perspective.

REFERENCES

Anderson, L. (2004). Exploring the paradox of autonomy: Federalism and secession in North America. *Regional & Federal Studies, 14*(1), 89–112.

Anderson, L. (2007). Federalism and secessionism: Institutional influences on nationalist policies in Québec. *Nationalism and Ethnic Politics, 13*(2), 187–211.

Andeweg, R. B. (2000). Consociational democracy. *Annual Review of Political Science, 3*, 509–536.

Athanassiou, P. (2009). *Withdrawal and expulsion from the EU and EMU: Some reflections.* Frankfurt: European Central Bank.

Bednar, J. (2009). *The robust federation: Principles of design.* Cambridge: Cambridge University Press.

Benson, D., & Jordan, A. (2008). Understanding task allocation in the European Union: Exploring the value of federal theory. *Journal of European Public Policy, 15*(1), 78–97.

Börzel, T., & Hosli, M. (2003). Brussels between Bern and Berlin: Comparative federalism meets the European Union. *Governance, 16*(2), 179–202.

Burgess, M. (2000). *Federalism and the European Union: The building of Europe, 1950–2000.* London: Routledge.

Burgess, M. (2006). *Comparative federalism: Theory and practice.* London: Routledge.

Burgess, M. (2012). *In search of the federal spirit: New theoretical and empirical perspectives in comparative federalism.* Oxford: Oxford University Press.

Chryssochoou, D. N. (2001). *Theorizing European integration.* London: Sage.

Costa, O., & Magnette, P. (2003). The European Union as a consociation? A methodological assessment. *West European Politics, 26*(3), 1–18.

Deutsch, K. W., with Burrell, S. A., Kann, R. A., Lee Jr, M., Lichterman, M., Lindgren, R. E., Loewenheim, F. L., & Van Wagenen, R. W. (1957). *Political community and the North Atlantic area: International organization in the light of historical experience.* Princeton, NJ: Princeton University Press.

Dion, S. (1996). Why is secession difficult in well-established democracies? Lessons from Quebec. *British Journal of Political Science, 26*(2), 269–283.

Elazar, D. (1987). *Exploring federalism*. Tuscaloosa, AL: University of Alabama Press.

Elazar, D. J. (1991). Introduction: Federalist responses to current democratic revolutions. In D. J. Elazar (Ed.), *Federal systems of the world: A handbook of federal, confederal and autonomy arrangements* (pp. i–xxi). Harlow: Longman.

Erk, J., & Anderson, L. (2009). The paradox of federalism: Does self-rule accommodate or exacerbate ethnic division? *Ethnopolitics, 19*(2), 191–202.

Etzioni, A. (2001). *Political unification revisited*. Lanham, MD: Lexington Books.

Fischer, J. (2000). *From confederacy to federation: Thoughts on the finality of European integration*. Retrieved July 8, 2017, from http://ec.europa.eu/dorie/fileDownload.do?docId=192161&cardId=192161

Filippov, M., Ordeshook, P. C., & Shvetsova, O. (2004). *Designing federalism: A theory of self-sustaining federal institutions*. Cambridge: Cambridge University Press.

Forsyth, M. (2007). Federalism, nationality, statehood: The problem of the European Union. In M. Burgess & J. Pinder (Eds.), *Multinational federations* (pp. 150–179). Abingdon: Routledge.

Franck, T. (1968). *Why federations fail: An inquiry into the requisites for successful federation*. London: University of London Press.

Genschel, P., & Jachtenfuchs, M. (2011). How the European Union constrains the state: Multilevel governance of taxation. *European Journal of Political Research, 50*, 293–314.

Glencross, A. (2009). *What makes the EU viable? European integration in the light of the antebellum US experience*. Basingstoke: Palgrave Macmillan.

Hale, H. (2000). The parade of sovereignties: Testing theories of secession in the Soviet setting. *British Journal of Political Science, 30*(1), 31–56.

Hale, H. (2004). Divided we stand: Institutional sources of ethnofederal state survival and collapse. *World Politics, 56*(2), 165–193.

Haldén, P. (2009). *Stability without statehood: Lessons from Europe's history before the sovereign state*. Basingstoke: Palgrave Macmillan.

Hechter, M. (1992). The dynamics of secession. *Acta Sociologica, 35*, 267–283.

Henderson, K. (2002). *Slovakia: The escape from invisibility*. London: Routledge.

Hicks, U. K. (1978). *Federalism: Failure or success, a comparative study*. London: Macmillan.

Hix, S. (1994). The study of the European community: The challenge to comparative politics. *West European Politics, 17*(1), 1–30.

Horowitz, D. (2003). The cracked foundations of the right to secede. *Journal of Democracy, 14*(2), 5–17.

Kelemen, R. (2003). The structure and dynamics of EU federalism. *Comparative Political Studies, 36*(1/2), 184–208.

Kelemen, R. D. (2007). Built to Last? The Durability of EU Federalism. In S. Meunier & K. R. McNamara (Eds.), *Making history: European integration and institutional change at fifty* (pp. 51–66). Oxford: Oxford University Press.

Kölliker, A. (2006). *Flexibility and European unification: The logic of differentiated integration*. Lanham: Rowman & Littlefield.

Kovačević, B., & Samardžić, S. (2016). Internal crisis of compound polities: Understanding the EU's crisis in light of the ex-Yugoslav federation's failure. *Journal of Balkan and Near Eastern Studies, 18*(3), 241–262.

Lijphart, A. (1977). *Democracy in plural societies: A comparative exploration*. New Haven and London: Yale University Press.

McGarry, J., & O'Leary, B. (2007). Federations and managing nations. In M. Burgess & J. Pinder (Eds.), *Multinational federations* (pp. 180–211). Abingdon: Routledge.

McGarry, J., & O'Leary, B. (2009). Must pluri-national federations fail? *Ethnopolitics, 8*(1), 5–25.

McKay, D. (2004). William Riker on federalism: Sometimes wrong but more right than anyone else? *Regional and Federal Studies, 14*(2), 167–186.

Nicolaidis, K., & Howse, R. (Eds.). (2001). *The federal vision: Legitimacy and levels of governance in the United States and the European Union*. Oxford: Oxford University Press.

Obinger, H., Leibfried, S., & Castles, F. G. (Eds.). (2005). *Federalism and the welfare state: New world and European experiences*. Cambridge: Cambridge University Press.

Papadopoulos, Y., & Magnette, P. (2010). On the politicisation of the European Union. Lessons from consociational polities. *West European Politics, 33*(4), 711–729.

Pavkovic, A. (2015). Secession: A much contested concept. In D. Kingsbury & C. Laoutides (Eds.), *Territorial separatism in global politics: Causes, outcomes and resolution* (pp. 13–28). London: Routledge.

Pavkovic, A., with Radan, P. (Eds.). (2009). *Creating new states: Theory and practice of secession*. Hampshire: Ashgate.

Riker, W. H. (1964). *Federation/federalism: Origins, operation, significance*. Boston: Little, Brown and Company.

Riker, W. H. (1975). Federalism. In F. I. Greenstein & N. Polsby (Eds.), *The handbook of political science, Volume V: Government institutions and processes* (pp. 93–172). Reading, MA: Addison-Wesley.

Scharpf, F. (1988). The joint-decision trap: Lessons from German federalism and European integration. *Public Administration, 66*(3), 239–278.

Slapin, J. (2009). Exit, voice, and cooperation: Bargaining power in international organizations and federal systems. *Journal of Theoretical Politics, 21*(2), 187–211.

Spinelli Group. (2012, June 28). *Only a European federal union can solve the crisis: Federal Union or disintegration*. Brussels: The Spinelli Group.

Stepan, A. (1999). Federalism and democracy. *Journal of Democracy, 10*(4), 19–34.

Taylor, P. (1990). Consociationalism and federalism as approaches to international integration. In A. J. R. Groom & P. Taylor (Eds.), *Frameworks for international cooperation* (pp. 172–184). London: Pinter.

Verdun, A. (2015). The federal features of the EU: Lessons from Canada. *Politics and Governance, 4*(3), 100–110.

Vollaard, H., Van de Bovenkamp, H., & Martinsen, D. S. (2016). The making of a healthcare union: A federalist perspective. *Journal of European Public Policy, 23*(2), 157–176.

Walter, B. (2006). Information, uncertainty, and the decision to secede. *International Organization, 60*(1), 105–135.

Watts, R. (1977). Survival or disintegration. In R. Simeon (Ed.), *Must Canada fail?* (pp. 42–60). Montréal: McGill-Queen's University Press.

Watts, R. (1998). Federalism, federal political systems, and federations. *Annual Review of Political Science, 1*, 117–137.

Watts, R. (2007). Multinational federations in comparative perspective. In I. M. Burgess & J. Pinder (Eds.), *Multinational federations* (pp. 225–247). Abingdon: Routledge.

Wood, J. (1981). Secession: A comparative analytical framework. *Canadian Journal of Political Science, 14*(1), 107–134.

Zbíral, R. (2007). Searching for an optimal withdrawal clause for the European Union. In M. Niedobitek & J. Zemánek (Eds.), *The constitutional treaty: A critical appraisal* (pp. 308–323). Berlin: Duncker & Humblot.

CHAPTER 5

Comparative Imperialism and European Disintegration

5.1 Introduction

Many political systems face the challenge of disintegration. Just think of Canada, the UK, Iraq, Spain, and Belgium. In contrast, the European Union (EU) has been undergoing a process of integration. A "genuine" economic and monetary union, banking union, capital market union, energy union, defence union, and innovation union are in the making. In addition to the EU, Germany, Vietnam, Yemen, and China (Hong Kong and Macau) are the only other instances of integrating pre-existing polities in a new formation over the last decades. Whereas these latter four countries did not expand any further after their unification, the EU does not have fixed geographical borders. In this way, the EU is an exception among the already exceptional category of examples of political integration. However, the EU does share its expansive nature with empires. World history has seen a large number of empires that expanded by force, but also by invitation, and that faced decline and fall, from the Roman, Swedish, and Polish-Lithuanian empires to the Habsburg and British ones. "Comparative imperialism" could thus be the source of an explanation of the possible disintegration of the EU.

Imperialism often has negative connotations and is associated with territorial conquest, colonisation, and repression. European Commission president José Manuel Barroso once discovered this first hand when he described the EU in imperial terms, in spite of the fact that he emphasised

H. Vollaard, *European Disintegration*, Palgrave Studies in European Union Politics, https://doi.org/10.1057/978-1-137-41465-6_5

the voluntary nature of its expansion (Die Welt, 2007; Mahony, 2007). His comparison received a rather critical response from British media (Charter, 2007; Waterfield, 2007). This chapter will not deal with the normative issue of whether empire and imperialism are inherently benevolent or evil. It uses these concepts only for analytical reasons, to learn from a comparison of empires and the EU. Empire has been somewhat neglected as comparative category in political science literature, however. In spite of this, several scholars have started to use imperial perspectives in their analyses of the EU (e.g., Wæver, 1997; Zielonka, 2006). They have done so particularly because of the EU's expansive nature and its fuzzy boundaries. However, the formal equality of EU member states clearly contradicts the asymmetric relationships found within previous instances of empire (Münkler, 2005). But even if empires and the EU are only remotely similar, comparative examination of empires may offer useful insights into the process and factors that can lead to the disintegration of vast, expansive, complex, and multilayered composite systems.

This chapter will first reflect upon on the questions of why empire has been neglected as comparative category and why it could still be of added value in Sect. 5.2. Based on the conceptualisation of empire presented in Sect. 5.3, it is shown in Sect. 5.4 that the EU shares sufficient commonalities with empires to seek an explanation of disintegration in comparative analyses of imperial decline and fall. As Sect. 5.5 concludes, however, these analyses provide a list of factors rather than a clear understanding of how these factors are interrelated in the processes of disintegration. The final section indicates which lessons might still be learned from comparative imperialism in the pursuit of an explanation of EU disintegration.

5.2   Empire as Comparative Category

The European Union has often been labelled unique (in Latin: *sui generis*). It may not be helpful to refer to a political system as one of a kind, as if any comparison with other types of political system would be null and void. Making comparisons does not mean that the political systems are the same. As such, the EU has been compared to federations and international organisations for descriptive and explanatory purposes, though there has been considerable debate as to whether it is either of them. Even if the EU only resembles certain key aspects of an ideal-type empire, theories of imperial fall and decline can be applied to it. Empires have been somewhat neglected as a comparative category in contemporary political science and

EU studies, however. This neglect may not only be due to the term's pejorative connotations but also to the broadly shared perception that empires and imperialism disappeared after decolonisation (Motyl, 2001). Additionally, empires do not fit in neatly with the predominance of state-centrism in political analysis. The Peace of Westphalia (1648) is often referred to as the moment at which "the state" was born—characterised by territorial sovereignty, a separation between the hierarchy of domestic politics and the anarchy of international politics and the designation of distinct societies by state borders (cf. Agnew, 1998, p. 49). The division in scholarly analysis between politics within states (Comparative Politics) and between states (International Relations) is based on this Westphalian template (Nexon & Wright, 2007, p. 254). If the world is neatly carved up into sovereign states, this division is not necessarily problematic in terms of political analysis. However, the Westphalian assumption can make scholars unaware of political structures and developments that deviate from the Westphalian template (Agnew, 1998; Paasi, 2003; Ruggie, 1993; Zielonka, 2006). Ironically, the Westphalian treaties constitute a striking example of this. Even if they are considered the foundation of the territorial, sovereign state, the treaties concerned foremost constitutional arrangements within the Holy Roman Empire after the ravages of the Thirty Years' War (1618–1648). The treaties thus determined, among other things, the rights and responsibilities of the emperor, the Empire, ecclesiastical and secular powers, the various estates, princely territories, and imperial circles (Haldén, 2009; Wilson, 2011). Instead of the eschewing external interference, Sweden and France were instituted as the formal guarantors of imperial peace, while Sweden and England remained indirectly involved in the Holy Roman Empire through their holding of German territories. Contrary to later interpretations, the treaties themselves dealt with what was clearly a non-state entity (Osiander, 2001; Teschke, 2003). The territorial, sovereign state only became a reality in the nineteenth century in some parts of Europe.

The possibility of overlooking non-state entities also holds for empires today. The very question is therefore whether empire and imperialism fully disappeared after decolonisation. Foreign powers may still be involved in the domestic politics of another entity, but by other means than annexation and war. Less state-oriented studies from a neo-Marxist and/or anthropological perspective have pointed at continuing patterns of economic exploitation and cultural subordination as instances of imperialism (see, e.g., Hardt & Negri, 2000). Additionally, the Soviet domination of

Central and Eastern European states during the Cold War has been described as an "informal empire" (Wendt & Friedheim, 1996). It was subordination rather than anarchy that characterised the relationship between the Soviet Union and Central and Eastern Europe. Regardless of the formal sovereignty the states possessed, imperial control of both foreign and domestic policies of the subordinated continued. The economic and military domination of Western Europe by the USA in the post-Second World War period has also been called an empire in spite of its voluntary, "by invitation" nature because of the unequal relationship between the USA and its Western European partners at that time (Lundestad, 2003). Furthermore, the concepts of empire and imperialism have been applied to the USA and its war on terror in the aftermath of the 9/11 attacks (see, e.g., Cox, 2003; Ferguson, 2004). In sum, even though the idea of a world carved up into territorial, sovereign states has dominated political practice and scholarly analysis, empire and imperialism have not disappeared from the world scene.

The concepts of empire and imperialism are often used as synonyms for hegemonic rule (Nexon & Wright, 2007). However, the concept of hegemony denotes only the (temporary) interference in the foreign policy of other states by a great power in order to restore the balance of power (Nexon & Wright, 2007). Hegemony thus blurs the distinction between domestic hierarchy of sovereign states and international anarchy, the absence of any overarching power above states. A hegemonic power supplies the public goods of security and order in the anarchic world of states because of its preponderant economic, socio-cultural, and/or military capabilities. It would therefore be unlike other states with respect to its capabilities, but also in terms of its function and form. Be that as it may, the territorial state remains fundamental in the ontology of realist and geopolitical analyses of hegemonic power (Gilpin, 1988; Waltz, 1979). An imperial structure in which a dominant entity is closely and permanently involved in the foreign *and* domestic realm of one or more other political entities, formally or informally, is of a different political nature. Empire has therefore been considered a necessary addition to existing state-based conceptual categories in analysing politics (Nexon & Wright, 2007). The obvious advantage here is that the concept of empire does not suffer from a state bias (Beck & Grande, 2011). If the EU were an empire-like system, it would render any attempt to describe it as a denial of anarchy or hierarchy, or as a hybrid of supranationalism and intergovernmentalism as unnecessary. It would simply be a different, non-state kind of political order. The EU may thus swing back towards being a region of mutually exclusive sovereign states, but it could also evolve further as a loosely connected, empire-like entity (cf. Wæver, 1997).

Another reason to compare the EU to empires is the significance of imperialism in European history. The idea of Eurafrica featured prominently in the negotiations of the European Economic Community (EEC) in the 1950s. Accordingly, the EEC had to bring about economic development and civilisation in Africa for the benefit of both (Hansen & Jonsson, 2012). Academically, the growing political interdependence and socio-economic interconnectedness across or even regardless of state borders in world politics and the EEC in particular have provided reason to refer to imperial rule. It reminded Hedley Bull (1977, p. 255) of the imperial order of mediaeval Europe with competing and overlapping authorities, crisscrossing loyalties and decentralised power (see also Friedrichs, 2001; Kobrin, 1998; Ruggie, 1993). Despite the considerable differences in terms of monopoly on violence, economic interdependencies, religious pluralism, and centralisation (Axtmann, 2003; Falk, 2000), others have also found inspiration in medieval times. Jan Zielonka (2006) referred to the Middle Ages to underline the EU's polycentrism, fuzzy boundaries, voluntary expansion, and low symmetry in core-periphery relationships. In his book *Europe as Empire: The Nature of the Enlarged European Union*, he argues that the eastern enlargement of the European Union was an "impressive exercise in empire-building", while the European Neighbourhood Policy constituted "quite an ambitious programme in a truly neo-medieval spirit" (Zielonka, 2006, p. 20, 112).

The Holy Roman Empire (800–1806), particularly in its *post*-mediaeval period, has also been a source of comparative inspiration given its similarities with the EU in terms of restrained jurisdiction of increasingly predominant territorial powers within an overarching constitutional order; its multireligious and multinational nature; the norm of seeking peaceful arbitration of mutual conflicts; a certain measure of constitutional patriotism; two imperial courts for settling legal disputes in which imperial law had supremacy over other laws; the myriad of decision-making procedures at the imperial level involving a variety of representatives adopting framework legislation on issues of public order, defence, economy and coinage; the predominance of lower levels in terms of legislation and implementation; the struggle to find balance between constraining internal domination and enabling common action; and the differentiated involvement of large parts of the present-day EU (Axtmann, 2003; Haldén, 2009; Osiander, 2001).

In addition to these European empires, Ole Wæver (1997) also referred to ancient ones such as the Sumerian Empire to highlight the radial pattern of authority in imperial structures, ranging from a core with direct rule in all policy areas towards an outer circle of suzerain entities. Wæver would not necessarily regret the EU becoming an empire. Looking back to the many instances of imperial systems, he has claimed that "[e]mpire is the best-proven peace model in world history" (Wæver, 1997, p. 64). Although empires are often associated with anti-democratic repression, political subordination, and military conquest, Wæver and other political scientists have argued that imperial systems have often provided internal peace among a plurality of cultures within a large trading area. It has therefore even been *recommended* to the EU (see, e.g., Münkler, 2005). According to Josep Colomer (2007), a European empire could even be good for democracy. It would provide security and trade agreements at an efficient scale. In this way, it facilitates the establishment of democratic, small-sized communities such as Catalonia that no longer have to bear the costs of maintaining their own defence and trade agreements. Moreover, the desires of individual citizens can be met more easily due to the assumed homogeneity of identity and interests in those small-sized communities. Robert Cooper (2004), an influential security advisor to British prime minister Tony Blair and the High Representative of the European Union for Foreign Affairs and Security Policy, argued that the EU should pursue "liberal imperialism" in its external policies. The EU should intervene in its neighbourhood and elsewhere if necessary by military means to protect itself against threats stemming from illegal immigration, terrorism, or organised crime and to stimulate human security and individual freedom. In contrast to previous colonial policies, liberal imperialism should be based on law, cosmopolitan values, multilateral approval and execution, and, above all, the voluntary agreement of those intervened upon. Imperialism also received recognition from other practice-oriented authors as benign interference by American or Western powers to reconstruct nations abroad (see, e.g., Ferguson, 2004; Ignatieff, 2003). Thus, empire and imperialism are even seen as beneficial to the world. Apparently, the concepts are losing their negative connotations. As stated above, this chapter will not deal with the normative issue of whether empire and imperialism are good or bad, but will seek an explanation of (dis)integration based on the comparative analyses of empires.

5.3   DEFINING EMPIRE AND IMPERIALISM

Prior to discussing European disintegration from an imperial perspective, it should be made clear whether or not the EU qualifies as an empire for the purpose of comparison. This section presents an ideal-type definition of empire. In reality, no empire will be fully consistent with this definition, but the list of features of an ideal-type empire should indicate whether a certain political system belongs to the family of empires or not. As a matter of fact, empire (*imperium*) has had a variety of meanings throughout history, such as the right to enforce the law, monarchy, new areas that had become subject to rule, universal rule, or full authority independent of some outside power (Axtmann, 2003, p. 129). Here, the focus will be on empire as a polity. Unfortunately, the concepts of empire and imperialism have been less developed than concepts that fit better within the Westphalian divide between Comparative Politics and International Relations, such as federations and hegemonies (Münkler, 2005; Nexon & Wright, 2007). Additionally, empires are often only studied individually, easily leading to idiosyncratic understandings of empire and imperialism (Zielonka, 2012). The political scientist Michael Doyle is a notable exception to this, as he discusses instances of empire from ancient Athens to the colonial powers from a comparative perspective. Even though Doyle's comparison is of maritime rather than continental empires such as the Holy Roman Empire and the Soviet Empire, analyses of these latter entities suggest Doyle's ideal-type definition also includes them (Motyl, 2001; Münkler, 2005).

First and foremost, Doyle emphasises the relational nature of empires: "Empire (...) is a relationship, formal or informal, in which one [polity] controls the effective political sovereignty of another political society" (1986, p. 45). Since an empire is more about the relationship between central and peripheral elites than about geographical control per se, the nature of empire has been described as "arterial" rather than "areal" (Motyl, 2001). An empire is not the equivalent of hegemonic power or the sphere of influence of a powerful state. In a hegemonic relationship and a sphere of influence, the dominant polity only controls or constrains the foreign policy of another polity (Doyle, 1986, p. 44). An empire, however, is a "system of interaction between two political entities, one of which, the dominant metropole, exerts political control over the internal and external policy—the effective sovereignty—of the other, the subordinate periphery" (Doyle, 1986, p. 12). The metropole thus controls "who rules and what rulers can do" in the domestic realm of a periphery as well (Doyle, 1986, p. 130). Political subordination is thus key to any imperial structure.

Another distinctive feature of an empire concerns the asymmetric and unequal relationships between the metropolitan core and the respective peripheries (see also Nexon & Wright, 2007). Peripheries are focused on the imperial centre and lack substantial mutual links. Thus, an empire resembles the hubs and spokes of a "rimless wheel" (Motyl, 2001, p. 4). An imperial relationship can be formal, in which the centre rules an annexed periphery directly through administrators from the centre (Doyle, 1986). However, annexation, conquest, and direct rule involve huge costs, particularly for non-contiguous empires, that were often too high for colonial empires of the past (Pagden, 1995). As a result, imperial centres often resort to informal, indirect rule. In this case, local rulers of a formally sovereign periphery are dependent from and controlled by the imperial centre in practice (Doyle, 1986). Multilayered and polycentric decision-making at both the imperial and peripheral levels and the management of heterogeneous bargains with the various peripheries often make imperial politics rather complex. The variety of identities, citizenship, and divisions of authority within the empire and from periphery to periphery contributes to this complexity. As a matter of fact, an emperor is not necessarily part of an imperial infrastructure, but he or she can have an important role as feudal overlord, military commander-in-chief or symbol of unity. In other words, empires can be without emperors.

The relationship between the centre and peripheries is key to an empire. So, what then is its basis? Present-day understanding of empire and imperialism is often informed by the Scramble for Africa in the late nineteenth century, when European powers expanded their colonial empires through territorial conquest. Many other empires also expanded by force, to protect the metropole and the peripheries by extending imperial borders, for example. However, empires can also expand by means other than force and for reasons other than security alone. "[Expansion] can be achieved by force, by political collaboration, by economic, social, or cultural dependence" (Doyle, 1986, p. 45). For instance, before the Scramble for Africa began, the Dominican Republic, Sarawak, and Togo requested that they become part of one or another empire, albeit to no avail (Doyle, 1986). Much earlier in history, pro-imperial factions in Greek cities invited the Roman Empire to support them. Furthermore, empires such as the Holy Roman Empire acquired and lost areas, titles, and rights because of

marriages and heredity (Wilson, 2011). Additionally, empires grew to support the foreign activities of private enterprises from the metropole or to
get hold of the economic surpluses from agricultural lands, trade hubs,
and commercial routes elsewhere. For example, the British and Spanish
empire grew more due to economic reasons than to immediate security
concerns (Doyle, 1986). Imperial aggrandisement was also achieved
through buying, as, for example, ownership of Louisiana, Alaska, and the
Virgin Islands switched by sale to the expanding USA. Expansion has also
been motived by reasons of prestige, military honour, or the glory of (certain factions in) the metropole (Doyle, 1986). A closely related driver of
imperial enlargement is the self-perception of an imperial centre being a
civilisation that is morally or culturally superior. The imperial civilisation is
both a reason for peripheries' attraction to the centre and the centre's
willingness to fight "barbarians" that are not willing to accept its civilisation. Whereas intra-imperial politics can be done in a civilised way, the
superiority of an imperial civilisation justifies interventions into domestic
politics to defend or spread its civilisation, if necessary by military force.
When the metropole perceives the civilisation's standards and values as
having been violated, it applies double standards, exhibited by a less
civilised response to the peripheries (cf. Behr, 2007). As a self-perceived,
self-legitimising superior force for good, empires do not unconditionally
recognise the principle of self-determination (Münkler, 2005). In principle, empires are therefore incompatible with democracy, in which people
rule themselves. In practice, though, imperialism and democracy have
been combined, as politicians do not necessarily act in a way that is fully
consistent from a conceptual standpoint.

Empires also sit rather uneasily with territorial states. States are based
on territorial control, for which they (at least implicitly) acknowledge the
right of rule by other entities outside their territory. Given its relational
rather than territorial nature, an empire is intrinsically unlimited in geographical terms and therefore often expansive. To be certain, empires use
territory as a *strategy* of control, as exemplified by the Hadrian Wall of the
Roman Empire and the Iron Curtain between the Soviet and American
empire (Vollaard, 2009). However, imperial boundaries are only the temporary delineation of its economic reach, marriage policy, military conquest, or civilisation. They thus remain unfixed, fuzzy, outer-oriented, and
inclusive buffer zones, in contrast to fixed and clearly demarcated state
borders that area designed to separate (Kristoff, 1959). Although a metropole may be more strongly present within imperial boundary zones for

reasons of protection, its inherently expansive nature lends itself to impe-rial rule creating a somewhat radial pattern of concentric circles, from direct and full rule in the core towards more indirect, partial, or informal control in peripheries (Wæver, 1997).

In sum, the components of the ideal-type definition of an empire con-sist of unequal and asymmetric relationships between a metropolitan cen-tre and peripheries arranged in a radial pattern; formal or informal imperial control of both foreign and domestic politics of the peripheries; multi-level and heterogeneous decision-making; and fuzzy, unfixed boundaries. Imperialism is just the intended or unintended creation and consolidation of an empire, be it by aggressive, exploitative, and military means or by persuasion, attraction, and soft power (Doyle, 1986). According to this definition, political actors in states, federations, international organisa-tions, or any other non-imperial polity can also pursue imperial policies. However, actors may be unaware of the imperial nature of their (external) policies or avoid explicit references to it. Thus, a distinction should be made between a specific actor, such as a government and the morphology of the political structure it is operating in (state, federation, empire, etc.) or what it is (unintentionally) developing.

Along similar lines, a polity that is explicitly called an empire might not necessarily be one. European history includes examples of political systems like the Holy Roman Empire (800–1806) that was christened an "empire" to borrow some of the prestige of the long-lasting Roman Empire and to denote its function as the universal, secular guardian of Christianity. The question remains as to whether or not these political systems, as well as the Roman Empire itself, have always been empires as defined above. When Emperor Caracalla equalised the still limited rights of inhabitants of both metropole and peripheries into a single political community, the Roman Empire lost one of the fundamental traits of an empire, inequality (Doyle, 1986, p. 97). And although the Holy Roman Empire and its components were clearly not sovereign states with a monopoly on the legitimate use of force within their respective territories, collectively, they increasingly resembled a rather federative system with consociational practices (Wilson, 2011). An argument against a categorisation of the Holy Roman Empire as federative, however, is that its underlying pact was not concluded by relative equals. It shares a sufficient number of the components of the above-mentioned ideal-type definition of empire—a relational nature, cen-tral involvement in the domestic sphere of its sub-units, many asymmetries, multi-level decision-making, and fuzzy boundaries—to qualify as one.

5.4   Is the EU an Empire?

Due to its low level of centralisation, the Holy Roman Empire seemed rather weak in comparison to contemporary states in the making, such as France, England, or Spain. In spite of its weakness, it lasted for about 1000 years. The political-legal constraints within its imperial order provided a certain measure of liberty to its members and protected others from anarchy (brought about by the Thirty Years' War, for example) or aggressive hierarchy (such as that which stemmed from the Habsburg dynasty). Given the fact that the EU is also often cast as (too) weak, it might be still be a sign of hope for those who favour its survival, that it might last for at least another 900 years; assuming the EU can be compared to empires at all, of course. Imperial descriptions of the EU often refer to its multinational and multilingual nature. Even though this is quite common in empires, it also holds true in many federations and consociations. As the ideal-type definition above indicates, empires distinguish themselves in terms of the way in which they are politically structured.

A first structural feature of the ideal-type empire is the relationship between the centre and the peripheries. So which entities are the peripheries and centre in the EU? To be sure, the EU is not led by an emperor or empress, even if the German chancellor Angela Merkel has occasionally been described as such, during the debt crises, for example (see, e.g., Nordhausen & Fras, 2013). Instead, the centre of the EU comprises the European Council, the Council of the European Union, the European Commission, the European Central Bank, and the European Parliament. Centres of empires in the past also consisted of a variety of actors, from a Senate in the Roman Empire to a House of Commons in the British Empire, but with the possible exception of the Holy Roman Empire, leadership of the EU centre is the most fragmented. That also holds in comparison to the informal empire of the USA. Even if democratic forces do play an important role, the president has more autonomy to pursue foreign or imperial policies than does the collective leadership of the EU. Peripheries can be identified by the involvement of the EU centre in their external *and* internal policies, which would distinguish the EU from a mere hegemonic power. In this respect, not only the EU member states but also (potential) EU candidate members, members of the European Economic Area (EEA), and neighbouring countries belong to the EU peripheries, given the EU role in issues such as agriculture, trade, corruption, environment, welfare, banking, terrorism, citizen rights, developmental aid, and diplomacy. This role includes prescriptions concerning policies as well as the way in which these should be implemented, as laid down in EU legislation, accession agreements, association treaties, and action plans.

At first glance, the EU is clearly an "areal" entity, in which the territories of the involved (member) states indicate the geographical delineation of its rule. However, this delineation is only a temporary limitation. The various rounds of enlargement illustrate the EU's expansive, geographically unfixed nature. In the relationship between the EU and its peripheries, national governments play a dual role. Not unlike the way in which the Holy Roman Empire was structured, national governments are both the elites of the peripheries *and* part of the EU centre. Their prominent role does not necessarily mean that the territorial, sovereign state is still the dominant political format. The involvement of the EU centre in the internal and external politics of states clearly constrains their effective territorial sovereignty, a key requirement of the ideal-type state. Additionally, national governments are prominent actors *collectively* in collegial bodies such as the Council, but are much less so individually. The word member state therefore indicates the status and role of certain representatives in EU decision-making rather than the specific political format of the represented entity.

The status and role of member states are different from those of candidate member states and other neighbours. This deviates from the strict Westphalian, territorial demarcation between the inside and outside of a political entity. Similar to empires, the EU also exerts influence in both domestic and foreign policies of its neighbours by exporting its legal norms and practices (Browning & Joenniemi, 2008). The legal boundary of the EU no longer fully coincides with the membership boundary (Lavenex, 2004, p. 694), creating a rather fuzzy zone of "intermediate spaces" between the inside and outside of the EU (Christiansen, Petito, & Tonra, 2000, p. 410). The European Neighbourhood Policy (ENP) is illustrative of these fuzzy boundaries. The EU launched the ENP in the early twenty-first century to deal more coherently with neighbours with no prospect of EU membership in the short run. It includes the Eastern Partnership directed at neighbours in the former Soviet Union's realm such as Belarus, Ukraine, Georgia, and Moldova and the Union for the Mediterranean involving the EU and countries such as Algeria, Israel, Egypt, and Palestine. The EU adopted a "hub-and-spoke bilateralism" by imposing its priorities onto each ENP agreement individually (Charillon,

2004, p. 259). Inequality between core and peripheries has also been reflected in the principle of conditionality in the ENP. The EU monitored the extent to which ENP states fulfilled certain criteria and was willing to use carrots or sticks (trade agreements, visa facilitation, prospects for EU membership) to correct a failing ENP participant. Even if the ENP failed to have much of an impact in the face of revolutions (Arab Spring) or revolts (Ukraine), it clearly reflects the inequality between the EU centre and some of its peripheries, another component of the ideal-type definition of an empire.

Conditionality has also been key in the accession processes of (potential) candidate member states over the last 25 years (Schimmelfennig & Sedelmeier, 2004; Zielonka, 2006, p. 13). The EU offered assistance and the prospect of EU membership to Central and Eastern European countries (CEECs) and Balkan countries in exchange for meeting the accession criteria and adopting EU legislation or policies related to the common market, justice, and home affairs and the common foreign and security policies. However, it was not an equal exchange. The EU decided which criteria applied, whether or not an applicant met the criteria to become a candidate and eventually a member as well as the set-up of the accession process. Whereas the accession criteria on fundamental issues such as democracy only had a limited effect on the democratisation of acceding countries, the "rule transfer" shaped their political infrastructure and policies significantly (Schimmelfennig & Sedelmeier, 2004). The European Commission could exert more influence on their political infrastructure than it could on existing member states. The inequality between the EU centre and the acceding countries and the asymmetries between acceding and neighbouring countries are consistent with still another component of the ideal-type definition of empire (Böröcz, 2001; Zielonka, 2006).

Inequality has also marked the relationship between the EU centre and countries that do not want to become EU member states, such as Norway, Iceland, and Switzerland. They have been basically "rule-takers" from the EU rather than equal partners in the agreements on the internal market, justice, and home affairs (Kux & Sverdrup, 2000). Even though Norway and Iceland participate in the EU decision-making apparatus through the arrangements of the EEA and contribute to candidate member states' and foreign EU missions, their policy autonomy is rather limited. However, full membership also does not guarantee equality. Romania and Bulgaria are still denied complete access to the arrangements of the Area of Freedom, Security and Justice (AFSJ). Furthermore, several relatively new member states are not sufficiently qualified to join the latest stage of the Economic and Monetary Union (EMU), the common currency. In the EMU, asymmetry and inequality in status among member states is institutionalised in the specific arrangements for those members with the Euro, such as the Eurogroup, a subset of the Council of Economic and Financial Affairs. Member states that do not want to join the Euro—the UK, Denmark, and Sweden—are also less involved in a key aspect of European policy-making as a result. Differentiated involvement of member states also concerns the partial participation in the AFSJ of the UK, Ireland, and Denmark.

Differentiated or asymmetric EU integration roughly follows a radial pattern from the member states around the German-French core, the member states with opt-outs from certain policy areas, the EEA members, and Switzerland, to the accession, association, and neighbouring entities, respectively (see also Lavenex, 2011). Even if the EU were to match another component of the ideal-type definition of an empire, the question remains as to whether or not all these asymmetric relationships between the centre and the peripheries are also based on inequality. In an empire, this relationship would be based on formal or informal control and dominance by the centre, however weak that control might actually be. If the relationships between the centre and peripheries are *not* based on control, the EU would be an instance of asymmetric federalism, in which relatively equal entities have made collective agreements about shared and divided rule that differs between the units. The units would thus cooperate together rather than be peripheries, individually dependent upon and controlled by the centre (cf. Gravier, 2009, p. 635). The partial opt-outs of member states from policy areas such as the EMU and the AFSJ have been accepted collectively, which exemplifies asymmetric federalism rather than imperial inequality. However, (potential) candidate member states and neighbouring entities in particular have not been in a position to decide on EU involvement on equal footing, even if they are, with the exception of Kosovo, fully recognised as formally independent states. This distinction between inside-federalism and outside-imperialism is not unlike how the informal US Empire operates, with a federation in North America at its core and peripheries such as Puerto Rico and Iraq under its control both in terms of internal and external policies.

As in other cases of imperial expansion, the EU has used means other than force to grow (Zielonka, 2006, p. 13). It has predominantly relied upon the soft power of persuasion and economic attractiveness. A constructivist understanding of EU expansion would emphasise its value-based nature. The European integration process started partly as a project to sustain the values of peace, political and economic liberty, rule of law, democracy, and human rights in Europe in response to the world wars and the Cold War. The European integration process can thus be understood as a "civilising process", in which the member states learn to live together more peacefully (Linklater, 2005; see also Behr, 2007). The barbaric past characterised by xenophobia, protectionism, war, authoritarianism, and political extremism had to be left behind. And the promise of a good life held for the entirety of Europe, including the Eastern part that was subjugated to the extremism and authoritarianism of communist rule for quite some time. After the end of Cold War, the Eastern part expressed its desire to "return to Europe", thereby reflecting the moral superiority of the values propagated in the European integration process (Böröcz, 2001). Entrapped in the rhetoric of an undivided Europe, the EU member states could not turn down the membership applications of Central and Eastern European states forever (Schimmelfennig, 2001; Sjursen, 1998). If a state is willing and able to live according to European values, in the long term, pleas for accession cannot be denied. The ability and actual adoption of European legislation has defined how much progress and development candidates have made in the eyes of the European Commission. The EU thus set the "standards of civilization" for the large-scale reform of domestic policies of candidate member states (Behr, 2007; see also Zielonka, 2011). According to European treaties, only European states can apply for EU membership. As such, the enlargement of the EU seems to be geographically limited. The issue here, however, is determining exactly where Europe's borders are. According to former European Commissioner for Enlargement, Olli Rehn, borders are a matter of values: "Europe's borders are defined rather by values than by geographical guidelines. Certainly, geographical borders set out the framework, but values define the borders" (quoted in Mahony, 2006). Following Rehn's logic, if a country were to adopt European values to a sufficient degree, Europe's borders would move. The conception of where Europe is may thus eventually include countries such as Turkey. EU member states have learned to live together in a more civilised way, which may increase its influence by shaping conceptions of what is considered normal: "...the most important factor shaping the role of the EU is not what it does or what it says, but what it is" (Manners, 2002, p. 252; see also Zielonka, 2006). Nevertheless, its civilised modes of politics also provide the moral justification or even obligation for the EU to intervene as a "force for good" in the domestic politics of entities beyond candidate member states (cf. Barbé & Johansson-Nogués, 2008; Duffield, 2007; Matlary, 2008). The EU has exported its governance, legislation, and values through the ENP and to the Balkans through quasi-protectorates in Bosnia-Herzegovina and Kosovo.

The expansive inclination of the European integration process not only results from its value-based nature but also from a changed understanding of threats. In the early 1990s, concerns about criminals, terrorists, and illegal immigrants roaming freely into and within a borderless internal market replaced fears of invading Soviet armies in Western Europe, particularly since the Iron Curtain no longer sealed off the east. Instead of desiring weak neighbours to keep security threats low for defensive reasons, well-organised and safe neighbours would be required for security (Howorth, 2007, p. 200). Initially, the EU sought to pacify its neighbourhood through peace-support operations and diplomatic interventions, largely within the framework of international organisations such as the UN, OSCE, Council of Europe, WEU, and NATO. The secure and wealthy future safeguarded by accession to EU and NATO also offered an instrument by which to limit instability and conflict in the EU's "near abroad" (Charillon, 2004).

The 2003 European Security Strategy reflected the redefinition of security, listing terrorism, the distribution of weapons of mass destruction, regional conflicts, failed states, and organised crime as the main security threats to the European Union. In particular, the prospect of enlargement shifted attention from settling conflicts to the "import" of crime from candidate member states and other neighbours. As a result, in the late 1990s, the EU sought to create temporary "law enforcement buffer zones" in Central and Eastern Europe against the infiltration of illegal immigrants, drugs, and criminals into the EU, as well as to curb the export of stolen goods from west to east (Andreas, 2003, p. 103). The full incorporation of the Schengen regime into the EU increased the requirements imposed upon new member states to invest in security measures (Mitsilegas, Monar, & Rees, 2003, pp. 34–35). António Vitorino, a former European Commissioner for Justice and Home Affairs (JHA), explained the expansive logic of the EU rather well in this respect: "…the best way to consolidate the security of the Union is not by erecting a barrier against our neighbours, but by spreading both stability and prosperity beyond our borders" (2002, p. 17). The external dimension of the EU's Justice and

Home Affairs policy therefore included "the promotion of the values of freedom, security and justice in third countries" through providing technical support for border management, strengthening law enforcement institutions, and supporting human rights in those countries (European Commission, 2005, p. 4). In the Balkans, the EU has also been active in instructing the judiciary and public prosecutors and in launching joint action plans to fight drug trafficking, organised crime, and illegal immigration. As a consequence, social order and threats defined by the EU glossed over local security concerns and practices in EU operations abroad quite easily (Merlingen & Ostrauskaite, 2005, p. 219; Barbé & Johansson-Nogués, 2008, p. 92). Similarly, EU security interests featured prominently in ENP action plans to create a protective buffer zone around the EU. The EU offered visa facilitation to its neighbours' citizens, but did so in exchange for readmission agreements and financial and institutional assistance to combat organised crime, illegal immigration, and terrorism (Wichmann, 2007).

The EU may also have expanded for other reasons, such as the creation of a larger internal market. What is important to underline here is the intrinsically unlimited nature of the EU project, kept at bay in practice only by internal resistance to EU enlargement and by other powers such as the Russian Federation. In the Ukraine, Georgia, and Moldova, peripheral elites have responded differently and in a divided manner to the foreign ambitions of the EU and the Russian Federation. The actual reach of EU control is, however, not only dependent on Russian influence. The EU has also been reliant on US power, in matters of high-intensity military capabilities and diplomatic sway in particular. This reliance is not only related to EU policies towards the former Soviet Union. The very launch of European integration relied at least in part on American security guarantees, diplomatic incentives, and a worldwide economic and monetary framework (Lundestad, 1998, 2003). The American "informal empire" aimed at balancing the Soviet Union, keeping communists out of power in Western Europe, maintaining free trade across the world, and containing Germany through supranational integration (Lundestad, 1998, p. 112). According to its own civilisation, the US Empire allowed considerable leeway in the democratic peripheries in Western Europe and used persuasion rather than blunt force as means of control. Nevertheless, it set clear limits on West European imperial ambitions outside Europe and turned against West European peripheries ganging up against it. It only accepted cooperation on foreign policy and defence within the EU if the EU would share the burden of providing security in the EU's backyard with the USA more equally. The fact that the EU is part of a US-led "informal empire" or, if that is an overstatement, just being subject to American hegemonic rule, does not eliminate the possibility that the EU is an imperial structure in and of itself. The Holy Roman Empire also depended on the protection of outside powers such as the French kingdom from time to time (Haldén, 2009; Wilson, 2011).

As stated previously, the EU centre is quite fragmented. Adding to this complexity is the fact that EU policy-making and implementation is exercised at various levels. Furthermore, the EU encompasses multiple identities and multilayered citizenship (national plus EU citizenship). Though this may also be common to federative systems, the EU is more heterogeneous and complex, as the various peripheries have different statuses and degrees of involvement they enjoy (see above). In sum, the EU does qualify as an empire, as it also meets many criteria of the ideal-type definition of empire, such as unequal and asymmetric relationships between the centre and peripheries in a radial pattern and EU involvement in both external and internal policies of member states. The EU is thus an instance of imperialism, the (unintended) creation and maintenance of an empire, even if only few practitioners acknowledge or consciously propagate EU imperialism (though see Barroso and Cooper above). The existence of imperialism does not preclude political actors from also practising "statism" or federalism in order to create an EU state or EU federation. But because the EU qualifies as an empire, explanations of imperial fall and decline can also be applied to it.

5.5   EXPLAINING THE DECLINE AND FALL OF EMPIRES

This chapter seeks to find a fruitful starting point for explaining EU disintegration in comparative analyses of disintegrating empires. EU studies have neglected the issue of European disintegration thus far. Additionally, only very few EU scholars have explicitly discussed the EU in imperial terms. Nevertheless, imperial features of the EU have been theorised, but by different names. The asymmetry that exists in terms of the rights and obligations of the EU member states is known as "differentiated integration" (Kölliker, 2006), while the EU's expansive nature is often reflected upon as being a trade-off between widening and deepening of integration (Kelemen, Menon, & Slapin, 2014a). Explanations of EU disintegration might still be derived from these analyses of differentiated integration and the relationship between widening and deepening. They will be discussed in subsection 5.5.1. The next section examines analyses of disintegrating empires a potential source of insight in explaining EU disintegration. Given the definitions of empire and imperialism presented above, these analyses include those of great powers in decline, kingdoms, security communities, and hegemonies (Davies, 2012; Deutsch et al., 1957; Gills, 1993; Gilpin, 1988; Kennedy, 1987).

5.5.1   EU Theories Concerning Enlargement

While issue of enlargement has been a common feature throughout EU history, its theorisation has only been developed fairly recently (Miles, 2004; Schimmelfennig & Sedelmeier, 2002). Instead, EU studies have largely provided descriptive analyses of enlargement or loose reflections on the repercussions of enlargement for the EU and European integration (Kelemen et al., 2014a). It has often been argued that widening the EU by including new member states with different preferences will impair decision-making and prevent the deepening of integration through the extension of supranational authority. Differentiated integration or flexibility has been suggested as a means of overcoming gridlock in decision-making and integration. Differentiated integration refers to a varying degree of integration between and within policy areas and the asymmetric involvement of member states and non-member states within the single institutional framework of the EU (Kölliker, 2006, p. 32; Schimmelfennig, Leuffen, & Rittberger, 2015, pp. 3–4).

Alkuin Kölliker (2001, 2006) was one of the first to engage in the sophistication of the theoretical analysis of differentiated integration. He focused on the member states that were not *willing* to take part in a step that would contribute to furthered integration (the UK regarding a common currency and Denmark concerning European defence policy), instead of temporary, transitional arrangements for member states not yet *able* to fully meet the requirements of EU membership or the introduction of the Euro. According to Kölliker, differentiated integration depends on the flexibility of EU institutions themselves, the willingness of the member states to integrate, and, most importantly, the type of issue area according to public goods theory. If a member state is excluded from the benefits of integration in a certain issue area that other member states enjoy, it will decide to join despite its initial unwillingness to do so. This will be even more the case if participation adds value for all participants. For example, the Schengen Information System (SIS) is a database on wanted or missing persons and objects that is accessible exclusively to participating member states (precluding freeriding) and is of greater value if more member states join (no rival consumption). This could explain why the UK sought to participate in SIS notwithstanding its initial reluctance to engage in any integration in the area of justice and home affairs. The case of tax harmonisation also illustrates that if effects of *non*-participation are perceived more positively, integration will not take off at all unless all participants are equally willing to integrate from the very beginning.

Primarily based on the type of issue area, Kölliker thus provides an explanation of why some (non-)member states would not initially join others' integrative initiatives, but might do so later. The advantage of this explanation is that it does not simply explain integration in light of patterns of interdependence (which has proven to be a rather indeterminate explanation), but takes into account the character of the issue area at stake. However, it is largely an explanation of why member states do not join an integrative initiative, as opposed to why they might leave such an initiative. In spite of this, disintegration can be explained by turning Kölliker's explanation upside down. Full or partial withdrawal from the EU could thus be explained by member states no longer willing to participate in a certain integrated issue area, having the flexibility to leave that issue area, the changing of an integrated issue area in terms of rivalry and exclusion of the consumption of goods, or the emergence of more beneficial policy arrangements within member states or those stemming from non-EU integration initiatives. As the level of rivalry in terms of the consumption of goods is particularly difficult to manipulate (cf. Kölliker, 2006, pp. 64–65), changes in the type of issue area are unlikely to be a source of disintegration. However, calculations based on continuing participants could turn negative with an increase in member states in the case of common pool resources such as fishing grounds, where consumption of goods is non-exclusive and competitive. As such, even if potentially fruitful building blocks for an explanation of European disintegration are provided here, problems remain. It is still unclear what the relative weights of these factors are in processes of disintegration and how they might be related to each other. Additionally, this explanation of differentiated integration is based largely on the results of the (re)calculation of costs and benefits of integration of member states. It would thus exclude the impact of non-material, non-calculable factors such as identity and values, which are perceived to have increased in importance in the European integration process over the last 25 years or so (Hooghe & Marks, 2008).

Another, more recent explanation of differentiated integration does factor identity in to some extent (Leuffen, Rittberger, & Schimmelfennig, 2013; Schimmelfennig et al., 2015). According to this explanation, international interdependence is a necessary, but not sufficient, impetus for member states to seek integration. Further integration of both member states and non-member states also hinges on the restraining effect of politicisation on the one hand (in particular if it is based on an exclusive national identity) and the stimulating force of powerful member states and the political interdependence created by supranational institutions on the other hand. As some authors themselves indicate, their "work is about European *integration*" (Leuffen et al., 2013, p. 12; emphasis in original), justifying their focus on why not all member states join subsequent integrative steps. At first sight, it seems logical to do this because "rollback has not yet taken place" in the EU (Leuffen et al., 2013, p. 6). However, if disintegration is understood in a broader sense and includes non-compliance, disintegration has actually been a fairly common feature of the EU's history. According to a more limited understanding of disintegration as the repatriation of competences from the EU level to the member states, the most important evidence of disintegration would be weakening interdependence, the declining facilitating influence of supranational institutions and leading member states, and, in particular, the growing politicisation of the EU. Similar to the previous explanation, it remains unclear how these various factors interrelate in processes of disintegration. Furthermore, why would politicisation necessarily always be constraining in nature? Particularly in (potential) candidate member states, polarisation on the issue of the EU can also reflect a growing willingness to join an integrative step. A complete explanation of EU disintegration derived from this theory of differentiated integration should at least indicate the level and nature of politicisation that would result in disintegration.

Differentiated integration emerged in the face of the various enlargements (Schimmelfennig, 2014). It has been seen as a way to overcome deadlock in the EU and in European integration more generally. This assumes, however, that an increasing number of member states would hamper decision-making in the EU. Recent analyses of the impact of EU enlargement have criticised the perceived trade-off between widening and deepening European integration. First of all, partisan heterogeneity, significant in budget negotiations, has resulted from changes in governments' composition rather than the inclusion of new member states

(Schneider, 2014). Additionally, if a new member state is in favour of European integration or shares its preferences with existing member states, no impediment to EU decision-making and European integration is expected (Kelemen, Menon, & Slapin, 2014b). Furthermore, EU institutions have changed the EU's decision-making rules and practices in advance to facilitate the functioning of the EU in the face of enlargement (Bressanelli, 2014; Kelemen et al., 2014b; Toshkov, 2017; Van der Veen, 2014). And even if political deadlock were to occur, non-elected, supranational actors such as the Court of Justice of the European Union and the European Commission could still move European integration forward (Kelemen et al., 2014b). Throughout the EU's history, deepening integration in terms of transfer of competences and a larger role of supranational centralisation has been accompanied by various rounds of enlargement (Leuffen et al., 2013, p. 6). Widening and deepening might thus have been a trade-off in some instances, but not in general. Nevertheless, the perception that widening and deepening have a negative relationship to one another is widespread (Kelemen et al., 2014a). Ongoing debates on the EU's capacity to absorb new member states also suggest that at some point in the future, the EU might no longer be able to deepen and widen. Studies of imperial disintegration have often referred to this point. This is not surprising, as all empires ultimately face the challenge of overextending their capabilities due to their inherently expansive nature. Comparative analyses of disintegrating empires could therefore provide a more comprehensive explanation than analyses that only focus on asymmetries (differentiated integration) or the EU's expansive nature (the widening-deepening trade-off).

5.6   Comparative Analysis of Disintegrating Empires

At least 210 diverse factors affecting its decline and fall have been identified in the manifold analyses the western part of the Roman Empire alone (Demandt, 1984). They range from incompetent leadership, moral decadence, corruption, distracting Christendom, declining fertility, lead poisoning, rising taxes, barbarian invasions, decreasing economic productivity, and long-stretched frontiers, to the ease with which quasi-autonomous elites switched loyalties to different powers. Closer scrutiny of these analyses indicates that attention to specific factors was at least as much a reflection of historical research as of political or ideological priorities of the day (Demandt, 1984). This should warn us against shallow comparisons between the Roman Empire and the European Union or any other empire-like entity based on a single analysis or on a set of analyses from a specific ideological or temporal framework. The overwhelming number of factors that have been identified might also in and of themselves prevent the emergence of a coherent explanation of disintegrating empires; as has been remarked, "a theory of empire that predicts the fall of empire is a theory of almost everything" (Marks, 2012, p. 15). However, *comparative* analyses of disintegrating empires have offered us a selection of the most relevant factors.

Studies of imperial disintegration often emphasise its irrevocability, irreversibility, and inevitability, as empires eventually overburden themselves as a result of their inherently expansive nature. Empires' histories are thus often described in cyclical terms of their rise, shine, decline, and eventual fall. The question remains, however, as to whether or not this holds for non-imperial entities too. For instance, the various polities that emerged from the western part of the Roman Empire (city states, feudal systems, city leagues) also fell apart or were incorporated into national states such as France, England, Spain, and Portugal (cf. Tilly, 1990). In other words, all political systems end at some point. Furthermore, these cyclical terms are rather indistinct with respect to the timing, evolution, and speed of processes of disintegration. The Napoleonic Empire and the Third Reich were rather short-lived in comparison to the Roman Empire. Empires may fall unexpectedly or swiftly such as the Soviet Empire, but also slowly, as was the case with the Holy Roman Empire. Additionally, empires might also be revived after a period of decline and decay (cf. Motyl, 2001). This is also evidence of the fact that empires do not necessarily fall apart into Westphalian states upon their decline.

The emphasis on the inevitable overburdening of the imperial system also suggests that there exists an optimal size of empire, beyond which it can no longer be maintained. The optimal size of an empire or any polity is, however, difficult to identify, if not impossible, since different functions require different scales of operation (Motyl, 2001, p. 34). For instance, citizens may be able to exert more influence in smaller political systems, but larger systems might be better able to meet certain citizens' demands (cf. Dahl & Tufte, 1973). Small, cohesive, and homogeneous communities may be able to facilitate efficient service provision and limit freeriding (Alesina & Spolaore, 2003), but a large-scale polity may be able to manage internal and external effects of certain economic and security issues more efficiently and effectively. Determining an optimal size is therefore in the eye of the beholder. Given the variety in size of states (think of Luxemburg and Singapore vs. Canada) and empires (compare the Swedish, Dutch, Danish, German, and the British empires), it appears that even if an optimal size can be calculated, an abstract notion of optimal size is not of much value in analysing historical reality.

Throughout history, empires did, in fact, weigh the pros and cons of extension vs. consolidation (Pagden, 1995, Chap. 5), as their expansive nature presented them with extra challenges in comparison to territorially delineated ideal-type states. All empires continuously face struggles of control at their edges. They may win these struggles, but will also occasionally cede some control in peripheries. This does not necessarily mean the end of the empire. Imperial disintegration should thus be distinguished from (temporary) decline or loss of control in some peripheries. Decline or loss of control in one or more peripheries is only a matter of failed expansion, not the disintegration of the empire as a whole. Imperial disintegration refers to the end of the hub-like structure between metropolitan centre and the peripheries (cf. Motyl, 2001, pp. 4–5). As a matter of fact, the end of empire can also occur as a result of the abolishment of imperial features such as expansion or symmetry and inequality through the full integration of all peripheries. In sum, empires face a challenge that is inherent to their expansive nature, but their lifespan and existence is not necessarily a predetermined, cyclical evolution.

In comparative analyses of imperial disintegration, external challenges such as the Barbarian invasions into the western part of the Roman Empire have often been pointed out as being a major factor contributing to the empire's demise. In his analysis of the rise and fall of great powers (which are at least partly empires according to the definition provided above), Paul Kennedy (1987) has emphasised the significance of relative strength vis-à-vis competing powers rather than absolute capacities. This competition could have arisen partly because a hegemon or empire bore the costs of providing order and peace (cf. Gilpin, 1988). The challenges to and transitions between leading powers are said to usually be accompanied by major warfare (Gilpin, 1988; Kennedy, 1987; Modelski, 1987; Organski, 1968; see also Davies, 2012, p. 729). Indeed, the Napoleonic, Ottoman, Habsburg, and Nazi-German empires all ended in large-scale wars. The issue debated is whether or not insufficient military power was the fundamental factor or (also) the lack of economic and financial resources to purchase and develop military capacities. Kennedy points to the significance of the latter factor. In other analyses of hegemonic and imperial transition, economic factors are attributed more significance (see, e.g., Gills, 1993, p. 123). The loci of accumulation would thus determine which power or powers would assume a leading role in shaping the world order. The present-day economic development of what often is somewhat indistinctly described as "Asia" has thus been deemed to be the precursor of a changing world order, which other (former) empires and hegemons can be a part of. Indeed, the US Empire did not fully replace the British Empire in the aftermath of the Second World War, but rather encompassed it. According to this latter interpretation, empires and hegemonic powers in decline can still survive even if another great power takes the lead in world or regional politics.

Whereas above the emphasis has been on external challenges, others have stressed the internal weaknesses of empires in explaining their eventual disintegration. External challenges and war are commonplace for empires because of their inherently expansive nature. These challenges and war are a sort of test of empires, which reflects rather than explains their disintegration. In comparative analyses of disintegrating empires, various factors have been identified that determine the internal strength of empires. A first factor is willingness of actors within the empire to bear the imperial burden. Several authors point to a lack of martial spirit, failing self-confidence, deficient feeling of pride, absent sense of honour, and no desire to seek glory as reasons why these actors are not or no longer committed to the expansion of empires (Doyle, 1986; Gilpin, 1988). A limited sense of legitimacy of the empire and an absent feeling of community and loyalty throughout the empire among a large share of the population are other ideational factors that contribute to the disintegration of empires (Doyle, 1986). Willingness can also be a product of the calculation of material interests, for which reluctance to support imperial membership and enlargement fatigue among parties and population depend on the economic and political gains or losses involved. In particular, this concerns the prospects for social and political mobility within the empire as perceived by peripheral elites, since they connect the imperial centre to the peripheries (Doyle, 1986). Closed elite circles could limit their responsiveness to demands from peripheries and frustrate peripheral elites' ambitions, which they might then seek to fulfil outside the empire (Deutsch et al., 1957, p. 86ff).

In addition to willingness, comparative analyses of disintegrating empires also point to the significance of the lack of capacity to maintain the empire. Factors such as a united and strong centre and an impartial, effective, and efficient bureaucracy and military are considered crucial to the establishment and maintenance of empires (Doyle, 1986, p. 128ff). A divided and weak metropole, the incapacity to mobilise resources, and the exploitation of the administration and the military for particularistic purposes are therefore considered to be detrimental to empires (Doyle, 1986). Closely related to an empire's politico-administrative capabilities is its capacity to efficiently obtain the necessary financial means to maintain the empire. This depends first of all on the presence of societies in which sufficient people can devote time and energy to economic growth and development (Doyle, 1986). The effective generation of economic growth is also dependent upon the availability of free-floating sources. An efficient imperial apparatus and system of taxation does not suffocate the production of economic surplus and allows the metropolitan centre to spend more resources directly on the maintenance or expansion of empire (Doyle, 1986; Gilpin, 1988). Limited public debt helps in this respect, too (Ferguson, 2004; Gilpin, 1988). If the taxing burden of the empire were to become too high, peripheries may protest, business might leave, and tax evasion could increase, with a growing taxing burden for the remaining peripheries as a result (Gills, 1993, pp. 134–138). Demography is considered a significant factor both in terms of the willingness and the capability to maintain an empire. An ageing population might reduce the population's ambitions and lead to a diminished capacity to defend the empire or generate economic growth. Additionally, declining population size might limit the number of military recruits and economic consumption.

Several comparative analyses have also pointed out that imperial disintegration cannot be explained by external challenges or internal weaknesses alone. Instead, it is a matter of the balance between the capacities and loads of empires (Deutsch et al., 1957, p. 86ff; Kennedy, 1987; Motyl, 2001). This balance is contingent upon the specific situation of an empire. Therefore, an internally weak empire can survive for a long time without dealing with the challenge of being overburdened, while an internally strong empire can collapse in the face of even stronger competitors. Paul Kennedy coined the concept of "imperial overstretch" to denote a situation in which the costs of controlling (new) peripheries exceed the profits. In particular, when empires import instability rather than export stability, the costs of maintaining the empire increase. Nevertheless, an empire can cope with these challenges if it is able to rely on economic productivity, a sound financial basis, and sufficient capacity to adapt, innovate, and flexibly respond to new circumstances. However, in times of economic down-turn in particular, all empires face the dilemma of choosing between spending to ward off imminent threats or investing in long-term economic productivity. In such a situation, decline is difficult to avoid. If an empire invests in fighting threats rather than in productivity, economic growth will slow and the empire will increase taxes to support its efforts to maintain itself. In response, business, peripheries, and the centre's citizens will protest against increasing financial pressure. As a result, peripheries may seek exit, while the centre's citizens will refuse to fund efforts to keep the peripheries on board, in particular if they have no say in the redistribution of imperial resources or differ strongly in terms of their perception of the goals of redistribution (see also Deutsch et al., 1957; Gills, 1993).

Whereas Kennedy emphasises an empire's economic underpinnings as fundamental to its survival, Alexander Motyl stresses the need for effective management of allotting resources and, even more importantly, the efficient collection and processing of information: "the efficient flow of resources is of overwhelming importance to the stability—or the self-maintenance—of empires. [...] The more peripheries there are, the larger the demands on information aggregation and resource allocation, the greater the likelihood of overload and disintegration" (Motyl, 2001, p. 48, 65). Given the expansive nature of empires, they all face the challenge of controlling an increasing diversity of peripheries. If imperial elites do not choose to increase their capabilities, the empire will decline irreversibly, according to Motyl (2001).

The factors mentioned above relate to a large degree to the core of the empire. In his comparative analysis, Doyle (1986, pp. 128–129) also points to the links between the imperial core and peripheries and the weakness of peripheries as factors crucial to establishing and maintaining empires. The more key actors in the peripheries that are connected to the culture, society, law, or economy of the imperial centre, the less likely disintegration is. Additionally, an imperial relationship can only be established if a periphery is available that is weak enough to be subordinated. This weakness can be the product of the limited availability of economic and financial resources. Political divisions can be exploited by an imperial centre to execute a divide-and-rule strategy within the peripheries as well. If the peripheries were to become powerful, they would be able to seek independence, but they could also form a united front against the imperial core and demand to be treated on an equal basis. In the latter case, the empire would be transformed into a federative system. The degradation of the hub-like structure of an empire may therefore lead to imperial disintegration, but it will also lead to a different type of polity.

External challenges to and internal weaknesses of the empire, the imbalance between the imperial burden and capacities, declining peripheral links with the imperial core, and the strength of peripheries are factors that have been identified in comparative analyses as being essential to understanding the disintegration of empires. The question remains, however, as to which factors are more and less significant to the process of disintegration. Similar to the explanations of failing federalism, a proper explanation of disintegration should also indicate when and how the identified factors interrelate. Another challenge is to identify which factors are crucial. As explained previously, empires have expanded by different means and for different reasons and the factors that contributed to their decline and fall also differ. Whereas economic productivity has often been argued to be the crucial factor that affected the disintegration of the Soviet Empire, the declining legitimacy of colonialism played a fundamental role in the end of the French, British, and Dutch empires. It might therefore be more fruitful to focus on the mechanisms at work in processes of integration and disintegration rather than specific factors, from population size to administrative efficiency, per se.

5.7   Conclusion

This chapter has shown that the EU shares sufficient commonalities with empires to justify exploring explanations of imperial decline and fall in an effort to find a full explanation of EU disintegration. The obvious advantage of an imperial perspective is its lack of state-centric bias. Furthermore, disintegration might also lead to resurrected empire, for example, as the disintegrating Soviet Empire evolved into a Russian one (Motyl, 2001). Empires are clearly non-state entities because of their unfixed boundaries and self-legitimation. They do not require mutual recognition of territorial sovereignty. The imperial perspective discussed in this chapter provides a few lessons that inform our exploration of EU disintegration. First, the Holy Roman Empire shows that even a relatively weak, divided entity can survive for quite a while. Thus, the end of an empire does not depend exclusively on strength or weakness, but on a combination of internal factors and external challenges. In addition, relationships with other economic or military hegemons and empires within the global sphere clearly matter in terms of the power and survival of an empire. This not only concerns its capacity to attract sufficient economic surplus, but also its reliance on the security and order provided by others. Similar to the reliance of the Holy Roman Empire on foreign powers to maintain internal peace, the EU depends on the USA for its external security. A third lesson from the imperial perspective is to include in the analysis political entities that are not formal members of the empire, but are still subordinate to the imperial core. An empire might lose or win these entities. Nevertheless, the loss of peripheries does not constitute imperial collapse. This should be distinguished from the disintegration of relationship of control between an imperial core and (remaining) peripheries. A final lesson is that a fruitful starting point for a comprehensive explanation of EU disintegration should be sought elsewhere because such an explanation should not just be a list of factors that affect disintegration, it should be able to demonstrate when, how, and which factors matter in processes of disintegration.

REFERENCES

Agnew, J. (1998). *Geopolitics: Revisioning world politics.* London: Routledge.
Alesina, A., & Spolaore, E. (2003). *The size of nations.* Cambridge, MA: MIT Press.
Andreas, P. (2003). Redrawing the line: Borders and security in the twenty-first Century. *International Security, 28*(2), 78–111.
Axtmann, R. (2003). State formation and supranationalism in Europe: The case of the Holy Roman Empire of the German Nation. In M. Berezin & H. Schain (Eds.), *Europe without borders: Remapping territory, citizenship and identity in a transnational age* (pp. 118–139). Baltimore and London: John Hopkins University Press.
Barbé, E., & Johansson-Nogués, E. (2008). The EU as a modest "force for good": The European neighbourhood policy. *International Affairs, 84*(1), 81–96.
Beck, U., & Grande, E. (2011). *Empire Europe: Statehood and political authority in the process of regional integration.* Oxford: Oxford University Press.
Behr, H. (2007). The European Union in the legacies of imperial rule? EU accession politics viewed from a historical comparative perspective. *European Journal of International Relations, 13*(2), 239–262.
Böröcz, J. (2001). Empire and coloniality in the "eastern enlargement" of the European Union. In J. Böröcz, M. Kovács, S. Engel-Di Mauro, A. Sher, K. Dancsi, & P. Kabachnik, (Eds.), *Empire's new clothes: Unveiling EU enlargement* (pp. 4–50). Shropshire: Central Europe Review e-books.
Bressanelli, E. (2014). Necessary deepening? How political groups in the European Parliament adapt to enlargement. *Journal of European Public Policy, 21*(5), 776–792.

Browning, C. S., & Joenniemi, P. (2008). Geostrategies of the European neighbourhood policy. *European Journal of International Relations, 14*(3), 519–551.

Bull, H. (1977). *The anarchical society: A study of order in world politics.* London: Macmillan.

Charillon, F. (2004). Sovereignty and intervention: EU's interventionism in its "near abroad". In W. Carlsnaes, H. Sjursen, & B. White (Eds.), *Contemporary European foreign policy* (pp. 252–264). London: Sage.

Charter, D. (2007, July 11). Call for vote on "Europe empire". *The Times.*

Christiansen, T., Petito, F., & Tonra, B. (2000). Fuzzy politics around fuzzy borders: The European Union's "near abroad". *Cooperation and Conflict, 35*(4), 389–415.

Colomer, J. M. (2007). *Great empires, small nations: The uncertain future of the sovereign state.* London: Routledge.

Cooper, R. (2004). *The breaking of nations: Order and chaos in the twenty-first century.* London: Atlantic Books.

Cox, M. (2003). The empire's back in town: Or America's imperial temptation – Again. *Millennium, 32*(1), 1–27.

Dahl, R., & Tufte, E. (1973). *Size and democracy.* Stanford: Stanford University Press.

Davies, N. (2012). *Vanished kingdoms: The history of half-forgotten Europe.* London: Penguin Books.

Demandt, A. (1984). *Der Fall Roms.* München: Beck.

Deutsch, K. W., et al. (1957). *Political community and the North Atlantic Area: International organization in the light of historical experience.* Princeton, NJ: Princeton University Press.

Die Welt. (2007, October 17). Dimensionen eines Imperiums.

Doyle, M. (1986). *Empires.* Ithaca: Cornell University Press.

Duffield, M. (2007). Development, territories, and people: Consolidating the external sovereign frontier. *Alternatives, 32,* 225–246.

European Commission. (2005). *Communication: Strategy on the external dimension of the area of freedom, security and justice* (COM (2005) 491 final). Brussels: European Commission.

Falk, R. (2000). A "New Medievalism"? In G. Fry & J. O'Hagan (Eds.), *Contending images of world politics* (pp. 106–116). Houndmills: Palgrave.

Ferguson, N. (2004). *Colossus: The price of America's empire.* New York: The Penguin Press.

Friedrichs, J. (2001). The meaning of new medievalism. *European Journal of International Relations, 7*(4), 475–502.

Gills, B. K. (1993). Hegemonic transitions in the world system. In A. G. Frank & B. K. Gills (Eds.), *The world system: Five hundred Years or five thousand?* (pp. 115–140). London: Routledge.

Gilpin, R. (1988). The theory of hegemonic war. *The Journal of Interdisciplinary History, 18*(4), 591–613.

Gravier, M. (2009). The next European empire? *European Societies, 11*(5), 627–647.

Haldén, P. (2009). *Stability without statehood: Lessons from Europe's history before the sovereign state.* Basingstoke: Palgrave Macmillan.

Hansen, P., & Jonsson, S. (2012). Imperial origins of European integration and the case of Eurafrica: A reply to Gary Marks' "Europe and its empires". *Journal of Common Market Studies, 50*(6), 1028–1041.

Hardt, J., & Negri, A. (2000). *Empire.* Cambridge: Harvard University Press.

Hooghe, L., & Marks, G. (2008). A postfunctionalist theory of European integration: From permissive consensus to constraining dissensus. *British Journal of Political Science, 39*, 1–23.

Howorth, J. (2007). *Security and defence policy in the European Union.* Basingstoke: Palgrave Macmillan.

Ignatieff, M. (2003). *Empire lite: Nation building in Bosnia, Kosovo and Afghanistan.* London: Vintage.

Kelemen, R. D., Menon, A., & Slapin, J. (2014a). The European Union: Wider and deeper? *Journal of European Public Policy, 21*(5), 643–646.

Kelemen, R. D., Menon, A., & Slapin, J. (2014b). Wider and deeper? Enlargement and integration in the European Union. *Journal of European Public Policy, 21*(5), 647–663.

Kennedy, P. (1987). *The rise and fall of the great powers: Economic change and military conflict from 1500 to 2000.* New York: Random House.

Kobrin, S. J. (1998). Back to the future: Neomedievalism and the postmodern digital world. *Journal of International Affairs, 51*(2), 361–386.

Kölliker, A. (2001). Bringing together or driving apart the Union? Towards a theory of differentiated integration. *West European Politics, 24*(4), 125–151.

Kölliker, A. (2006). *Flexibility and European unification: The logic of differentiated integration.* Lanham: Rowman & Littlefield.

Kristoff, L. K. D. (1959). The nature of frontiers and boundaries. *Annals of the Association of American Geographers, 49*, 269–282.

Kux, S., & Sverdrup, U. (2000). Fuzzy borders and adaptive outsiders: Norway, Switzerland and the EU. *European Integration, 22*, 237–270.

Lavenex, S. (2004). EU external governance in "wider Europe". *Journal of European Public Policy, 11*(4), 680–700.

Lavenex, S. (2011). Concentric circles of flexible "European" integration: A typology of EU external governance relations. *Comparative European Politics, 9*(4/5), 292–305.

Leuffen, D., Rittberger, B., & Schimmelfennig, F. (2013). *Differentiated integration: Explaining variation in the European Union.* Basingstoke: Palgrave Macmillan.

Linklater, A. (2005). A European civilizing process? In C. Hill & M. Smith (Eds.), *International relations and the European Union* (pp. 435–457). Oxford: Oxford University Press.

Lundestad, G. (1998). *"Empire" by integration: The United States and European integration, 1945–1997.* Oxford: Oxford University Press.

Lundestad, G. (2003). *The United States and western Europe since 1945: From "Empire" by invitation to transatlantic drift.* Oxford: Oxford University Press.

Mahony, H. (2006, April 10). *Rehn says EU borders are not fixed.* Retrieved from www.euobserver.com

Mahony, H. (2007, July 11). *Barroso says EU is an "empire".* Retrieved from www.euobserver.com

Manners, I. (2002). Normative power Europe: A contradiction in terms? *Journal of Common Market Studies, 40*(2), 235–258.

Marks, G. (2012). JCMS annual lecture 2011: Europe and its empires: From Rome to the European Union. *Journal of Common Market Studies, 50*(1), 1–20.

Matlary, J. H. (2008). Much ado about little: The EU and human security. *International Affairs, 84*(1), 131–143.

Merlingen, M., & Ostrauskaite, R. (2005). ESDP police missions: Meaning, context and operational challenges. *European Foreign Affairs Review, 10*, 215–235.

Miles, L. (2004). Theoretical considerations. In N. Nugent (Ed.), *European Union enlargement* (pp. 253–265). Basingstoke: Palgrave Macmillan.

Mitsilegas, V., Monar, J., & Rees, W. (2003). *The European Union and internal security: Guardian of the people?* Basingstoke: Palgrave Macmillan.

Modelski, G. (1987). *Long cycles in world politics.* Basingstoke: Macmillan.

Motyl, A. (2001). *Imperial ends: The decay, collapse, and revival of empires.* New York: Columbia University Press.

Münkler, H. (2005). *Die Logik der Weltherrschaft: Vom Alten Rom bis zu den Vereinigten Staaten.* Berlin: Rowohlt.

Nexon, D. H., & Wright, T. (2007). What's at stake in the American empire debate. *American Political Science Review, 101*(2), 253–271.

Nordhausen, F., & Fras, D. (2013, September 25). Die Kaiserin von Europa: Auslandpresse über Merkel. *Berliner Zeitung.*

Organski, A. F. K. (1968). *World politics.* New York: Alfred Knopf.

Osiander, A. (2001). Sovereignty, international relations, and the Westphalian myth. *International Organization, 55*, 251–287.

Paasi, A. (2003). Territory. In J. Agnew, J. K. Mitchell, & G. Toal (Eds.), *A companion to political geography* (pp. 109–120). Malden, MA: Blackwell.

Pagden, A. (1995). *Lords of all the world: Ideologies of empire in Spain, Britain and France c. 1500 – c. 1800. New Haven.* London: Yale University Press.

Ruggie, J. G. (1993). Territoriality and beyond. *International Organization, 47*(1), 139–174.

Schimmelfennig, F. (2001). The community trap: Liberal, rhetorical action, and the eastern enlargement of the European Union. *International Organization, 55*(1), 47–80.

Schimmelfennig, F. (2014). EU enlargement and differentiated integration: Discrimination or equal treatment. *Journal of European Public Policy, 21*(5), 681–698.

Schimmelfennig, F., Leuffen, D., & Rittberger, B. (2015). The European Union as a system of differentiated integration: Interdependence, politicization, and differentiation. *Journal of European Public Policy, 22*(6), 764–782.

Schimmelfennig, F., & Sedelmeier, U. (2002). Theorizing EU enlargement: Research focus, hypotheses, and the state of research. *Journal of European Public Policy, 9*(4), 500–528.

Schimmelfennig, F., & Sedelmeier, U. (2004). Governance by conditionality: EU rule transfer to the candidate countries of central and eastern Europe. *Journal of European Public Policy, 11*(4), 669–687.

Schneider, C. (2014). Domestic politics and the widening-deepening trade-off in the European Union. *Journal of European Public Policy, 21*(5), 699–712.

Sjursen, H. (1998). *Enlargement and the common and security policy: Transforming the EU's external policy?* (ARENA Working Paper 18). Oslo: Centre for European Studies.

Teschke, B. (2003). *The myth of 1648: Class, geopolitics and the making of modern international relations.* London and New York: Verso.

Tilly, C. (1990). *Coercion, capital and European states: AD 990–1990.* Cambridge, MA: Blackwell.

Toshkov, D. (2017). The impact of the Eastern enlargement on the decision-making capacity of the European Union. *Journal of European Public Policy, 24*(2), 177–196.

Van der Veen, M. A. (2014). Enlargement and the anticipatory deepening of European integration. *Journal of European Public Policy, 21*(5), 761–775.

Vitorino, A. (2002). New European borders and security cooperation: Promoting trust in an enlarged Union. In M. Anderson & J. Apap (Eds.), *Police and justice cooperation and the new European borders* (pp. 11–17). The Hague: Kluwer.

Vollaard, H. (2009). The logic of political territoriality. *Geopolitics, 14*(4), 687–706.

Wæver, O. (1997). Imperial metaphors: Emerging European analogies to pre-nation-state imperial systems. In O. Tunander, P. Baev, & V. I. Einagel (Eds.), *Geopolitics in post-wall Europe: Security, territory and identity* (pp. 59–93). London: Sage.

Waltz, K. (1979). *Theory of international politics.* Readings, MA: Addison-Wesley.

Waterfield, B. (2007, July 18). Barroso hails the European "empire". *Telegraph.*

Wendt, A., & Friedheim, D. (1996). Hierarchy under anarchy: Informal empire and the east German state. In C. Weber & T. J. Biersteker (Eds.), *State sovereignty as social construct* (pp. 240–277). Cambridge: Cambridge University.

Wichmann, N. (2007). *The intersection between justice and home affairs and the European neighbourhood policy: Taking stock of the logic, objectives & practices* (CEPS Working Document no. 274). Brussels: CEPS.

Wilson, P. H. (2011). *The Holy Roman Empire, 1495–1806* (2nd ed.). Basingstoke: Palgrave Macmillan.

Zielonka, J. (2006). *Europe as empire: The nature of the enlarged European Union.* Oxford: Oxford University Press.

Zielonka, J. (2011). The EU as an international actor: Unique or ordinary? *European Foreign Affairs Review, 16*, 281–301.

Zielonka, J. (2012). Empires and the modern international system. *Geopolitics, 17*(3), 502–525.

CHAPTER 6

Towards a Proper Explanation of European Disintegration

6.1 Introduction

A crumbling European Union would not be a unique case of disintegration. Many other political systems have broken down before. An explanation of European disintegration can thus be based on a more general account of disintegrating political systems, such as federations, empires, currency areas, and regional organisations. The additional advantage of a more general explanation is that the story of European disintegration is then not simply written in more abstract theoretical terms, but is one that can be approached comparatively and empirically. As discussed in the previous chapters, theories of European integration and international politics and comparative approaches to federalism and imperialism all face problems in terms of providing an explanation of (European) disintegration. For instance, some suffer from state bias, whereas others neglect the multicausal nature of the process of disintegration. Be that as it may, valuable lessons can be learned from the discussion of these theories and approaches that inform a proper explanation of European disintegration. Section 6.2 provides an overview of these lessons learned. The subsequent sections demonstrate how the political scientist Stefano Bartolini offers a more promising starting point for explaining European disintegration, as his account avoids the problems associated with the theories and approaches discussed in the previous chapters. In his book, *Restructuring Europe* (2005), he presents a theoretical framework on polity formation derived

© The Author(s) 2018
H. Vollaard, *European Disintegration*, Palgrave Studies in European
Union Politics, https://doi.org/10.1057/978-1-137-41465-6_6

from the political sociologist Stein Rokkan's understanding of state building in Europe. Rokkan's ideas are addressed in Sect. 6.3. As described in further detail in Sect. 6.4, Bartolini's framework is applicable to the formation of all political systems, including the European Union. Whereas Bartolini focused on disintegrating national states and European integration, this chapter employs his theoretical framework to address European disintegration as well. In Sect. 6.5, the way in which the framework can be used to do so is discussed, providing the theoretical basis for the chapters that follow.

6.2   Lessons Learned

This section provides an overview of the lessons learned based on the problems previously discussed theories and approaches faced in seeking to explain European disintegration. Two lessons concern the conceptualisation of European disintegration. A first lesson is that *European disintegration is multifaceted* and involves political, economic, institutional, territorial, socio-cultural, and legal dimensions (Eppler & Scheller, 2013). Additionally, disintegration in one dimension need not be accompanied by disintegration in another. For instance, a formal expansion of the EU's competences does not necessarily coincide with trends in patterns of trade and intercultural trust. Moreover, a closer E(M)U might even be an obstacle to trade and mutual understanding among Europeans (Zielonka, 2014). Processes of disintegration should therefore be disentangled to explain how each and every dimension changes. As indicated in the introduction, this book focuses on the political dimension of European disintegration. It seeks to explain the disintegration of the EU polity understood as a system of interactions through which authoritative allocations of values are made and implemented (cf. Easton, 1965). According to this conceptualisation, the EU polity is not necessarily limited to formal EU membership, as (potential) candidate member states can also be part of a European system of value allocation.

Also, political integration involves many dimensions, including the scope of policy areas affected and the demand flow for European regulation. According to the neo-functionalist Leon Lindberg (1971), these dimensions do not necessarily evolve in the same direction and are not necessarily explained by the same logic either. Similarly, political *dis*integration is expected to consist of various dimensions. For instance, a decrease in the number of member states might not necessarily coincide with a repatriation of competences from the European to the national level. This applies to politico-administrative compliance as well. Along similar lines, comparative analyses of disintegrating states, empires, and federations point at the various manifestations of disintegration at both the system and the actor levels. For example, disintegration refers not only to the decline or dissolution of an entire empire or federation, but also to the secession of a single unit (full exit), as well as partial exits including the growing ignorance of the basic rules of a polity and a refusal on the part of any actor to share the polity's financial burden (Bednar, 2009; Kelemen, 2007; Motyl, 2001). Moreover, actors other than states (such as groups of states, companies, regions, or groups of citizens) can also fully or partially exit from a political system of allocating values like the EU. Exit from a political system by one actor can happen simultaneously with (partial) entry by another actor of whatever type to the system of allocating values. Additionally, an actor's exit does not necessarily imply the breakup of the complete system. In other words, the (partial) withdrawal of an individual EU member state does not necessarily mean that the entire EU will fall apart. The various dimensions of (dis)integration at the system and the actor levels should therefore be distinguished and thus require distinct explanations.

A second lesson is that *political disintegration is not necessarily integration in reverse*. Whereas, up until the 1980s, European integration might have been a largely behind-the-scenes, technocratic process that aimed to solve common policy problems, a full and up-to-date understanding of the EU's evolution should also account for the politicisation of identity and the growing public dissensus on the EU (Hooghe & Marks, 2009). Neo-functionalists introduced the concept of spillback to capture the "withdrawal from a set of specific obligations", which may result from nationalistic resistance, exogenous shocks, too much and too quick integration, or changing interest coalitions, among other things (Lindberg & Scheingold, 1970, pp. 137, 121–122; Niemann & Bergmann, 2013; Schmitter, 1971, pp. 242–243). The conceptualisation and explanation of spillback have not been sufficiently elaborated upon, however. It has been operationalised as the decrease of the EU's scope of action and institutional capacities. But how does spillback distinguish between the rearrangements of competences common to any multi-level system and the more destructive notion of disintegration? Additionally, neo-functionalists understand disintegration as the reversal of integration. However, disintegration is not necessarily the opposite of territorial states becoming or being integrated. Instead, the EU's authoritative allocation of values can also be (partially) divided into a northern and southern zone or be (partially) merged into a larger transatlantic scheme. A straightforward return to traditional notions of the territorial state should, therefore, not be assumed to be the only possible outcome of a process of European disintegration (Vollaard, 2014). As a result, classic theories of European integration and international cooperation (not only neo-functionalism but also realism and intergovernmentalism) simply turned on their head are problematic in terms of conceptualising and explaining European political disintegration. State-centric bias should be avoided, even if a return to sovereign states may still be a possible outcome empirically.

The next set of lessons learned relates to the explanation of European disintegration. The third lesson is that *political disintegration is not a mono-causal process*. European disintegration is not just a question of changing balances of power, diminishing economic interdependencies to be managed, or failing requirements of an optimal currency area (cf. Mearsheimer, 1990; Rosato, 2011; Sadeh & Verdun, 2009; Vollaard, 2014). Instead, comparative analyses of integrating and disintegrating empires, monetary unions, and federations show that a multitude of factors are at play, including ineffective decision-making, administrative corruption, military ineffectiveness, judicial and party-political safeguards, a lack of social and political mobility, economic decline, barbarian invasions, changing demography, cultural heterogeneity, linguistic diversity, and incompatible values or ideologies (see, e.g., Deutsch et al., 1957; Doyle, 1986; Elazar, 1987, p. 240ff; Etzioni, 2001; Filippov, Ordeshook, & Shvetsova, 2004; Franck, 1968; Motyl, 2001; Riker, 1964). A wide variety of factors, both material and ideational in nature, external and internal, systemic and those at the actor level, should thus be taken into account.

Comparative analyses of disintegrating polities also emphasise that all polities face a continuous struggle between integrative and disintegrative, centripetal and centrifugal forces. For example, empires face a tension between their expansive nature and their internal capacity to sustain growth (Deutsch et al., 1957, p. 86ff; Kennedy, 1987). Federations are characterised by permanent conflicts between member states that shirk on their commitments and the systemic safeguards that are in place to prevent such transgressions (Bednar, 2009; Kelemen, 2007). The fourth lesson is, therefore, that *disintegrative and integrative forces are always present in a polity* (see also Eppler & Scheller, 2013). Exclusive focus on one of them would lead to too rosy or too gloomy a conclusion regarding the sustainability and survival of a polity. As a result, a complete explanation of European disintegration must also account for the evolution of the entire EU polity, including its integrative forces.

Another lesson gleaned from comparative analysis of disintegrating systems in the past and present is that the *same factor can be both conducive to integration and disintegration*, depending on the specific context. For instance, decentralisation of competences from the highest level can foster further claims for repatriation, but may also temper calls for (partial) exit. With respect to the EU polity, Euroscepticism can, therefore, account for both why an electorate would vote in favour of exit and for the growing involvement of anti-system parties and citizens in EU politics. Additionally, the disintegrative potential of processes like enlargement can also be an impetus for further integration (Eppler & Scheller, 2013, p. 318). Moreover, the disintegration of political systems in the past and present cannot always be explained by the same factors; rather, it depends on the existence of a specific constellation of several, dynamically interrelated factors. The sixth lesson is, therefore, that *a proper explanation should not be based upon a static list of potential factors contributing to European disintegration*. A checklist of potential integrative and disintegrative factors cannot fully explain disintegration. The interrelationship between the manifold factors at work should be indicated. Therefore, a proper explanation must describe a mechanism that can account for the dynamic and dialectic process involving context-specific disintegrative and integrative factors, indicating how macro-dynamics and micro-components of the EU's machinery are causally connected (cf. Hedström & Swedberg, 1998; Mason, Easton, & Lenney, 2013). A mechanism should be seen as an analytical instrument that helps us grasp the process of European disintegration, in which a variety of factors and actors play a role, at both the macro and the micro levels, and in which different factors than those at work in the instances of disintegrating federal systems, empires, and common currency areas discussed before may play a role. The additional advantage of identifying such a mechanism is that it would offer a relatively concise, parsimonious explanation rather than simply producing an unwieldy list of factors that may explain European disintegration. Furthermore, it would allow for the factoring in of the impact of new evolutions, such as the digitalisation of society and the growing financialisation of the economy, in which processes of European (dis)integration are embedded (cf. Zielonka, 2014).

6.3   ROKKAN: THE MECHANISM OF STATE FORMATION

The lessons learned set the bar high for a proper explanation of European disintegration. A comprehensive understanding is required. In one of the first and few theoretical publications that tackles European disintegration head on, Douglas Webber (2013) suggests combining theories of hegemonic stability and domestic politics to account for European disintegration. For the sake of parsimony, a single theoretical foundation would be preferable, however. Bartolini (2005) offers such a foundation in his book, *Restructuring Europe*. As said, his theoretical framework is based on Rokkan's understanding of the history of state formation. Despite the fact that it is focused on the history of *states*, state borders are not taken for granted in Rokkan's analysis (Mjøset, 2000, p. 388). In particular, the book *Exit, Voice and Loyalty: Responses to Decline in Firms, Organizations and States*, by the political economist Albert Hirschman (1970), taught Rokkan to perceive the formation and evolution of states as a function of the interdependence between boundary transcendence and boundary control, between centrifugal and centripetal forces. State borders have been a means and temporary outcome of this interdependence, rather than a given or an inevitable result. Rokkan integrated Hirschman's focus on the way actors respond at the micro-level to a situation of deterioration based on a macro-level perspective on the way states have evolved.

Before explaining Rokkan's line of thinking in more detail, the key concepts of boundaries and borders should be defined here. Borders and boundaries can have distinct meanings depending on discipline (e.g., political anthropology and political geography), but are often used interchangeably. Following Bartolini (2005, p. 13), "borders" refers here to the physical-territorial delineation of states, whereas "boundaries" refers to the delineation of any manner of system (*in casu*, a system of allocation of values) that can be based on function, territory, or person (Vollaard, 2009). Boundaries thus distinguish between the inside and the outside of a political system, functioning as filters and selectors, regulating exit and entry of persons, goods, capital, services, or whatever else (Moisio & Paasi, 2013; Popescu, 2012). They can vary in degree of permeability. The higher the barrier to enter or leave, the less permeable they are. These barriers can be geographical or physical, but also coercive and socialising mechanisms and institutional arrangements anywhere (Popescu, 2012). For instance, people can be inculcated through educational or media programmes where the political system and its boundaries are or can be required to ask for approval to travel or obtain goods across boundaries under the threat of punishment if approval is not sought. Borders delineating "geographical space" do not necessarily coincide with boundaries indicating "membership space" (Rokkan, 1999). For instance, travellers may be able to access states' territories, but not their welfare arrangements or education systems. Additionally, the boundaries of a political system should not only be understood in horizontal, spatial terms but also in "vertical" terms that delineate the extent to which the political system penetrates society and individual space.

Rokkan's main argument is that the closure of states by boundary control has allowed for the establishment of a coercive and politico-administrative centre that penetrates societal and individual spaces by means of taxation, policy implementation, and law enforcement, for nation-building and for setting up systems of redistribution and participation: "[y]ou cannot build states without controlling borders" (Rokkan, 1975, p. 589). In Rokkan's view, in the absence of boundaries, actors can easily escape from compulsory taxation or democratic agreements (see also Finer, 1974) among other things. Stuck *within* state territories, however, actors have to make political deals and exchange resources to address a situation of deterioration. Thus, external closure facilitates the extraction of resources necessary to build up a power centre with the means to address actors' dissatisfaction. These resources could also be used by the state centre in the making to enhance its boundary control, be it by enforcing laws in societal and individual spaces, enhancing socio-cultural adherence to the state in the making or regulating exit and entry more tightly in more and more domains, from economic to even ideological. This allows the centre to lock actors and resources further into the state system, preventing actors from escaping from the system and steering them towards addressing their dissatisfaction within the system, which allows it to expand its scope of policy involvement.

Rokkan used Hirschman's triad of exit, voice, and loyalty in his analysis of the mutual dependence between a state's external consolidation and its internal construction (Rokkan, 1999, p. 100ff). Hirschman argues that actors are less inclined to voice their dissatisfaction with the values allocated in any (political) system when they have the option to exit. With mobility constrained by boundary control and loyalty to the system, dissatisfaction with the allocation of whatever value would be primarily expressed by voice, which refers to a wide array of individual, organised, and collective activities of political articulation intended to express dissatisfaction, including petitioning, voting, and protesting (Hirschman, 1970, p. 30). As actors became increasingly locked into their states, voice took on more structural patterns. These have been expressed along territorial, corporate, and/or electoral lines, involving centre-periphery relations, interest mediation, and cleavage systems. As previous investments in voice can be used again within the same membership space, the relative cost of voice drops, fostering its use. Eventually, voice structures can thus be built up across geographical divides within states in the making:

> Functional oppositions can only develop after some initial consolidation of the national territory. They emerge with increasing interaction and communication across the localities and the regions, and they spread through a process of "social mobilization." (Rokkan, 1970, p. 101)

Thus, the closure of states resulted in an increasingly differentiated voice arena. Sub-state authorities, political parties, and interest groups reflected the fundamental political conflict lines that resulted from the processes of state formation and nation-building, as well as the Reformation, the Industrial Revolution, and the Russian Revolution. In sum, external consolidation, the extent to which actors and resources are "locked in", facilitated resource extraction, voice structuring, and the development of system-wide loyalty. As such, internal construction depended on external consolidation. However, internal construction also impacts external consolidation, as it affects the (relative) costs of exit and also the means of control of boundaries.

A variety of power centres attempted to establish and maintain political systems when the military-coercive and politico-administrative constructions of the Roman Empire unraveled. Despite the fact that the mechanism of external consolidation and internal construction operated in all these instances of polity formation, geographical and social factors shaped the specific conditions and outcomes of this causal process of integration. Polity formation, thus, depended on factors like where and when the Roman Empire lost its military and political control, distance from the economically rich Lothringian trade belt, ranging from the Low Countries to Lombardia, and the remaining cultural and religious unity between Roman culture and Christianity (Rokkan, 1999). Additionally, geography mattered in terms of the way in which resources could be extracted for the purpose of making a polity and in terms of the opportunities for exit and voice that existed in response to this extraction. For instance, the geography of the British Isles allowed the English power centre to rely predominantly on maritime forces for boundary defence and control, with the surrounding seas providing a buffer against outside interventions (Finer, 1974; see also Hintze, 1975, p. 159). Power centres in the French areas were forced to maintain much larger and more expensive land armies, which in turn required more taxation and broader administrative and control arrangements (Finer, 1974, p. 114). In contrast to those in French areas, internal competitors in the British Isles also had fewer opportunities to escape fully from London's power, and there were fewer outsiders capable of providing support for their escape. As a consequence, the political agenda of the British Isles is characterised by persistent disagreements with the Scottish, Welsh and Irish parliamentarian and lords' claims for more say in British politics (voice) or in their own areas (partial exits). Whereas French kings faced the continuous threat of regional magnates escaping from the French political system with the support of other power centres, English kings struggled first and foremost with regional powers over their say in the goings on the British Isles. As such, Samuel Finer (1974, p. 115) stated that French historiography "is obsessed by the demon of exit", while the English is marked "by the angel of voice."

Although external consolidation and internal construction were mutually dependent in all states-in-the-making, they followed different trajectories that were contingent on various conditions. This concerned not only geographical and material factors, but institutional arrangements as well. In some states, such as Italy, dissatisfaction could be alleviated by allowing emigration. This exit by dissatisfied actors released states from certain amount of pressure to adopt economic, political, or social reforms (Hirschman, 1981, p. 258ff). Therefore, the specific conditions did matter in terms of the way the mechanism of internal construction and external consolidation worked in states. And this also determined their evolution. For instance, limited participation allowed rulers to establish and extend political systems without conceding unmanageable levels of voice:

> The decisive thrust toward the consolidation of the machineries of territorial control took place (...) before the lower strata could articulate any claims for participation. This gave the national elites time to build up efficient organizations before they had to face the next set of challenges: the strengthening of national identity at the mass level, the opening of channels for mass participation, the development of a sense of national economic solidarity and

the establishment of a workable consensus on the need for a redistribution of resources and benefits. (Rokkan, 1975, pp. 597–598)

As Hirschman himself also observed, the limitation of voice and exit options thus facilitated the making and functioning of states:

> Every state [...] requires for its establishment and existence some limitations or ceilings on the extent of exit or of voice or of both. In other words, there are levels of exit (disintegration) and voice (disruption) beyond which it is impossible for an organisation to exist as an organisation. (Hirschman, 1981, pp. 224–225)

However, rulers in the French areas not only sought to curtail exits, they also continued to limit the voice of the lower strata of society. When the latter felt dissatisfied with the level of taxation, the only option left was to raise their voices more forcefully:

> [...] the absolutist-centralist states not only tried to close their borders, they also choked the channels of representation within the territory. [...] you cannot reduce both the exit and the voice options at the same time without endangering the balance of the system. This is what happened in the absolutist-mercantilist states. They had to go through much more violent transitions to mass democracy than the states which managed to keep a better balance between exit controls and voice channelling during the crucial phases of state-building. (Rokkan, 1975, p. 589)

The French Revolution is a prime example of "disruption" by less-structured and excessive voice. Disruption did not mean disintegration, however, which would have meant an exit from the French state (Hirschman, 1981, p. 224).

Rokkan combined Hirschman's focus on the micro-level behaviours of exit, voice, and loyalty with the dialectic dynamics of external consolidation and internal construction at the macro level. According to this characterisation of the mechanism, boundaries are not fixed, but variable. The mechanism suggests commonalities in the causal processes of state formation, but also accounts for the particular geographical and social factors at play in specific instances of state formation. As such, it appears to be a fertile base for further exploration of processes of European integration and also disintegration, despite its initial focus on the formation of states: "At first glance, [Rokkan's concepts] appear closely tied to his analysis of the development of the nation-state, but a closer look reveals promising perspectives also for examining the process of European unification" (Flora, 1999, p. 89). Hirschman (1974, p. 15, 1981, pp. 224ff, 282ff) himself showed some hesitance in applying his triad of exit, voice, and loyalty to European integration, despite his acknowledgement of how illuminating Rokkan's use of his triad to analyse processes of state formation had been. His triad was primarily aimed at explaining the reform and recuperation of existing "fully established" organisations in decline and not to the quasi-unique instance of regional integration. However, as of now, the European Union might be also considered a fully established organisation struggling to maintain satisfactory value delivery. Additionally, the EU is not unique in the sense that it *can* be compared to other political systems, integrating or disintegrating, as they all share the same mechanisms of external consolidation and internal construction and exit, voice, and loyalty.

Rokkan used his ideas first and foremost to map the historical evolution of states in Western Europe (Flora, 1999). Based on the social and geographical factors influencing the internal and external forces of polity formation, he drew maps of the European continent's polities:

> The essential rationale for my 'typological-topological' model of Europe is that it generates hypotheses about the interaction between external and internal boundary-building strategies in the history of the organization of the different territorial systems: the policies pursued in controlling external transactions also affect internal channelling of voice. (Rokkan, 1974, p. 49)

These typological-topological maps are merely suggestive in nature and, as the historical sociologist Charles Tilly (1990, p. 13) argued, "[i]t is hard to see how Rokkan could have gotten much farther without laying aside his maps and concentration on the analysis of the mechanisms of state formation" in order to explain the specific organisation of states. Rokkan himself did not have the opportunity to develop his notions extensively into a consistent set of propositions to indicate and detect the internal-external mechanism in any political system through empirical research. Fortunately, as will be explained below, Bartolini (1998, 2004, 2005) as well as Peter Flora (1999, 2000) and Maurizio Ferrera (2003, 2004, 2005) strengthened the analytical potential and rigour of Rokkan's ideas.

6.4   THE BOUNDING-BONDING MECHANISM IN ALL POLITICAL SYSTEMS

As with Rokkan, the key notion in Bartolini's framework is the mutual dependence between the external consolidation and the internal construction of a political system.[1] A system's external consolidation, the locking-in of actors and resources by means of boundary control and loyalty, facilitates its internal construction. This internal construction involves the development of voice structures, further exchanges, the growth of political alignments and mutual loyalty, as well as the extraction of resources for the formation of a power centre to address sources of dissatisfaction, including the accretion of the administrative, coercive, legal, political, or fiscal means to decide upon, legitimise, and implement policies (Bartolini, 2005, p. 27ff). In turn, internal construction provides the resources to strengthen boundaries and to generate more loyalty to the system, further increasing the costs of exit from the political system.

In addition to the degree of loyalty, external consolidation also refers to the strength of boundaries. This can be expressed in terms of permeability and congruence. As explained before, permeability refers to the barriers to entry and exit in a system. The less permeable a formation's boundaries are, the higher the costs are of leaving it. The more congruence, the more boundaries of a different nature (coercive, administrative, legal, cultural, social, economic) coincide with each other in one and the same political formation, making the costs of fully leaving that formation higher. The establishment and control of boundaries, territorial or non-territorial, constitute the systemic counterpart of the actor-level act of exit. Exit is defined as "the act of transcending a boundary" (Bartolini, 2005, p. 13). As said, political boundaries delineate a system of allocation of values. Exit, therefore, means that an actor leaves such a system. The act of exit can be carried out by individuals or companies, as well as by institutional actors, such as subnational regions. In Bartolini's understanding, exit comprises not only the complete and permanent transfer from one political formation to another, by means of regional secession or an individual's emigration, for example. Actors can also remain part of a political formation, but temporarily use public goods from another political formation (e.g., by consuming healthcare elsewhere) or withhold resources or refuse

---

[1] Despite being based on Bartolini's theoretical framework, the choice of wording here may differ slightly so as to express as clearly as possible the political phenomena at hand.

to comply with orders from the centre, in other words, failing behavioural conformity with the system's rule. For instance, France withdrew from NATO's military command structure between 1966 and 2008, whereas it remained a member of the political branch of the organisation. The latter types of behaviour are defined as "partial exits" (Bartolini, 2005, p. 7). As a matter of fact, exits may be used according to formal arrangements for exits (for instance, through an exit clause in a federal constitution), as well as illegally executed (for instance, by non-compliance). In sum, exit is about partial or full withdrawal from a system's allocation of values. Entry is the opposite of exit (see Table 6.2). Entry also has another opposite, non-entry. In the start-up phase of a political system or when a political system takes further integrative steps, actors can choose between entry and non-entry, fully or partially. In EU-speak, partial non-entries are often called opt-outs.

Whether or not actors use (partial) exit when they are dissatisfied with the values and goods allocated depends on a variety of considerations. Exit is a somewhat risky option when it is unclear whether membership in another system would offer superior goods and values. The more political systems resemble each other, the greater the chance of exit, as uncertainty around exit is diminished (Hirschman, 1970, p. 81). Exit also depends on other costs. The penalty for avoiding taxes may be different than that for consuming publicly insured healthcare in another system. Furthermore, in a region that borders on another system, it is easier to find external support for escape than in "system-locked" regions. These considerations also underline the fact that exits are differentiated among the members of any political formation, be they individual or institutional. One member may be able to bear the costs of exit more readily than another.

Dissatisfaction is not only expressed in terms of exit, but also through voice. Among other things, the use of voice depends on the benefits and costs involved. Voice can be rather costly if rulers forcefully retaliate against dissent (Hirschman, 1981). However, members may still seek to use voice because of the value of the act of (democratic) voice in and of itself (Bartolini, 2005, p. 36; Hirschman, 1970, p. 77). For individuals, gaining effective influence on the allocation of values can be a huge challenge. Nevertheless, the collective action required to use voice more effectively also demands a great deal of effort and carries with it the risk of freeriding amongst members (Barry, 1974; Hirschman, 1981, pp. 215–216). In this respect, collective action not only depends on the presence of eloquent political entrepreneurs but also on the existence of organisations and institutional infrastructure for voice that greatly enhances the efficient and effective use of voice. In other words, voice depends on "political structuring" (Bartolini, 2005, p. 36). When a political formation is highly structured, voice can be fairly easily (re-)mobilised at a low cost. Political voice can be directed vertically at rulers, but also horizontally at other actors in an effort to prevent their entry (when they are perceived to be competing for jobs and social benefits, for example) or exit (when they are perceived to be avoiding taxation, for example) (cf. Dowding et al., 2008).

Hirschman emphasises that exit and voice are not necessarily mutually exclusive. Someone can employ voice from outside (Hirschman, 1970, p. 104) or they can leave while voicing their dissatisfaction (Dowding, John, Mergoupis, & van Vugt, 2000, p. 73). A dissatisfied actor would thus face two questions: (a) should I stay or go? and (b) should I raise my voice or keep silent? (Ferrera, 2005, p. 29; cf. Hirschman, 1970, p. 98ff). The calculus of when to exit and when to express dissatisfaction depends on the benefits and costs at play. In line with Hirschman's and Rokkan's thinking, Bartolini (2005, p. 53) underlines that the availability of exit options has an impact on the expression of dissatisfaction through voice: "As closure and structuring are linked theoretically, the same applies to exit and de-structuring. This is the nucleus of a theory of boundary-building and political structuring and exit-options and political de-structuring." The use of exit and voice also depends on the type of good (Bartolini, 2005, pp. 6–7). If it is possible to withdraw from the production of a certain good (e.g., taxation), while still enjoying consumption (e.g., security), exit will be more likely. If, however, consumption of a good or value involves negative externalities, using voice would be the more likely choice.

The use of exit and voice is not only a matter of a calculation of costs and benefits. Loyalty also intervenes, a psychological factor that impacts actual behaviour (Dowding et al., 2000, p. 481). "Loyalty" can be defined as attachment to an organisation built upon feelings of solidarity, trust, and common identity within the organisation and among its members (Bartolini, 2005, p. 31). Loyalty may prevent members from exiting and also from voicing criticism, since their commitment to the organisation prevents them from doing so. Even if actors are somewhat dissatisfied with the allocation of a specific value, they may still stay and remain silent out of loyalty to the political system as a whole. Bartolini describes the systemic counterpart to loyalty as "system building", which refers to the development of identity, trust, solidarity, and social capital through cultural integration, social-sharing institutions, and participation rights (Bartolini, 2005, pp. xiv, 31). Boundary maintenance is closely related to system building and its subsequent impact on exit and voice behaviour: "[h]igh fees for entering an organization and stiff penalties for exit are among the main devices generating or reinforcing loyalty in such a way as to repress exit or voice or both" (Hirschman, 1970, p. 93).

In sum, the use of exit and voice depends on an actor's level of dissatisfaction, the opportunities available to employ exit and voice, as well as the degree of loyalty. As Bartolini (2005, p. 40ff) emphasises, in line with Rokkan, systemic conditions at the macro level shape the expression of dissatisfaction by actors within a system to allocate values. First, the more actors are locked into a political system and the more difficult and costly an exit is, the more likely they are to express dissatisfaction using voice (Hirschman, 1970, p. 34). In other words, without the option of mobility, actors look for mobilisation. Actors are more locked-in when the permeability of a formation's boundaries decreases, loyalty increases and boundaries of a different nature (coercive, economic, cultural, etc.) are more congruent. In short, it would require more effort for an actor to leave fully. Second, when actors become more locked-in to a political system, they are more inclined to put their resources into political exchanges with a variety of strategic allies in the political centre to address their dissatisfaction, thereby expanding the centre's political infrastructure and scope of involvement. Third, when actors remain more locked-in to an externally consolidated political system, a stabilisation of patterns of political exchange emerges that is reflected in more permanent alignments across the political system. When voice behaviour is repeated, uncertainty and even distrust may gradually disappear, being replaced by standardised expectations or even mutual loyalty. In a situation of "full exit", political structuring like this would not occur to the same degree, as actors (be they individuals, companies, or investors) can easily escape from and destabilise political exchange and alignments (Bartolini, 2005, p. 48). Thus, the establishment of boundaries is a fundamental prerequisite for political structuring. This interdependence between internal construction and external consolidation has been aptly summarised as the "bounding-bonding nexus" (Ferrera, 2005). Table 6.1 presents the systemic components of the bounding-bonding mechanism.

With the bounding-bonding mechanism, Bartolini developed a "holistic" theoretical framework (2005, p. xv) dealing with the formation of

Table 6.1 The systemic components of the bounding-bonding mechanism

External consolidation	*Internal construction*
• Greater congruence of boundaries • Increasing impermeability of boundaries • Building of loyalty towards system	• Institutionalisation of voice • Further exchange of resources • Centre formation: widening scope of involvement and more resources to reinforce boundaries and strengthen loyalty • Stabilising alignments • Increasing mutual expectations and loyalty

political systems, involving external and internal factors of various nature, playing out both at the systemic and the actor levels. The mechanism of internal construction and external consolidation, comprising the relationships between exit, voice and loyalty and their systemic counterparts, offers the necessary coherent and focused orientation on the dialectic between the ever-present multitude of disintegrative and integrative factors. Additionally, the framework is sufficiently abstract to apply it to any polity in time and space, not only states, but also non-state entities like the European Union (Ferrera, 2007). As its general theoretical premises meet the high standard set in light of the lessons learned presented above, the framework constitutes a fine starting point for explaining the specific case of the EU. Though Bartolini focused primarily on European integration (Bartolini, 2005, p. 3), as will be explained in the following section, his framework can also be used to explain disintegration.

6.5   THE BOUNDING-BONDING MECHANISM AND EUROPEAN (DIS)INTEGRATION

The bounding-bonding mechanism features in all political systems, but that does not mean that these systems should be expected to follow the same trajectory or adopt the same morphology, for example, due to the differentiated opportunities available to establish and transcend boundaries and to organise voice. Unless these opportunities are exactly the same as those that were at play in French or British history, the European Union is not expected to end up as a territorial state (Bartolini, 2005, p. 390). The outcome of processes of integration and disintegration is contingent on the material, geographic, social, institutional, and epistemic settings in which political actors operate. Thus, Bartolini's framework does not follow structural-functionalist or systemic determinism with respect to the specific functions or direction of polity formation (such as self-sufficiency, stability, survival, or equilibrium). Consequently, polities are not necessarily seen as fulfilling certain functions or striving for a certain equilibrium or stability. No isomorphism is expected, unless the circumstances, mechanisms of exit, voice and loyalty, and underlying reasons for dissatisfaction are similar. This reflects the analytical potential of Rokkan's ideas as developed by Bartolini. They do not take the territorial state for granted, but also did not exclude it as a potential outcome of processes of political formation or deformation (Karvonen, 2007). As such, it would be empirically unlikely that European disintegration would be simply integration in reverse, even though it is theoretically not outside of the realm of possibility.

Bartolini (2005) applies the bounding-bonding mechanism to the process of European integration at length. He describes European integration as a "process of boundary re-definition"; state boundaries are transcended, while the boundaries of the EU are constructed. The concept of "European integration" thus refers not only to the process of integration at the EU level but also to processes of disintegration at the national level. To eliminate potential confusion here, this book understands European integration (and disintegration) exclusively in terms of the making (or unmaking) of the EU system of allocating values.

So, how should European disintegration be understood in Bartolini's terms? European disintegration refers here at the actor level to full and partial exits from the EU polity's authoritative system of allocating values (whereas European integration at the actor level is the opposite: the entry into such a system) (see Table 6.2). The explanatory mechanism behind exit (or entry for that matter) is the consideration of exit and voice opportunities and loyalty in case of dissatisfaction. The more an actor is locked into a system by loyalty bonds and boundary control, the more an actor will be inclined to opt for voice if it is dissatisfied, in particular if there is an elaborate voice infrastructure. The less attractive the exit, the more inclined an actor will be to stay and vice versa.

At the systemic level, European disintegration fundamentally concerns the locking-in capacity of a political system. In other words, it is not necessarily about more or fewer competences, institutional capacities, policy areas, activities, or expectations or more or less enforcement *per se*, but about the capacity to keep actors within a system of allocating values. The locking-in capacity can be indicated by the permeability and congruence

Table 6.2   Conceptualisation and explanation of European disintegration

Dimension of political disintegration	Conceptualisation	Explanation
Actor level	Partial or full exit from system of allocating values (opposite: partial or full entry)	Mechanism of exit, voice, and loyalty if actor is dissatisfied
Systemic level	Declining locking-in capacity of a system of allocating values Expressed in terms of permeability and congruence of boundaries, boundary control, and loyalty building (=external consolidation) and institutionalisation of voice, exchange of resources, and centre building (=internal construction) (opposite: strengthening locking-in capacity)	Bounding-bonding mechanism: Mutual dependence between external consolidation and internal construction

of boundaries of various natures, boundary control, and loyalty building, which all serve to increase exit costs, as well as by the institutionalisation of voice, which lowers the costs of voicing dissatisfaction within the political system. The explanatory mechanism behind a system's locking-in capacity is the mutual dependence between external consolidation and internal construction. A system can be in a disintegrative spiral of weakening external consolidation and declining internal construction, but also find itself in an opposite integrative spiral. The mutually reinforcing relationships in the process of integration have been explained above, with more voice, political exchange, stabilisation of political alignments, and mutual loyalty as successive integrative components and with less voice, less political exchange, de-stabilisation of political alignments, and declining loyalty due to external de-consolidation as the steps of disintegration (cf. Bartolini, 2005, p. 53). Table 6.2 summarises this conceptualisation and explanation of European disintegration.

Both integration and disintegration involve processes that take place in the context of complex networks of relationships, in which independent and dependent variables are not necessarily fixed (Bartolini, 2005, p. 4). With this in mind, how can this framework be altered to provide a suitable foundation for carrying out coherent empirical research on European disintegration (or other processes of political (de)formation)? According to Bartolini's line of thinking, every polity is expected to function according to the bounding-bonding mechanism, involving exit, voice, and loyalty and their systemic counterparts. The process of European integration, which unfreezes internal borders and lays down new external boundaries, *must*, therefore, affect the internal construction of polities within the EU area. If European integration had not opened state borders and allowed member states to exit and enter more freely, then the member states would have taken different formation paths. Dissatisfaction may always exist. The key question is whether and how it will be dealt with, particularly in the member states and the European Union, both of which are unsettled by the "unbounding" effects of integration and enlargement. Thus, the obvious advantage of the Bartolini framework is that it offers a basis upon which to select the crucial historical causes and dynamics that determine the evolutions of and in the EU. As a result, a description and an explanation of European disintegration need not rely on an *ad hoc* reconstruction of the EU's history, rather it should rely on a general explanation of political disintegration. Bartolini's analytical framework of (dis)integration at the systemic level is foremost a combination of structural and institutional explanations, indicating how material and man-made constraints dictate the behaviour of actors, as opposed to their specific ideas or psychological conditions (cf. Parsons, 2007). At the actor level, the psychological conditions of loyalty also matter.

The overarching mechanism in Bartolini's framework is the bounding-bonding mechanism. Bartolini shows how external consolidation and internal construction are causally related in any political formation, including the European Union. His framework allows us to examine how this systemic relationship structures actors' exit, voice, and loyalty, and how actors' aggregate behaviour has systemic impact. According to Bartolini's framework, political systems are the collective result of actors' individual choices, but they are also partly purposefully constructed by authorities. This neo-institutional approach comprises both the mutual shaping of actors' individual choices and the opportunity structures. This leads to the observation that initial preferences expressed through exit or voice do not necessarily correspond to the final outcome of the game. For example, popular or partisan Euroscepticism may still result in an (grudging) acceptance of the EU, if people and parties lack any viable exit option, are bribed by side payments, or can express their voice sufficiently in the EU. Additionally, actors themselves may not be aware of structural processes of a polity's (dis)integration. Depending on the configuration of exit, voice, and loyalty and their systemic counterparts, dissatisfaction can lead to both further integration and disintegration of a political system. Even if these deep structural relationships between partly social phenomena are not fully and directly observable, the bounding-bonding mechanism allows us to reconstruct how they unfold. The evolution of these processes can be inferred from aggregated, quantitative data on exit, voice, and loyalty and behavioural conformity, as well as from qualitative observations of the systemic elements of boundary control, system building, enforcement of compliance, and political structuring. The framework is thus of a realist nature in terms of its ontology and epistemology (Marsh & Furlong, 2002). Though even this study may influence the perceived realities of political actors on the way the European Union does or does not function, it may also flounder on material and intersubjectively accepted facts. In the end, scientific studies may err profoundly regarding big issues such as European disintegration in particular. A study should therefore phrase propositions in such a way that they can check and test the bounding-bonding mechanism in the EU.

Bartolini's framework points to the various interrelationships that can and should be disentangled and examined separately to try and test it empirically. Problematic in this respect is that Bartolini did not put forward rigorously phrased, testable hypotheses (Morgan, 2006). This book therefore seeks to *develop* his framework by presenting testable propositions (see also Vollaard, 2014). They are called propositions instead of hypotheses to indicate the somewhat tentative nature of this stage of theory-building. For the purpose of theoretical fine-tuning, more extensive empirical evidence is also still required (Ferrera, 2007). To this end, this book presents four propositions on the key interrelationships in the processes of European integration and disintegration.

Proposition 1 The EU and its predecessors have always faced the challenge of non-integrative and disintegrative forces. Many national and international options for non-entry to and exit from the EU and its predecessors have been available, also just after the Second World War. So, what was it that made European integration take off at that time, in spite of all this? Obviously, there was no European polity with a capacity to lock-in resources and actors. It would therefore require an actor-level explanation according to the mechanism of exit, voice, and loyalty to identify why states decided to launch a European system of allocating values. It is therefore expected that the relative unattractiveness of national and international alternatives explains why some states opted for European integration, whereas others did not. As Hirschman (1981, pp. 224–225) has argued with respect to the formation of states, a certain limitation of voice also facilitates the establishment of a new political organisation. These considerations lead to the first proposition concerning the initial phase of European integration: *the unattractiveness of alternatives and limited voice allowed European integration to take off.* This proposition will be the focus of Chap. 7.

Proposition 2 As said, the EU and its predecessors have always faced non-integrative and disintegrative forces. Additionally, they have faced external de-consolidation time and time again, not the least being generated by the various rounds of enlargement. This must have had an impact on internal construction according to the bounding-bonding mechanism, challenging the integrative spiral involving the stabilisation of political alignments, increasing mutual exchange of resources, the ensuing growing power of the European centre required to maintain and strengthen its boundaries, and increasing mutual loyalty. The continuous challenges of external de-consolidation are expected to have limited the build-up of the EU's locking-in capacity, as expressed in Proposition 2: *the weak external consolidation of the EU and its predecessors has restrained its internal construction.* This proposition will be examined in Chap. 8. With its limited locking-in capacity, the EU and predecessors have had limited means to contain actor-level disintegration. If the integrative spiral still moved on, as it did, it should therefore be explained in large part at the actor level, in the same vein as the first proposition. Chapter 8 therefore also examines whether or not and how the relative unattractiveness of national and international alternatives and constrained voice have kept European integration moving on.

Proposition 3 The focus of the first two propositions is on the integrative spiral at the European level. The third proposition, however, deals with the impact of European integration at the national level. The creation of a European market and the pooling of sovereignty have required the external de-consolidation of the member states. State boundaries have become less congruent with certain policy areas that are partially or fully dealt with at the EU level. State boundaries have also become more permeable. At least some citizens, companies, and regions can use (partial) exits from their member states to seek better conditions elsewhere in the

EU. Following the bounding-bonding mechanism, this external de-consolidation has put the internal construction of the member states under pressure. With more exit options, citizens, companies, and regions can seek to exchange their resources elsewhere in the EU, providing member states with fewer means with which to maintain boundaries, among other things. Additionally, non-national EU citizens and companies can access member states on the basis of the rights of residence and free movement of labour. As a result, political alignments can be unsettled by antagonisms with regard to these new exit and entry options. This line of thought above is laid down in Proposition 3: *the external de-consolidation of the EU's member states has weakened their internal construction*. This third proposition is the central theme of Chap. 9.

Proposition 4 Chapters 7, 8, and 9 provide the background required to find out where and how dissatisfaction is and will be expressed within the multi-level EU. These chapters show how European integration has changed the constellations of exit, voice, and loyalty and how it has also generated dissatisfaction. Dissatisfaction is the starting point for all political dynamics. Dissatisfaction about EU membership might stem both from the ongoing integrative spiral at the EU level, whether or not it is sustained or constrained by voice, and the weakening internal construction of member states. Even if it is growing, this EU-induced dissatisfaction does not necessarily translate into full European disintegration, however. Dissatisfaction is a normal condition in any political formation. Without dissatisfaction, there would be no politics. The key issue is how dissatisfaction is and can be processed in the multi-level EU. This will play out differently from actor to actor according to the mechanism of exit, voice, and loyalty. As opposed to the EU itself, many member states can still rely on a substantial locking-in capacity, based on widespread and deep national loyalty and a sizeable law enforcement apparatus. Citizens, companies, and regions that fear the external de-consolidation of member states can call upon their member states to counter external de-consolidation by European integration. These citizens, companies, and regions can also use well-developed national voice structures for this purpose. Whether EU-related dissatisfaction leads to full EU disintegration will therefore depend first on the opportunities available to exert effective voice to compensate (perceived) losers of European integration within member states. Secondly, the prospect of European disintegration depends on the opportunities available in the EU for (perceived) losers of European integration to address their dissatisfaction effectively within the EU. As mentioned previously, the internal construction of the EU has been constrained by the continuing challenges of external de-consolidation, with limited EU loyalty, voice structures, and means with which to compensate dissatisfaction as a result. EU voice is therefore expected to have limited effectiveness. Thirdly, the international context should be taken into account: are there better alternatives outside the EU? This leads to Proposition 4a: *The stronger the EU-directed dissatisfaction, the lower the EU loyalty, the less (perceived) options to effective voice at the EU level, the less compensation for EU-directed dissatisfaction, the lower the perceived costs to leave the EU, and the better the perceived provision of values and goods by national or international alternatives to the EU, the more likely full exit is.* This proposition offers the opportunity to spell out cross-country variation more precisely and to take external circumstances more seriously into account, both of which were lacking in Bartolini's analysis (Ferrera, 2007, p. 218; Morgan, 2006).

When exit options outside the EU are considered too uncertain, too risky, or too costly, dissatisfied actors are stuck within the EU. This makes *partial* exits *within* the EU more likely. Eurosceptic member states, citizens, companies, and regions thus seek certain opt-outs from the EU (e.g., more possibilities to reinstate national border control within the Schengen area) or withhold their resources by refusing to comply with EU legislation or by limiting budgetary solidarity within the EU. Additionally, lacking a viable exit option outside the EU, Eurosceptic actors might seek improvement in terms of the goods and values allocated in the EU by excluding (future) malfunctioning member states. They can do this by blocking further enlargement, rejecting member states who want to join the Schengen area, or by calling for the expulsion of states from the EMU, Schengen, or EU. In other words, dissatisfaction with the EU also increases the likelihood of voice *for* exit. This reasoning is summed up in Proposition 4b: *With high costs for leaving fully, and without high EU loyalty, effective voice in the EU, compensation for EU-directed dissatisfaction, and attractive full exit options, EU-directed dissatisfaction induces partial exits within the EU and voice for the exit and non-entry of others.* Chapter 10 analyses a variety of actors, from member states to citizens, companies, and regions, to examine this proposition. It will also deal with whether the EU still has some time to recuperate or if it has already entered into a disintegrative spiral.

6.6   Conclusion

Bartolini's framework sensitises us to the causal mechanisms underpinning both processes of European integration and disintegration, as it follows the lessons learned from previously discussed theories and approaches. The framework is therefore a sound starting point from which to explain the case of the EU. Whereas Bartolini focused foremost on integration, this chapter has made the necessary steps to account for European disintegration as well. Four propositions have been derived from the framework. The basic argument is that an integrative spiral may have started and continued in the EU (and its predecessors) due to a lack of better alternatives and constrained voice. However, continuous challenges related to external de-consolidation, such as enlargement, have constrained the EU's capacity to lock-in resources and actors like member states. Ongoing European integration has also weakened the capacity of member states to lock-in resources and actors. The ensuing dissatisfaction will not necessarily lead to member states leaving the EU fully, as this calculation depends on exit costs and the attractiveness of alternatives outside the EU. The next chapters assess the four propositions. They offer a selective reading of the history of European integration, not presented in strictly chronological way, as the analytical focus here is on checking the propositions.

References

Barry, B. (1974). Review article: "Exit, voice, and loyalty". *British Journal of Political Science, 4,* 97–107.

Bartolini, S. (1998). *Exit options, boundary building, political structuring.* Working Paper 98/1. Florence: EUI.

Bartolini, S. (2004). Old and new peripheries in the processes of European territorial integration. In C. K. Ansell & G. di Palma (Eds.), *Restructuring territoriality: Europe and the United States compared* (pp. 19–44). Cambridge: Cambridge University Press.

Bartolini, S. (2005). *Restructuring Europe: Centre formation, system building and political structuring between the nation-state and the European Union.* Oxford: Oxford University Press.

Bednar, J. (2009). *The robust federation: Principles of design.* Cambridge: Cambridge University Press.

Deutsch, K. W., with Burrell, S. A., Kann, R. A., Lee Jr, M., Lichterman, M., Lindgren, R. E., Loewenheim, F. L., & Van Wagenen, R. W. (1957). *Political community and the North Atlantic area: International organization in the light of historical experience.* Princeton, NJ: Princeton University Press.

Dowding, K., John, P., Mergoupis, T., & van Vugt, M. (2000). Exit, voice and loyalty: Analytic and empirical developments. *European Journal of Political Research, 37*, 469–495.

Doyle, M. (1986). *Empires*. Ithaca: Cornell University Press.

Easton, D. (1965). *A framework for analysis*. Englewood Cliffs, NJ: Prentice-Hall.

Elazar, D. J. (1987). *Exploring federalism*. Tuscaloosa, AL: University of Alabama Press.

Eppler, A., & Scheller, H. (2013). Zug- und Gegenkräfte im Europäischen Integrationsprozess. In A. Eppler & H. Scheller (Eds.), *Zur Konzeptualisierung Europäischer Desintegration* (pp. 11–44). Baden-Baden: Nomos.

Etzioni, A. (2001). *Political unification revisited: On building supranational communities*. Lanham, MD: Lexington Books.

Ferrera, M. (2003). European integration and national social citizenship: Changing boundaries, new structuring? *Comparative Political Studies, 36*(6), 611–652.

Ferrera, M. (2004). Social citizenship in the European Union: Towards a spatial reconfiguration? In C. Ansell & G. Di Palma (Eds.), *The restructuring of territoriality* (pp. 90–121). Cambridge: Cambridge University Press.

Ferrera, M. (2005). *The boundaries of welfare: European integration and the new spatial politics of social protection*. Oxford: Oxford University Press.

Ferrera, M. (2007). Book review: Restructuring Europe. *Comparative Political Studies, 40*, 215–218.

Filippov, M., Ordeshook, P. C., & Shvetsova, O. V. (2004). *Designing federalism: A theory of self-Sustainable federal institutions*. Cambridge: Cambridge University Press.

Finer, S. (1974). State-building, state boundaries and border control: An essay on certain aspects of the first phase of state-building in Western Europe considered in the light of the Rokkan-Hirschman model. *Social Science Information, 13*(4/5), 79–126.

Flora, P. (1999). Introduction and interpretation. In S. Rokkan (Ed.), *State Formation, Nation-Building and Mass Politics in Europe: The Theory of Stein Rokkan* (ed. by P. Flora) (pp. 1–91). Oxford: Oxford University Press.

Flora, P. (2000). Externe Grenzbildung und Interne Strukturierung: Europa und seinen Nationen: Eine Rokkanische Forschungperspektive. *Berliner Journal für Soziologie, 10*, 157–166.

Franck, Th. M. (Ed.). (1968). *Why federations fail: An inquiry into the requisites for successful federalism*. New York: New York University Press.

Hedström, P., & Swedberg, R. (1998). Social mechanisms: An introductory essay. In P. Hedström & R. Swedberg (Eds.), *Social mechanisms: An analytical approach to social theory* (pp. 1–31). Cambridge: Cambridge University Press.

Hintze, O. (1975). In F. Gilbert (Ed.), *The historical essays of Otto Hintze*. New York: Oxford University Press.

Hirschman, A. O. (1970). *Exit, voice, and loyalty: Responses to decline in firms, organizations and states.* Cambridge: Harvard University Press.

Hirschman, A. O. (1974). "Exit, voice, and loyalty": Further reflections and a survey of recent contributions. *Social Science Information, 13*(1), 7–26.

Hirschman, A. O. (1981). *Essays in trespassing: Economics to politics and beyond.* Cambridge: Cambridge University Press.

Hooghe, L., & Marks, G. (2009). A postfunctionalist theory of European integration: From permissive consensus to constraining dissensus. *British Journal of Political Science, 39*(1), 1–23.

Karvonen, L. (2007). Europe's spaces and boundaries. *Comparative European Politics, 5,* 441–460.

Kelemen, R. D. (2007). Built to last? The durability of EU federalism. In S. Meunier & K. R. McNamara (Eds.), *Making history: European integration and institutional change at fifty* (pp. 51–66). Oxford: Oxford University Press.

Kennedy, P. (1987). *The rise and fall of the great powers: Economic change and military conflict from 1500 to 2000.* New York: Random House.

Lindberg, L. (1971). Political integration as multidimensional phenomenon requiring multivariate measurement. In L. Lindberg & S. Scheingold (Eds.), *Regional integration: Theory and research* (pp. 45–127). Cambridge, MA: Harvard University Press.

Lindberg, L., & Scheingold, S. (1970). *Europe's would-be polity: Patterns of change in the European community.* Englewood Cliffs, NJ: Prentice-Hall.

Marsh, D., & Furlong, P. (2002). A skin not a sweater: Ontology and epistemology in political science. In D. Marsh & G. Stoker (Eds.), *Theory and methods in political science* (pp. 17–41). Basingstoke: Palgrave Macmillan.

Mason, K., Easton, G., & Lenney, P. (2013). Causal social mechanisms: From the what to the why. *Industrial Marketing Management, 42,* 347–355.

Mearsheimer, J. (1990). Back to the future: Instability in Europe after the Cold War. *International Security, 15*(1), 5–56.

Mjøset, L. (2000). Stein Rokkan's thick comparisons. *Acta Sociologica, 43*(4), 381–397.

Moisio, S., & Paasi, A. (2013). Beyond state-centricity: Geopolitics of changing state spaces. *Geopolitics, 18*(2), 255–266.

Morgan, G. (2006). The nation-state, European (dis)integration, and political development. *European Political Science, 5,* 341–351.

Motyl, A. (2001). *Imperial ends: The decay, collapse, and revival of empires.* New York: Columbia University Press.

Niemann, A., & Bergmann, J. (2013). Zug- und Gegenkräfte im Spiegel der Theorien der Europäischen Integration. In A. Eppler & H. Scheller (Eds.), *Zur Konzeptualisierung Europäischer Desintegration* (pp. 45–70). Baden-Baden: Nomos.

Parsons, C. (2007). *How to map arguments in political science.* Oxford: Oxford University Press.

Popescu, G. (2012). *Bordering and ordering in the twenty-first century: Understanding borders.* Lanham, MD: Rowman & Littlefield.

Riker, W. H. (1964). *Federation/federalism: Origins, operation, significance.* Boston, MA: Little, Brown.

Rokkan, S. (1970). *Citizens, elections, parties.* Oslo: Universitets Forlaget.

Rokkan, S. (1975). Dimensions of state formation and nation-building: A possible paradigm for research on variations within Europe. In C. Tilly (Ed.), *The formation of national states in western Europe* (pp. 562–600). Princeton, NJ: Princeton University Press.

Rokkan, S. (1999). *State formation, nation-building, and mass politics in Europe: The theory of Stein Rokkan* (P. Flora, S. Kuhnle, & D. Urwin, Eds.). Oxford: Oxford University Press.

Rosato, S. (2011). *Europe united: Power politics and the making of the European Community.* Ithaca: Cornell University Press.

Sadeh, T., & Verdun, A. (2009). Explaining Europe's Monetary Union: A survey of the literature. *International Studies Review, 11,* 277–301.

Schmitter, P. (1971). A revised theory of regional integration. In L. Lindberg & S. A. Scheingold (Eds.), *Regional integration: Theory and research* (pp. 232–264). Cambridge, MA: Harvard University Press.

Tilly, C. (1990). *Coercion, capital and European states: AD 990-1990.* Cambridge, MA: Blackwell.

Vollaard, H. (2009). The logic of political territoriality. *Geopolitics, 14*(4), 687–706.

Vollaard, H. (2014). Explaining European disintegration. *Journal of Common Market Studies, 52*(5), 1142–1159.

Webber, D. (2013). How likely is it that the European Union will disintegrate? A critical analysis of competing theoretical perspectives. *European Journal of International Relations, 19*(4), 1–25.

Zielonka, J. (2014). *Is the EU doomed?* Cambridge: Polity Press.

CHAPTER 7

How European Integration Started Despite Ever-Present Disintegrative Forces

7.1 Introduction

Many attempts have been made in European history to establish and maintain political systems of value allocation, such as empires, city leagues, national states, and, also, regional organisations. These efforts have often been in vain. Political systems have fallen apart, been lost in oblivion, or have been merged with other ones, even in their early stages. The European Union has avoided this fate, until now. This chapter shows how the EU's predecessors came into existence, in spite of having faced virtually continuous, non-integrative and disintegrative forces. These forces will be discussed in Sect. 7.2. Subsequently, the early steps of European integration will be discussed in light of the first proposition: *the unattractiveness of alternatives and limited voice allowed European integration to take off.* The relevant data are derived from existing accounts of the EU's history. Though it would be preferable to test the propositions on the basis of evidence from primary sources, in this preliminary stage of theory development, secondary literature has been used to explore how the bounding-bonding mechanism has functioned throughout the history of European integration. Wherever possible, a variety of accounts have been used to avoid potential selection bias (cf. Lustick, 1996).

© The Author(s) 2018
H. Vollaard, *European Disintegration*, Palgrave Studies in European Union Politics, https://doi.org/10.1057/978-1-137-41465-6_7

7.2   NON-INTEGRATIVE AND DISINTEGRATIVE FORCES ALWAYS PRESENT AT ACTOR LEVEL

The main argument of this section is that the EU and its predecessors have always faced non-integrative and disintegrative forces. Alternatives to full or partial entry to the EU or its predecessors have been propagated time and time again and have been acted upon too. After the launch of European integration, calls for and attempts at partial or full exit from the allocation of values established by the EU and its predecessors have also frequently been made. These alternatives and exit options, constituting non-integrative and disintegrative forces respectively, can be divided into two types: international and national.

International alternatives or exit options refer here to the international organisations or regimes that an actor can join in order to receive certain values, as alternatives to the EU or its predecessors. In post-war Europe, a variety of international organisations have served as possible alternatives to the EU and its predecessors, providing options to actors that could have fully or partially switched membership, such as the Council of Europe, the Commonwealth, the Benelux, the Nordic Council, the Western European Union (WEU), the North Atlantic Treaty Organization (NATO), the European Free Trade Area (EFTA), the Organisation for European Economic Cooperation (OEEC) and its successor from 1961 onwards, the Organisation for Economic Cooperation and Development (OECD), the World Trade Organization (WTO), the Organization for Security and Cooperation in Europe (OSCE), and the Eurasian Economic Union (EEU). The presence of these international alternatives or exit options could and have been used to support the claim that membership in the EU or its predecessors is not or no longer (fully) required. For instance, the International Ruhr Authority, which regulates the heart of the German coal and steel industry, the Council of Europe, the OEEC, and the WEU's predecessor were considered by France as alternatives to the European Coal and Steel Community (ECSC), which came into effect in 1952 (Parsons, 2003, Chap. 1). A combination of the transatlantic security organisation, NATO, and the Western European organisation for collective security, WEU, offered an alternative to manage the rearmament of the Federal Republic of Germany (hereafter West Germany) in the mid-1950s, after the initiative for a European Defence Community (EDC) did not achieve sufficient support in France. Also, after the launch of the European Economic Community (EEC) in 1958, its dissolution into a free trade area within the framework of the OEEC initially saw considerable support from free market, liberal parties in West Germany and the Netherlands. The EFTA, established in 1960, functioned as an alternative to the EEC, although many EFTA members, such as the UK, Portugal, and Finland, switched to EEC or EU membership later on. Furthermore, the existence of NATO has often provided the basis of the argument that there is no real need for the EU to develop full-fledged security and defence capacities. And to mention just one more example of international alternatives, it has been suggested in recent debates on Brexit that (a combination of) a special relationship with the USA, the Commonwealth, NATO, EFTA, G8, OECD, IMF, the United Nations, and WTO provides sufficient cushion in terms of international arrangements to soften the blow of an exit from the EU (see, for instance, Mansfield, 2014, p. 22).

The availability of international options in terms of seeking value delivery elsewhere, to withdraw partially or fully from the EU's allocation of values, is different from actor to actor. Only some states are eligible to opt into regional organisations such as the Benelux, the Nordic Council, or the Eurasian Economic Union. Actors' preferences also have an impact on the selection of international exit options available at any given time. These preferences may relate to the tasks, structure, leadership, or scale of an international organisation. For instance, the market-oriented liberal parties in West Germany and the Netherlands preferred trade arrangements on a much wider scale than the high external tariffs surrounding the "Little Europe" comprised of the original six member states. Furthermore, governments from states such as Denmark and Norway preferred intergovernmental organisations such as EFTA over the supranational EEC for some time.

The EU and its predecessors have not only faced non-integrative and disintegrative forces that favour the allocation of values by other international arrangements. There have also been many calls for and attempts to keep or return the allocation of values to the national level. From the very start, right-wing conservatives, like the French Gaullists, have often demanded the maintenance or reclamation of full, formal national sovereignty. The French president Charles de Gaulle threatened to leave the EEC in an effort to strengthen the French voice in the negotiations on a Common Agricultural Policy (CAP) in the early 1960s (Dinan, 2005, p. 48). Furthermore, left-wing parties like the Communists and even the British Labour Party and the Greek PASOK resisted EEC membership for some time in part as a result of the fear that the creation of a European market might hamper national economic planning policies (Verney, 2009).

The vote of the Norwegian electorate against EEC membership in 1972 showed how referendums can result in non-integration, whereas the British referendum on EEC membership in 1975 reflected the way in which a full exit from the EEC could still be on the political agenda after accession. In 1982, Greenland's vote to leave the EEC showed that referendums can also be the start of disintegration, an exit from the EU's allocation of values. The adoption of an exit clause for member states in the EU treaties in the 2000s meant that the prospect of a full exit was not entirely unimaginable, even after several decades of integration. Nationalist and populist parties, like the UK Independence Party, the Dutch Freedom Party, and the French *Front National*, have proposed the full exit of their countries.

National exit options can also be partial. The French government withdrew its representatives from the Council of Ministers during the so-called Empty Chair Crisis (1965–1966), thereby hampering the EEC's allocation of values. The introduction of non-tariff trade barriers in the 1970s, by the then EEC member states, constituted partial exit from the internal market. Governments of the EEC member states did not live up to the mutual exchange rate agreements made in the 1970s; the French government withdrew twice from the so-called Snake, indicating the margins of the mutual conversion rates of their currencies. In 1981, the new socialist government in France considered exiting from European monetary arrangements (Parsons, 2003, p. 171), whereas the UK and Italy withdrew from the European exchange rate mechanism in 1992. Subsequently, the UK did not fully take part in the Economic and Monetary Union in the early 1990s and Denmark also opted out of defence cooperation. Right-wing French politicians campaigned against the Economic and Monetary Union that was agreed upon by the French government in the Maastricht Treaty (1991) and went so far as to briefly consider exiting from the monetary arrangements when they were in government in 1993 (Parsons, 2003, p. 224). Additionally, West Germany and Greece have been criticised for their refusal to comply with the Stability and Growth Pact of the Economic and Monetary Union, and Austria, Poland, and Hungary have been blamed for not complying with EU values such as the rule of law and freedom of speech. Furthermore, the UK government used a block opt-out of certain aspects of justice and home affairs in 2014, even though it did select certain measures it wished to adhere to. And as a last example of partial exit, several parties across the EU have pleaded for leaving the Eurozone, but not the EU as a whole.

It may not be a surprise that the EU has faced these calls for and attempts to suspend the allocation of values by the EU in some or all of its tasks. National loyalty has generally been much stronger than loyalty to the EU and to fellow people in the EU when it is expressed in terms of identification and trust (Polyakova & Fligstein, 2016; Thomassen & Bäck, 2009). In contrast to European identity, national identity has been (re)generated by extensive national welfare state arrangements and through national education and media systems in post-war Europe. The national exit option is also the better-known option, at least with regard to the political infrastructure and the delivery of goods and services, which might convince those who prefer the known evil over the unknown good. The nature of calls for and attempts at national exit differ from actor to actor and also fluctuate over time per actor. These calls and attempts depend on the perception of whether or not the national state can do better than the EU in terms of the allocation of certain values, whether they are related to security, democracy, welfare, or environmental protection. As both preferences and the (perceived) capacities of national states and the EU to deliver them have changed over time, so too have the considerations about national exit options, partial or full. If the EU's evolution brings the state further away from the preferences of its relevant actors than does the state itself, calls for and attempts at national exit may grow, in particular in areas where EU loyalty is weak.

7.3   One European Alternative That Garnered Sufficient Support and One That Did Not

Despite the competition between national and international alternatives, European integration still started. How did that happen? Why did actors invest in the making of the EU's predecessors, even thought they had other options for addressing their dissatisfaction? Just after the Second World War, dissatisfaction was pervasive among governments, political parties, interest groups, and citizens in Western Europe. It stemmed from their past experiences with the economic crisis in the 1930s and the destabilising rivalry between France and Germany, as well as from a widespread desire to revitalise national societies after two devastating world wars and from concerns about the power of individual states or Western Europe collectively vis-à-vis Germany, the Soviet Union, the USA, and the rest of the world (Urwin, 1997). As will be argued below, the relative unattractiveness of alternatives and constrained voice allowed for the EU's predecessors to emerge and develop as a (partial) means of addressing these sources of dissatisfaction.

Even if adherence to national sovereignty was still prevalent among many Western European actors and the revitalisation of national societies constituted a core political object, exclusively national options obtained less support than before the wars. The disadvantages of national protectionism in response to economic crises in the 1930s and the two world wars made Western European governments, particularly those of defeated states, more willing to accept international cooperation as instruments for national security and national wealth (cf. Milward, 1992). Although national alternatives were less favoured in the calculation of the costs and benefits of the various options, a wide array of international possibilities to deal with the unsatisfactory situation remained available. Should international arrangements be supranational or intergovernmental? Which states should be part of these arrangements? What policy areas should they cover? And how deep should cooperation or integration go?

Soon after the end of the Second World War, Europe was again divided by the Cold War. The Iron Curtain between Western and Eastern Europe limited entry into integrative initiatives. States under the influence of the Soviet Empire could not take part in a Western initiative. Also, Austria and Finland did not have an opportunity to engage very closely with Western organisations. As a nuclear power, the lead entity of the Western block, the USA, provided protection to Western Europe against (military-coercive) attempts by the Soviet Union to capture resources and actors (Lundestad, 2003). In other words, the American security umbrella provided a certain measure of external consolidation of Western Europe. In particular, the Communist Party's involvement in strikes in France and a Soviet-supported coup in Czechoslovakia made a growing number of elites in Western Europe increasingly susceptible to international options to contain the communist influence that seemed to be spreading unencumbered. Acknowledging their dependence on the USA to keep the Soviet Union at bay, Western European governments soon embraced the US-led NATO. The US government pressed for political integration in Western Europe as part of its Marshall plan to foster economic prosperity in an effort to counter communist expansion, provide humanitarian relief, and strengthen a market for American products (Dinan, 2010, pp. 13–14).

The Cold War thus brought about a certain delineation of international options and membership. Nevertheless, many questions remained as to how to address the sources of dissatisfaction more fully, in particular with respect to Germany. Resistance movements had put forward the idea of a federal Europe as a means of overcoming the nationalist animosity cultivated during war (Dinan, 2010, p. 9ff; Urwin, 1997, p. 17ff). Furthermore, Christian-democratic networks and beliefs were instrumental in the process of fostering mutual reconciliation, a shared aversion of communism and political thought open to supranationalism among the dominant political movements in many continental states (Gehler, 2004; Kaiser, 2004; Pulzer, 2004). This loyalty to the ideal of reconciliation through supranationalism had the capacity to provide a measure of credible commitment among the prospective members of a cooperative or integrative scheme, as it could have limited the inclination of these members to make a quick exit from mutual agreements and exchanges. Nevertheless, this loyalty resonated much less in the UK and Scandinavia, for which supranational integration initiatives limited membership even further to continental Western Europe. Nevertheless, continuing distrust of Germany, strong pleas to involve the UK in European cooperation arrangements, and enduring attachment to national sovereignty prevented the supranational initiative from taking hold in continental Western Europe immediately.

Actors in continental Western Europe took various positions in response to the question of which international alternative(s) would best address the various sources of dissatisfaction. These positions did not necessarily follow existing political cleavages and bureaucratic orientations, and they left governments, administrations, interest groups, political parties (including Christian-democratic ones), and citizens divided. For instance, three positions could be distinguished in France, with each of them finding support on both ends of the political and administrative spectrum (Parsons, 2003). Some, indeed, preferred a supranational community, but many others favoured traditional foreign policy to balance threats to French sovereignty and power, such as (temporary) alliances, whereas still others sought loose intergovernmental arrangements like the Council of Europe and the OEEC. Some preferred to work closely with West Germany, whereas others sought to prevent any rehabilitation of West Germany; some were reluctant to accept American or Anglo-Saxon leadership, whereas others perceived British and American involvement as essential to creating peace and prosperity on the continent.

The intergovernmental nature of organisations like the Council of Europe rendered voice rather ineffective, according to Jean Monnet, head of the government body tasked with developing plans to revive France economically. Instead, he conceived of a supranational community that included West Germany (and if necessary, excluded the UK) as the best option available to effectively address French dissatisfaction. In line with previous plans issued elsewhere, he suggested commencing integration in the area of coal and steel. In the years immediately following the Second World War, the occupying powers curtailed Germany's muscle. Through the establishment of an international authority that ruled the Ruhr area, with its coal and steel industry, more traditional French governments had tried to control important sources of Germany's economic and military power and maintain easy access to essential energy sources for French industries. However, the US government pushed for West Germany's political and economic reconstruction to prevent politically extreme forces from taking hold again and to build up a bulwark against Soviet influence in Europe. This push could have meant bringing an end to international rule over the Ruhr area. Additionally, French elites feared West Germany might seek a neutral course, and, in response, they aimed to lock West Germany more strongly into the Western alliance. Therefore, in 1950, Monnet proposed launching an ECSC with a supranational High Authority that could enforce compliance regardless of national objections. The ECSC would thus provide a supranational constraint on West Germany.

According to Monnet, a supranational coal and steel community would be best positioned to address the several sources of French dissatisfaction, in particular with respect to the role of Germany. But his plan did not receive overwhelming support in France and not only because of traditionalist or intergovernmentalist objections. The costs and benefits of such an innovative supranational arrangement were difficult to determine, and it was near impossible to compare the outcome with what would happen otherwise. So, how did they still reach this arrangement and why did discussions on an ECSC not continue endlessly as a result of the seemingly intractable positions of the actors involved and the uncertainty around its outcome? Here, limitations on voice facilitated the adoption of the ECSC. Foreign policy making and international (treaty) negotiations were less democratised at that time (Everts, 1985, p. 9). Governments enjoyed considerable discretion in this realm. Monnet had been able to convince the French minister of foreign affairs, the Christian-democratic Robert Schuman, of his ideas. Schuman put his weight behind these ideas after receiving only minimal support from his own government and, as a result, the ideas became known as the Schuman plan. During the negotiations on the ECSC, Schuman neglected the voices of traditionalist and intergovernmentalist groups, and, at the ratification stage, his government was able to cobble together a supportive coalition for the final treaty within the government and parliament by making concessions on unrelated issues and by exerting political pressure (Parsons, 2003, p. 63ff). Similarly, in the West German system of *Kanzlerdemokratie*, the Christian-democratic chancellor, Konrad Adenauer, was able to press ahead with the Schuman plan, despite considerable resistance from the social-democratic opposition, which prioritised reunification of divided Germany, from industries resisting the cartel policy of the ECSC and even from politicians in his own party who favoured greater economic cooperation, in the framework of the OEEC, for example. Adenauer, however, perceived the ECSC as a necessary step towards international rehabilitation of West Germany, regardless of the costs (Dinan, 2010, p. 17). The avoidance of ratification referendums also limited the voice of the masses, which would have otherwise complicated approval of the Schuman plan.

A delineation of its membership and constrained voice allowed for the adoption of a supranational ECSC in France and West Germany. Apart from their rejection of supranational integration, the UK, as a major economic and geopolitical power with a large coal and steel sector, and the agricultural economies of Ireland and Scandinavia were much less interested in cooperation on coal and steel. In contrast, the Italian government, led by the Christian-democratic Alcide de Gasperi, embraced the plan as a means of regaining voice in European politics and containing domestic communist influence through international cooperation. The Benelux governments were, however, more reluctant to join. They felt that the economic reconstruction of West Germany was necessary, given their trade dependence. Additionally, they believed that stronger trade links with West Germany would pave the way to becoming less dependent upon American markets (Milward, 1992). But, the Dutch government preferred trade liberalisation on a larger scale via the OEEC, whereas the Belgian government faced domestic hostility to supranational interference into its important coal and steel sector. Moreover, both governments favoured UK participation. However, they did not want to leave the settlement of Western European affairs exclusively to their larger neighbours. Out of fear of being overshadowed by the larger states or being dominated by the High Authority, they insisted successfully on a stronger Council of Ministers in order to obtain sufficient voice within the ECSC. In their eyes, as well as Germany's, the supranational High Authority had to be kept accountable by a common assembly that would have not only a consultative role, like that of the assemblies of international organisations, but also a scrutinising role (Rittberger, 2005). A Court of Justice completed the set of institutions charged with keeping the High Authority accountable. The legitimation of a novel, partly

supranational allocation of values thus brought about a specific voice structure with a council, a proto-parliament, and a court. Rather than preserving
a particular form of a political organisation, *in casu* the sovereign state,
national governments sought to effectively address sources of national dissatisfaction in the context of a partly supranational organisation.

In spite of the fact that the ECSC faced a competitive market of national
and international alternatives, it was launched based on estimates of the
costs and benefits of creating a partly supranational, partly intergovernmental organisation of six continental, Western European states. It offered
more effective voice to its participants and a measure of mutual loyalty in
the new organisation that prevented exit. The adoption of the ECSC was
facilitated by the ability to contain opposing domestic voices. This did not
hold for the simultaneously launched initiative, the EDC, a European
army that was to include West German troops. In that case, divisions and
uncertainty about the relative costs and benefits of supranational European
arrangements featured more strongly. For instance, the two largest parties
in the Dutch parliament favoured another step towards federal Europe
and Franco-German reconciliation, whereas the Dutch government, supported by the very same parties, even initially declined to take full part in
the negotiations (Van der Harst, 1990; Vollaard & Voerman, 2015). It
feared that the EDC would make autonomous foreign policy impossible
and would undermine the unity of the transatlantic alliance, as well as the
security protection offered by the USA, which it trusted more than its
larger neighbours. The Dutch government accepted the proposal partly
due to pressure from the US government, which perceived the rearmament of West Germany as necessary to containing the Soviet Union more
effectively and as a precondition for its contribution to protect Western
Europe. The EDC proposal originated in France in 1950, where Monnet
and some ministers, including Schuman, saw it as a European safeguard
against the rearmament of West Germany and as a means of providing sufficient conventional defence against the preponderant, non-nuclear Soviet
power. The proposal once again divided the governments, administration,
political parties, interest groups, and citizens of France (Parsons, 2003,
Chap. 2). Opponents objected to the rearmament of a former aggressor,
the exclusion of the UK as anti-German ally, the creation of an anti-Soviet
power, the deviation from a pacifist and neutral course for Western Europe,
and the partial cession of sovereignty on a key function of the French state.
Alternatives, such as intergovernmental arrangements that included the
UK, did not see a great deal of support. This time, changes in parliament

and government that were by and large unrelated to the EDC and the replacement of Schuman as foreign minister prevented supporters of the EDC from once again shielding a supranational proposal from the voices of a substantial, anti-supranational majority. The French assembly refused to vote on the EDC proposal in 1954, effectively vetoing it. In doing so, the attempt to launch a European Political Community, which would have provided the political infrastructure to draft an accompanying foreign policy and more, also died. Instead, an intergovernmental alternative prevailed, with a combination of the WEU (with British participation) and NATO (with the USA as well) encapsulating West Germany militarily. In the eyes of the Dutch government in particular, this combination provided more effective voice for its security concerns.

7.4   Continuing the Mutual Exchange: Towards the European Economic Community

Whereas the relative attractiveness of alternatives in terms of effective voice and loyalty and the constraints on opposing voices led to the emergence of the ECSC, the EDC failed because of its relative unattractiveness and the failing constraints on opposing voices. European integration did not stop after the failure of the EDC, however. The ECSC provided the political infrastructure for further exchange. Its administrative apparatus was instrumental to bringing people together to discuss further European integration in a setting of mutual understanding and shared commitment (cf. Seidel, 2010). An important push for further integration came from the Dutch minister of foreign affairs, Jan Willem Beyen (1952–1956). Given the shifting trading patterns of the Netherlands vis-à-vis the other ECSC member states in the 1950s, since 1952, he pushed for the creation of a customs union of the six that would be based on automatic procedures and supervised by a supranational body, laid down in a treaty (Milward, 1992, p. 185ff). According to his calculations, this would be a better option in terms of Dutch exports (in agricultural products in particular) than waiting for some intergovernmental agreement in the framework of the OEEC that would be bogged down by national vetoes. Beyen had successfully kept economic integration on the political agenda in exchange for Dutch participation in EDC and EPC negotiations. Partly thanks to his discretion as foreign minister, he was able to push forward with this option, despite deep reservations in his own government about supranational institutions. After the failure of the EDC, he also managed to keep his option as part of the political exchanges among the ECSC-six. These exchanges continued in spite of the EDC debacle because of the mutual desire to save the existing Franco-German rapprochement in the ECSC by accepting talks on further integration (Milward, 1992, p. 208). The costs of abandoning the ECSC were perceived to be too high, even in France. As such, some willingness existed in France to accept a European arrangement on atomic energy, which could have also brought about (financial) support for the advanced French nuclear industry and control over German initiatives in this area. Beyen's idea of a customs union met widespread resistance in France, however, although some perceived it to be a welcome incentive for the French industry and agricultural sector to modernise. But many argued that if there had to be international arrangements, loose liberalisation with national vetoes in the framework of the OEEC would be preferable to a supranational and automatic economic community as proposed by Beyen. The eventual compromise at the conference in Messina in 1955 resulted in a study committee tasked with both exploring integration on atomic energy and the establishment of a common market among the six. Thus, the availability of the ECSC and the political costs of exit from the ECSC allowed for the continuation of discussions on further political exchange.

The West German chancellor, Adenauer, favoured talks on more integration among the ECSC-six as part of West Germany's rehabilitation and Franco-German reconciliation (Milward, 1992, p. 197ff). Given resistance to atomic energy integration at home, he focused on a customs union, instead. This had the potential to open French and Italian markets to German industry, which at that time maintained important trade links outside the ECSC area. For that reason, many West German actors advocated arrangements for currency convertibility and the reduction of quota and tariffs, such as those maintained by the OEEC. The Italian government saw the establishment of an economic community as instrumental to containing the domestic power of the Communist party, gaining greater market access elsewhere, and to exporting its unemployment (Urwin, 1997, p. 72). The governments in the smaller Benelux countries supported a supranational community as an instrument that would prevent their underlying position in bilateral relations with larger states. In other words, they perceived that their voice would be more effectively heard in a supranational arrangement than in bilateral ones.

The Belgian government expressed concerns that its economy would be disadvantaged in a customs union because of its higher wages, partly due to welfare state arrangements. In France, similar concerns existed. The idea of a loose, intergovernmental arrangement in the OEEC received more support at that time than the idea of a supranational European customs union did (Parsons, 2003, p. 110). In the end, the French government and parliament still accepted a supranational economic community, as it offered provisions to save certain welfare arrangements such as equal payment, preferential access for the French colonies to the customs union, a relatively high external tariff protecting French industry, and temporary trading guarantees for the French agricultural sector, in spite of the fact that it remained unclear how this would be arranged in the long run. Additionally, the EEC treaty received support as an effort to further Franco-German reconciliation and because it was seen as an incentive to modernise the French economy. Against the background of the Suez crisis and the Soviet intervention in Hungary, it was also seen as being instrumental to invigorating France's and Western Europe's sway in international politics (Milward, 1992, p. 215). Though the idea of the European atomic energy community helped to keep French support for integrative initiatives alive, it had been stripped of its essence at the request of the French because other ECSC governments were fairly reluctant to contribute to it (Parsons, 2003, p. 113). The French government lobbied intensively for support among interest groups for the EEC as the best, or the least bad, option to reinforce France. Even with much grumbling about the concessions made, all governments and parliaments of the ECSC-six accepted the political exchanges made. Opposing voices remained somewhat limited as there were no referendums held to ratify the treaties establishing the European Economic Community (EEC) and the Atomic Energy Community (EURATOM), which both came into force in 1958. These supranational arrangements had similar voice structures to the ECSC to legitimise its supranational allocation of values and to enforce the agreements made, even against the will of individual members.

7.5   PARTIAL EXITS FROM THE EEC

It is no surprise that dissatisfaction with the EEC lingered on after its establishment. Many politicians in West Germany and the Netherlands still sought trade liberalisation within the framework of OEEC, which would have required the dissolution of the EEC. The new French prime minister and later president De Gaulle disliked the supranational nature of the entire EC,[1] seeing intergovernmental arrangements as being more effective

---

[1] EC refers here to the three communities, ECSC, EURATOM, and EEC, whereas EEC refers to the European Economic Community.

for empowering French voice. Furthermore, he preferred a much stronger Western European voice under French leadership on matters of foreign policy to enhance Western European autonomy from the US-dominated transatlantic alliance. Both the market-oriented politicians and De Gaulle had two options to address their dissatisfaction: (a) full or partial exit from the EC and (b) to voice it within the EC. Given the very existence of the EEC in addition to the ECSC, the costs of exit had increased, at least in terms of political reputation. Indeed, De Gaulle quickly decided to accept the EC in order to gain trust from the other governments in the EEC, despite his aversion to its supranational nature (Parsons, 2003, p. 127). Furthermore, according to De Gaulle's calculations, the EEC could still serve as a vehicle to modernise French industry. More economic power would re-energise the grandeur of the French state. In addition, speeding up liberalisation among the six could create a greater distance between the continental and British economies. De Gaulle thus tried to prevent closer association between the EEC and the UK, which he perceived as being too supportive of US leadership in international politics. For this purpose, De Gaulle also blocked the creation of a free trade area between the EC-six and other Western European countries, as proposed by the UK. It left the dissatisfied, market-oriented politicians in West Germany and the Netherlands with one international exit option less. The buoying economic growth and talks on further trade liberalisation in the framework of the General Agreement on Tariffs and Trade (GATT) assuaged their dissatisfaction somewhat, however. Moreover, the Dutch government also accepted De Gaulle's move in exchange for building up a CAP, which De Gaulle had started to see as a means of strengthening the French agricultural sector at the expense of others (Parsons, 2003, p. 131). Meanwhile, with his threat of full disintegration from the EEC, De Gaulle strengthened his voice in the negotiations on CAP, extracting a great deal of funding for French farmers in exchange with the German government in particular, which still saw, if more grudgingly, close ties with France as being necessary to its rehabilitation, as well as protection from ongoing Soviet threats (Parsons, 2003, p. 137).

De Gaulle attempted to initiate cooperation on foreign policy among the EC-six outside the framework of the EC or NATO to enhance the French voice in international politics. He pursued traditional instruments, such as a Franco-West German treaty and a more confederal arrangement in the form of regular meetings of the governments of the EC (the so-called Fouchet plan). After these attempts failed due to resistance on the part of governments that favoured the transatlantic alliance, the EEC became an increasingly important option for advancing French (agricultural) interests in De Gaulle's eyes. Yet he still resisted its supranational nature, which would be increased by the foreseen introduction of qualified majority voting in the council, own resources for the EC, and the accompanying budgetary control by the European Parliament. De Gaulle expressed his objection in 1965 in a partial exit: the boycott of meetings of the Council of Ministers, the so-called Empty Chair Crisis. With increasing attention on the costs of leaving the EEC and its agricultural funds on the part of the French electorate and administration, plus the lack of real international alternatives (Piers Ludlow, 2006, pp. 91, 114ff), De Gaulle eventually returned to the negotiation table, accepting the Luxembourg compromise in 1966, which allowed a government to veto a decision if vital interests were at stake, notwithstanding formal decision-making procedures based on qualified majority voting. In this way, the voice of the French and other national governments could still be secured at the European level.

Therefore, the limited alternatives to the EC and the increasing costs of exit options forced actors, be they market-oriented politicians in Germany or the Netherlands or French Gaullists, to continue seeking satisfaction *within* the EC. The resultant external consolidation allowed political exchange among the EC-six to continue, which kept the integrative spiral moving. The internal construction of three European Communities was subsequently strengthened. The European Commission, the EEC's equivalent to the High Authority, developed a certain *esprit de corps*, with its employees believing in further integration (Seidel, 2010). Furthermore, a sort of cross-national stabilisation of political alignments slowly emerged in the European Parliament, with parliamentary groupings emerging along ideological lines and also European party federations as a result. This indicated that national political parties had been sufficiently locked-in to the EC to seek cross-national coalitions. Further voice structuring also took place in the Council of Ministers and its supportive apparatus of permanent representatives in the Committee of Permanent Representatives (COREPER) and working groups of national civil servants. A norm of consensus-seeking emerged among the political and administrative representatives of the six participating states, which had already been helpful in overcoming the Empty Chair Crisis (Piers Ludlow, 2006). A certain level of external consolidation indicated the governments with which deals had to be made, allowing deals to be crafted that were beneficial to all, even if the benefits were only enjoyed in the long run. Meanwhile, the merger of the institutions of

EEC, EURATOM, and ECSC in 1967 was illustrative of the ongoing internal construction. Additionally, the customs union went into force eighteen months ahead of schedule, in 1968, in which the European Commission had relatively strong powers to enforce compliance with EC competition law. European institutions also limited partial exits on the part of member states, with the European Court of Justice (ECJ) establishing the direct effect and supremacy of Community rules and the European Commission's right to make international agreements (Weiler, 1999, p. 34ff). The European Commission participated on behalf of the EEC member states in trade negotiations on the GATT and with decolonised countries. The EC itself had primarily legal and regulatory means at its disposal with which to maintain and reinforce its boundaries in terms of compliance.

In sum, with the relative unattractiveness of national and international alternatives in the eyes of those who were in charge of foreign policy in the six Western European states, European integration could start and disintegrative behaviour was kept at bay. Their investments made to establish voice structures and to set up political infrastructure to address dissatisfaction changed the calculus on integration and disintegration, making the states less inclined to withdraw, even when dissatisfied with integrative tendencies like supranational decision-making. Nevertheless, the Empty Chair Crisis and its resolution also clearly showed the (financial) dependence of the EC on member states. As a consequence, the EC did not have many resources or competences to enhance European loyalty through social sharing or fostering a common identity among the greater public. It had to rely foremost on the member states themselves for decision-making, legitimisation, implementation, and compliance both with EC legislation and ECJ case law, whereas any means of enforcement to keep member states in was completely out of the question. The strength of its external consolidation remained, therefore, relatively frail, with low congruence of boundaries of economic (only partially EC), cultural (mostly national, but also Western/transatlantic), and coercive-military (states and NATO) natures. It was the relative attractiveness of the EC vis-à-vis the various other national and international options, rather than its weak locking-in capacity, that kept European integration moving.

7.6   Conclusion

The EU's predecessors emerged in a competitive situation with a variety of national and international alternatives available to address the various sources of dissatisfaction. Political actors in Western Europe had different understandings of what would best serve their national interests. In spite of this, European integration was still able to start, as the actors in six Western European states perceived it to be the best option in terms of effectively addressing sources of discontent, and the effectiveness of voice and the measure of mutual loyalty played a role in the case of the ECSC. The first step towards European integration had been facilitated by the containment of voices in favour of the alternatives to the ECSC, as was laid down in Proposition 1. The supporters of the EDC did not manage to quash calls for its alternatives. However, European integration could still move forward, as the ECSC provided a platform upon which to continue political exchange, not to mention the fact that the political costs of exit were considered to be too high. The exchanges eventually resulted in the launch of the EEC, which was accepted on the basis of it being the least unattractive option among the various national and international alternatives available. Excluding the masses from directly participating in the European integration process facilitated the making of exchanges and building of political alignments among the six continental Western European states. The locking-in capacity of the EEC remained limited, however, for which it remained highly reliant on the willingness of its member states to support its continued existence. Its relative attractiveness vis-à-vis other national and international options kept member states in. The EC's limited locking-in capacity not only resulted from the reluctance to provide it with the means to build mutual loyalty and reinforce its boundaries, but also from its welcoming stance towards new member states. Governments of neighbouring states had taken notice of the economic growth within the EEC and surmised that entry might be more beneficial than their national and international alternatives. Their membership applications would challenge the formation of the EC, as the ensuing external deconsolidation of the EC would also have an impact on its internal construction. This will be focus of the next chapter.

REFERENCES

Dinan, D. (2005). *Ever closer union? An introduction to European integration* (3rd ed.). Basingstoke: Palgrave Macmillan.

Dinan, D. (2010). *Ever closer union? An introduction to European integration* (4th ed.). Basingstoke: Palgrave Macmillan.

Everts, Ph. (Ed.). (1985). *Controversies at home: Domestic factors in the Foreign policy of the Netherlands*. Dordrecht: Nijhoff.

Gehler, M. (2004). The Geneva circle of western European Christian democrats. In M. Gehler & W. Kaiser (Eds.), *Christian democracy in Europe since 1945* (Vol. 2, pp. 207–220). London: Routledge.

Kaiser, W. (2004). Transnational Christian democracy: From the Nouvelles Equipes Internationales to the European People's Party. In M. Gehler & W. Kaiser (Eds.), *Christian democracy in Europe since 1945* (Vol. 2, pp. 221–237). London: Routledge.

Lundestad, G. (2003). *The United States and western Europe since 1945: From "empire" by invitation to transatlantic drift.* Oxford: Oxford University Press.

Lustick, I. S. (1996). History, historiography, and political science: Multiple historical records and the problem of selection bias. *American Political Science Review, 90*(3), 605–618.

Mansfield, I. (2014). *A blueprint for Britain: Openness not isolation.* London: IEA.

Milward, A. (1992). *The European rescue of the nation-state.* London: Routledge.

Parsons, C. (2003). *A certain idea of Europe.* Ithaca, NJ: Cornell University Press.

Piers Ludlow, N. (2006). *The European Community and the crises of the 1960s: Negotiating the Gaullist challenge.* London: Routledge.

Polyakova, A., & Fligstein, N. (2016). Is European integration causing Europe to become more nationalist? Evidence from the 2007–9 financial crisis. *Journal of European Public Policy, 23*(1), 60–83.

Pulzer, P. (2004). Nationalism and internationalism in European Christian democracy. In M. Gehler & W. Kaiser (Eds.), *Christian democracy in Europe since 1945* (Vol. 2, pp. 10–24). London: Routledge.

Rittberger, B. (2005). *Building Europe's parliament: Democratic representation beyond the nation-state.* Oxford: Oxford University Press.

Seidel, K. (2010). *The process of politics: The rise of European elites and supranational institutions.* London: I.B. Tauris.

Thomassen, J., & Bäck, H. (2009). European citizenship and identity after European enlargement. In J. Thomassen (Ed.), *The legitimacy of the European Union after enlargement* (pp. 184–207). Oxford: Oxford University Press.

Urwin, D. W. (1997). *A political history of western Europe since 1945.* London: Routledge.

Van der Harst, J. (1990). The pleven plan. In R. T. Griffiths (Ed.), *The Netherlands and the integration of Europe, 1945–1957* (pp. 137–164). Amsterdam: NEHA.

Verney, S. (2009). An exceptional case? Party and popular Euroscepticism in Greece, 1959–2009. *South European Society and Politics, 16*(1), 51–79.

Vollaard, H., & Voerman, G. (2015). De Europese opstelling van Nederlandse Politieke Partijen. In H. Vollaard, J. van der Harst, & G. Voerman (Eds.), *Van Aanvallen! naar verdedigen? De opstelling van Nederland ten aanzien van Europese integratie* (pp. 99–182). Den Haag: Boom Bestuurskunde.

Weiler, J. J. H. (1999). *The constitution of Europe.* Cambridge: Cambridge University Press.

CHAPTER 8

How European Integration Has Continued, Despite the EU's Limited Locking-in Capacity

8.1 Introduction

The previous chapter showed how the lack of better alternatives allowed European integration to begin. Key decision-makers facilitated the making of this choice for Europe by circumventing voices from politics and society that argued in favour of national or international alternatives to European integration. Thus, members remained within the European Communities (ECs), providing the latter with a certain measure of external consolidation. This, in turn, fostered the internal construction of these communities, following the logic of the bounding-bonding mechanism. However, the EC soon faced the challenge of external de-consolidation after their launch in the 1950s. For instance, various requests for accession and the fear of Germany going-it-alone were indicative of the permeable nature of their boundaries. According to the bounding-bonding mechanism, external de-consolidation serves to unsettle political exchanges, coalitions, and alignments in the making, thereby disturbing processes of voice structuring, centre formation, and loyalty building. This chapter traces how the EU and its predecessors have developed since the 1960s in order to examine Proposition 2: *the weak external consolidation of the EU and its predecessors has constrained its internal construction.* As a result of constrained internal construction, the locking-in capacity of the EU and its predecessors has remained limited. They have therefore not been able to forcefully counter the ever-present non-integrative and disintegrative forces. Nevertheless, European integration did move on. The actor-level explanations highlighted in Proposition 1—the lack of better alternatives and constrained voice—are thus also examined again. Sections 8.2, 8.3, 8.4, and 8.5 show how the integrative spiral continued despite the impact of the various rounds of enlargement and other forms of external de-consolidation.

8.2   The Impact of North-Western Enlargement and an Assertive West Germany

In the 1950s, British governments had suggested on various occasions that the negotiations on coal and steel and on the common market should be held with the intergovernmental Council of Europe or the OEEC. In 1956, the British government also proposed the creation of a free trade area excluding agriculture for the six ECSC member states and seven non-ECSC states in Western Europe. For various reasons, it could count on considerable support in West Germany, the Netherlands, France, and Belgium. The British proposal also remained on the negotiating table after the start of the EEC. However, De Gaulle and Adenauer eventually turned it down, as they believed that the EEC was the better alternative in terms of moving forward with Franco-German rapprochement or a France-dominated power in international politics. By keeping the EEC boundaries closed and thus maintaining its external consolidation, they allowed the nascent EEC to develop its internal construction:

> Community and member states officials feared that an early agreement between the Six and the Seven would thwart proper implementation of the Treaty of Rome. Instead, they resolved to press ahead with closer Community integration... (Dinan, 1994, p. 44)

Nevertheless, the EEC boundaries remained relatively permeable as the EEC treaty welcomed other European states as members. Soon after the launch of the EEC, the British government considered the EEC the best (or the least bad) option to restore the economic and international position of the UK (Dinan, 2005, p. 61). Lacking sources of European loyalty, such as Christian-democratic supranationalism, national loyalty, and pragmatic calculations on entry and non-entry featured even more strongly in the British case than it did in those of the original six. Similar considerations marked governments with close (trading) ties with the UK—Denmark, Ireland, and Norway, which also filed application requests

(Nicholson & East, 1987; Petersen & Elklit, 1973). Even though these governments also considered the alternative of national sovereignty plus free trade arrangements with the EEC, they saw EC membership as a way of strengthening the trading options and international standing of their relatively small countries.

The very possibility of British entry constrained further internal construction of the EEC, however, as expected in light of the bounding-bonding mechanism. To start, De Gaulle's attempt to initiate intergovernmental European foreign and defence policy in the early 1960s could have been delayed by the Dutch government, in particular, which could have argued in favour of waiting for the membership of the UK. If UK membership were out of the question, it would have been much harder for the other five governments to postpone political cooperation in the French way (cf. Segers, 2010). The actual British application for membership in 1961 was met with outright refusal by De Gaulle in early 1963. According to De Gaulle, the UK was historically, geographically, economically, and culturally too different to join the European Communities at that time (see Nicholson & East, 1987, p. 30ff). He resisted membership of the pro-Atlantic UK, as it would otherwise make his plans for a *European* Europe, less dependent on US leadership, more difficult. By refusing the UK's entry, De Gaulle maintained the EEC's external consolidation. The accession of new member states would have had a weakening impact on the EEC's internal construction at this early stage:

...allowing Britain to join in the early 1960s would in all likelihood have thwarted the CAP, undermined the Community, and turned the customs union into a broad free trade area. (Dinan, 2005, p. 39)

Thus, De Gaulle's first refusal had a rather positive effect on the EC's internal construction. The CAP could be elaborated upon and interest groups of farmers organised their voices at the European level. Though at times grudgingly, the EC-six accepted the mutual political exchanges, thus continuing the integrative spiral. With the growing strength of the EC's internal construction, concerns about the unsettling impact of British membership diminished. When the UK filed another membership request in 1967, it was up to the applicant rather than the EC itself to adapt (Piers Ludlow, 2006, pp. 139–140). Moreover, the British government accepted the CAP by and large, despite it being rather unprofitable for the UK. De Gaulle's second veto of the British application was therefore of more limited significance, if any, in terms of the preservation of the EC. Yet, the prospect of British membership continued to constrain the EC's internal construction. The governments of Belgium, the Netherlands, and Italy were reluctant to deepen European integration and sought to limit the threshold for potential applicants, in particular for the UK (Piers Ludlow, 2006, p. 155). As reforms of the EC became conditional on UK accession, the French government began to reconsider its position, as it also had something to gain from these reforms. Thus, UK membership became part of the mutual exchange between the EC-six.

After De Gaulle's demise in 1969, the British government soon reactivated its membership application as did its counterparts in Ireland, Denmark, and Norway. British accession had always been favoured by many actors in the EC. Some perceived it as a necessary Atlantic corrective to the continental foreign policy of the EC-six, as pursued by De Gaulle. Others favoured British entry as a free-market barrier against overly *dirigiste* economic policies in the customs union. Close trading links with the EFTA made many West German actors particularly amenable to UK accession. Governments from the Benelux and Italy saw the UK's accession as a possible counterweight to a Franco-German directorate of the EC. In spite of De Gaulle's vetoes, support for British membership was present in France. For instance, British EC participation provided a welcome antidote to supranationalism, particularly in the eyes of De Gaulle's successor, Georges Pompidou. The EC reforms and electoral calculations that would accompany UK membership also made their accession worthwhile in his eyes. Many within and outside France also considered British EC membership to be a necessary counterbalance to an increasingly powerful West Germany. When West German engagement with Eastern Europe increased in the context of *Ostpolitik* after the social-democrats returned to government in 1966, concerns had grown about the possibility of its (partial) exit from the EC and the Western bloc. Meanwhile, a dynamic economy bolstered West Germany's growing political self-confidence, whereas a weak dollar and an unsuccessful war in Vietnam undermined trust in the USA as provider of stability and security in Europe and in terms of its ability to lock West Germany into the transatlantic alliance. UK membership was thus seen as being helpful to the project of containing West Germany.

Even if UK membership were to be warmly welcomed, the inclusion of new members would have certainly meant a shift in possible political exchanges and alignments between the existing member states and party groups. The governments that feared being disadvantaged by the new alignments tried to secure their interests in anticipation of enlargement (Van der Veen, 2014). Thus, widening of the EC is not antagonistic to internal reform deepening the EC (cf. Kelemen, Menon, & Slapin, 2014), even if the bounding-bonding mechanism would suggest as much at first sight. One important precondition should not be forgotten in this respect, however. The EC member states continued political exchanges within the framework of the EC, as national and other international exit options were relatively unattractive in comparison, given previous investments in the EC, the relative effectiveness of seeking satisfaction through the EC as opposed to exiting and the benefits accrued in the EC. Given the lack of better alternatives, the EC-six made political exchanges to maintain their gains insofar as possible from EC membership in the face of external de-consolidation by enlargement, as well as *Ostpolitik*. At their summit in The Hague in 1969, they agreed to complete the CAP, through which the French government managed to make an advantageous deal on agricultural funds before enlargement. At that summit, the governments of the EC-six also launched an initiative for monetary cooperation to stabilise mutual trade in agriculture and to lock in the West German currency. Furthermore, they also agreed on a new intergovernmental initiative for common foreign policy-making, European Political Cooperation (EPC), enlargement, and a declaration of the "irreversibility" of their union, also in an effort to lock in West Germany (Dinan, 1994, p. 70). Prior to accession, the existing member states also agreed on a common fisheries policy that served their own interests, much to the irritation of the prospective member states that had to agree to it as part of EC legislation (Van der Veen, 2014, pp. 766–767). In the absence of better options elsewhere, the integrative spiral continued, with an exchange of resources widening the scope of the European allocation of values and even a declaration of mutual loyalty. However, internal construction was *not* maintained in the face of external de-consolidation due to the EC's locking-in powers to prevent full or partial exits, but rather by the EC's attractiveness relative to national and international alternatives.

British approval of EC membership did not come about without domestic protest. Supranational encroachment upon parliamentary sovereignty, the impact of the EC market on national economic planning, food prices, links with the Commonwealth, EFTA members, and the Third World made Labour MPs, in particular, reluctant to accept EC membership. The budgetary consequences of the deal of the EC-six on EC budgets for the UK further undermined support. The limit to voice imposed by parliamentary ratification without a referendum and the lack of viable alternatives to EEC membership in terms of resolving the unsatisfactory British economic situation in the eyes of the Conservatives in particular helped secure a majority nevertheless. In Norway, the masses did have the opportunity to express their opinion on EC membership. A majority consisting of voters from the radical left, peripheral areas and the agricultural and fisheries sectors preferred looser ties with the EC to maintain national sovereignty and to protect the social-economic order from the allegedly capitalist EC, among other things (Valen, 1973). The government abided by the resultant rejection of EC membership. Although similar concerns existed in Denmark and Ireland about the EC's impact on national sovereignty and the social-economic order, popular calculations of the pros and cons of EC membership resulted in different outcomes in referenda. Fears about economic viability and international influence outside the EC, especially in light of the fact that their most important trading partner (the UK) was to join regardless, led to a resounding yes. Alternatives such as (a combination of) national sovereignty, EFTA, or Nordic cooperation were deemed less attractive, by the agricultural sector in particular (Nicholson & East, 1987; Petersen & Elklit, 1973).

In spite of the fact that the EC governments had managed to maintain the EC's internal construction in advance of enlargement, the actual accession of three new member states by 1973 unsettled it. After entry, the British government tried to make a better budgetary deal (Dinan, 2010, p. 55). The leaders of the EC governments agreed to develop a corrective mechanism in the event of unacceptable situations, access to certain products from Commonwealth and developing countries, and expanding funds for backward regions (Nicholson & East, 1987). To deal with internal divisions on EC membership, a new Labour government called for a referendum on EC membership in 1975, suggesting that a full national exit option was still clearly on the table. A majority of the UK voters still accepted EEC membership, most probably for pragmatic bread-and-butter reasons (Smith, 1999). After the referendum, British governments still expressed their dissatisfaction with their budgetary position in the EC, in particular after the Conservatives, led by Margaret Thatcher, returned to power in 1979. They did so not by seeking exit from the EC, but by voicing their dissatisfaction loudly and clearly *within* the EC. Reflecting the limited solidarity with the British within the EC, the discussions continued until 1984, when the French and German governments eventually agreed to foot the bill for a permanent reduction in the British EC contribution to unblock political exchange in the EC on other issues (Parsons, 2003, p. 188). Thus, the key alignment underpinning the European integration process, the French-German axis, had survived the unsettling effect of enlargement. Be that as it may, the exchange of resources and subsequent centre formation in the EC had been severely hampered by British entry. It also strained the mutual loyalty between the "awkward partner" and its continental counterparts (George, 1998). The relatively low level of European attachment between the new member states in comparison to the original six ones (Thomassen & Bäck, 2009) also made efforts to foster a common European loyalty at the mass level more difficult. The accession of new member states also weakened internal construction by increasing the diversity of national policies within the EC, making the harmonising of EC legislation and also the EC's scrutiny of the growing diversity more difficult, thereby limiting its means of maintaining its boundaries in terms of compliance. In sum, the first round of enlargement weakened the EC's internal construction, as well as its external consolidation.

8.3   LACKING BETTER ALTERNATIVES, GOVERNMENTS CONTINUED EUROPEAN INTEGRATION

Meanwhile, despite the unsettling impact of enlargement, the lack of appealing alternatives outside the EC kept its external de-consolidation at bay. It also allowed for some continuation of internal construction, however slowly. At their summit in Copenhagen in 1973, the governments of the EC member states attempted to describe their common values and identity in an effort to express their mutual loyalty more explicitly in foreign policy. They also coordinated their efforts in the Conference on Security and Cooperation in Europe (CSCE), in which the EC governments, the USA, Canada, the Soviet Union, and its vassals and the non-aligned and neutral European states came together to discuss Europe's political order. The conference had been intended to be another means of locking in West Germany's *Ostpolitik*, but it also served to decrease tensions at the eastern EC boundaries by acknowledging the current division between East and West. Although the US government pursued tougher policies regarding the Soviet Empire, Western European governments preferred warmer relations to consolidate the boundaries of their states and thus the EC. It showed that the EPC could function, albeit only when governments of larger member states such as France perceived it to be instrumental to strengthening its voice in international politics.

These governments used other national or international options when it suited them better (Krotz & Schild, 2012, p. 217).

In an attempt to increase the efficiency of an increasingly sclerotic decision-making machine, hampered by the Luxembourg compromise, in 1974, heads of states and governments decided to meet regularly in the so-called European Council. It requested that various committees suggest improvements to the institutional construction of the EC. For instance, the Tindemans committee put forward the suggestion of a two-speed Europe (in other words, an EC with partial non-entries) to deal with increased differences between EC member states after the first enlargement. References to "two-speed Europe" were subsequently made whenever certain more pro-integration governments felt that reluctant counterparts would block further integration. The latter governments were expected to join in the end, as they would eventually consider the costs of non-entry to be too high due to exclusion from the allocation of certain goods (cf. Kölliker, 2006). In order to maintain a balance in voices at the EC level and to legitimise the EC's allocation of values, the European Council also agreed to launch direct elections of the European Parliament (EP), which, since 1979, have provided citizens of EC member states with another modest voice in EC decision-making, in addition to elections and referenda at the national level. Meanwhile, the Court of Justice gradually increased the impact of European law through its verdicts, coining the idea of mutual recognition of national market regulations rather than European harmonisation. Internal construction also moved forward when alternatives to Interpol and the Council of Europe appeared less attractive in terms of coordinating the fight against political terrorism due to their intergovernmental nature, their size, and diverse opinions on the definition of terrorism. Given the international nature of terrorism, the EC-nine used their existing connections to launch an intergovernmental and informal platform to share information about terrorism and related issues. Later, it also served as a platform to deal with international hooliganism, immigration, and organised crime.

Meanwhile, new sources of dissatisfaction had made their way onto the political agenda of Western European states. The breakdown of the Bretton Woods system of fixed exchange rates in the early 1970s prompted them to look for an international alternative to achieve exchange rate stability in a financially turbulent situation. Because trade in (agricultural) goods and capital had become increasingly international, exclusively national alternatives in terms of monetary agreements received less support. In addition to monetary instability, the EC-nine also faced the challenges of economic decline and unemployment as well as deteriorating relations with the Middle East, upon which they were dependent for oil. The choice they faced in terms of solving this unsatisfactory situation was between seeking an alternative for international coordination on monetary, economic, and energy issues by making further exchanges among the EC-nine and building a new political infrastructure. Due to divergent preferences vis-à-vis the Middle East, a common energy policy did not emerge. In response to the economic downturn, many governments also relied on non-tariff barriers to protect their domestic industries, even if this undermined the establishment of a common market as was specified in the EEC treaty.

Only after the Bretton Woods exchange rate system broke down fully did West German governments accept an alternative monetary arrangement between the EC member states. They faced domestic opposition to the establishment of close monetary ties with France and other countries with weak currencies, out of fear of the potential inflationary pressure on the German Mark and the requirement to support these countries. Thus, solidarity between the EC-nine had its limits. The monetary agreements between EC governments made to limit fluctuations in mutual exchange rates failed, however, after the French government had to withdraw from them. Nevertheless, many French actors perceived some kind of European monetary agreement as being necessary to locking West Germany in, restoring exchange rate stability with its major trading partners, and keeping some independence from the still-dominant US influence on monetary policies (Parsons, 2003, Chap. 5). Differences of opinion existed as to how this should be arranged and reluctance to accept supranational arrangements was widespread. Limited opportunities for voice allowed the West German chancellor, Helmut Schmidt, and the French president, Valéry Giscard-d'Estaing, to launch the European Monetary System (EMS) by 1979. Their close friendship and the European Council allowed them to circumvent domestic opposition and get their plans adopted. Among other things, Schmidt considered the EMS to be a means of sustaining Franco-German ties and to increasing the competitiveness of German exports by decreasing the German Mark's value somewhat. With the lack of a better alternative elsewhere, governments of other member states accepted the EMS. Only the British government decided upon non-entry, which indicated that the EC's locking-in capacity depended foremost on its relative attractiveness as perceived by member states. A two-speed Europe had thus emerged.

The EMS created considerable policy problems for the socialist government that came to power in France in 1981. The high value of the Franc, being linked to the highly valued German Mark, hampered the international competitiveness of French goods and services. Defence of the Franc's high value also required huge amounts of foreign currency reserves. Also, because of the international mobility of capital, the EMS constrained opportunities to foster economic growth by means of government spending or unilateral devaluation. Not surprisingly, the French government initially supported an exit from EMS (Parsons, 2003, p. 173). However, the previous investments made to remain within the EMS and the economic and political uncertainties surrounding a possible exit, in particular in relation to West Germany, prompted the socialist government to stay. In exchange for another devaluation of the Franc, the West German government obtained the commitment of the French government to adopt domestic policies of non-Keynesian nature, which were more in keeping with the EMS. The avoidance of a partial exit thus resulted in further political exchange within the framework of the EC.

8.4   The Entry of Mediterranean Countries and Locking in a Reunified Germany

While the internal construction of the EC continued, it remained highly dependent on its member states. It had not been empowered to maintain its boundaries or enforce compliance using coercive means. As such, the means at the EC's disposal to foster European loyalty were rather marginal, as national governments still dominated cultural, educational, and welfare programmes. To prevent full and partial exits, the EC had to rely primarily on the willingness of member states' governments to stay. Thus, the EC's locking-in capacity remained limited. As long as the EC remained relatively attractive from the standpoint of key decision-makers, external de-consolidation could be kept at bay and the integrative spiral could continue. Another enlargement round constituted a new de-consolidation challenge, however. The wealth and values of the EC attracted the governments of the recently (re)democratised states of Greece, Portugal, and Spain. They requested accession in 1975, 1977, and 1978, respectively. Common loyalty in terms of democratic values provided an impetus for starting the talks. Concerns about Greece's economic immaturity expressed by the European Commission were subsequently overrun by the governments of the existing member states, in part because they considered Greek accession to be a means of stabilising the southern boundaries of the Western alliance (Krotz & Schild, 2012, p. 143). In 1981, Greece joined the EC. Even more so than was the case with Greece's accession, various governments of member states feared the changing political alignments and exchange that would result from further enlargement, seeking deals to secure their share of funding, agricultural trade, and fishing before Spain and Portugal entered the EC. It delayed the accession negotiations until French president, François Mitterrand, accepted enlargement at the Fontainebleau summit in 1984, despite considerable domestic protest after he made the deal (Parsons, 2003, p. 189). After a promise of more European funding in early 1985, the Greek government also accepted the entry of Spain and Portugal the following year. The increasing diversity of systems brought about by the southern enlargement also posed challenges in terms of effectively scrutinising the implementation of EC law. It left the door open for non-integration or disintegration by means of no (longer) complying with European law.

Another source of external de-consolidation resulted from the relative *un*attractiveness of the EC and its member states. Capital and knowledge were expected to flow to the booming economies of Japan and the USA. An initiative to launch research and development policies and to intensify the EC's regional market made up of almost 300 legislative initiatives to be implemented by 1992 was therefore able to count on support from EC governments seeking sources of economic growth, including both the German and the British ones. More favourable to economic interventionism designed to protect industries and preferring to secure social rights, the socialist government in France had been much more reluctant to engage in economic liberalisation and deregulation, however (Parsons, 2003, p. 192). When French president, Mitterrand, pushed for supranationalist institutional reforms, in spite of a domestic preference for intergovernmentalism, a deal was still struck between the EC member states' governments to launch treaty revisions providing for both economic and institutional changes in 1985. Opinions had differed among member states about the necessity of institutional reforms, such as the principle of mutual recognition of national market regulations and qualified majority voting in the council for market regulation in an enlarged EC. A larger role of the European Parliament in EC decision-making had been advocated as being a legitimisation of this more supranational allocation of values, indicating that the voice of the masses and their representatives gained increasing prominence on the EC agenda (Rittberger, 2005). The British, Danish, and Greek governments opposed the decision to engage in treaty revision. Being outvoted in the council, they decided to stay in the EEC in order to influence the revision as far as they could. In other words, they perceived staying *plus* voice as being more beneficial than exit. The exchange of trade liberalisation and institutional reform had been laid down in the Single European Act (SEA), which had been in force since 1987. It also included a reference to cooperation on foreign policy, partly at the request of the French government in an effort to increase the say of the EEC governments in international politics.

Given the disagreements and compromises on the EC's future in France, as well as other EC member states, there were plenty of reasons for dissatisfaction among specific groups of voters with regard to the EC. In elections for national parliaments, key actors were involved in ratifying treaties; however, European issues had played only a very limited role, if any, with elections in the period of accession in Denmark, Norway, and the UK as the very few exceptions (De Vries, 2007; Van der Eijk & Franklin, 2004). And when European issues did feature in campaigns for the European parliamentary elections, which they hardly ever did (Franklin, Van der Eijk, & Marsh, 1996), the impact was rather limited. In the end, at that time, the European Parliament had no binding say on the founding treaties. Voice thus remained limited to a relatively closed circle of interested parliamentarians, which involved ministers, civil servants, and interest groups. As such, they had some leeway to move on with the internal construction of the EC, if they wanted to. Where referenda had been held on the SEA, in Ireland and Denmark, the economic benefits of the SEA convinced a majority to support the treaty, despite continuing left-wing objections to the EC's capitalist nature in Denmark in particular. The expansion of the EC's political infrastructure through the SEA and its ratification reflected the way in which member states continued to accept further internal construction, given the sole fact that they lacked an attractive alternative outside the EC on the issues dealt with in the SEA. Meanwhile, member states' political and financial investments in the EC increased the cost of their exit.

Given that European integration had been a product of calculation of the benefits and costs of non-entry and exit rather than one of outright mutual loyalty, suspicion still loomed large in discussions on the removal of border controls within the EC and the EC budget. The governments of France, West Germany, and the Benelux countries excluded their Southern European counterparts in negotiations on the Schengen framework on common border control, due to a lack of trust in the latter's capacity in that respect (Dinan, 2010, p. 531). Acrimonious conflicts on the budget revealed the limited inclination of EC governments to share financial resources. Only when a budgetary deal had the potential to become part of larger exchanges or had been considered necessary to enjoying the benefits of EC participation did governments that were hesitant to accept a larger budget acquiesced, if grudgingly. Locked into the EC by the lack of better alternatives at the national or international level, they calculated that an exchange of resources, which would expand the EC's political centre, would still be advantageous to them.

The SEA also included a reference to the goal of economic and monetary convergence, at the request of the French government in particular. Mitterrand saw a common monetary union as a way to regain some influence on West German monetary policy and its central bank in particular (Dinan, 2010, pp. 86–87). The reunification of West and East Germany as a result of the end of the Cold War constituted an extra impetus to maintain political control over a more powerful neighbouring state. In the framework of the Maastricht Treaty, West German chancellor, Helmut Kohl, accepted further monetary cooperation as means of anchoring his country solidly in European institutions, being afraid of what a German exit might mean (Krotz & Schild, 2012, p. 192). Kohl's acceptance came in exchange for free movement of capital, an independent central bank, strict limits on national budget deficits and debts, no bailout arrangements, and no monetisation of sovereign debts in the run-up to the monetary union. These attempts to prevent the mutualisation of debts, among other things, which would later also apply after entry to the common currency zone, reflected the limited solidarity among member states in terms of sharing the burden in the event of asymmetric shocks. Kohl did not manage to prevent the adoption of a fixed date for the introduction of a common currency in the Maastricht Treaty (in force since 1993). The establishment of the Economic and Monetary Union in the Maastricht Treaty met with considerable opposition in both France and Germany. Many French actors preferred a confederal arrangement that would not require ceding too much formal sovereignty and that would involve more political influence on monetary policies (Parsons, 2003, Chap. 7). Giving up a key symbol of national loyalty in the post-war period did not see much support in West Germany either. Furthermore, the fixed date raised fears that Germany would end up in a monetary union with member states with weak currencies, resulting in inflation and pressure to support economically and fiscally weaker states. In the end, the relatively closed circle of actors involved, with

Mitterrand and Kohl playing a key role in the European Council, kept voice at bay, allowing for the adoption of the monetary proposals. Participants in the European Council did have an effective voice though. Thus, the governments of poorer member states such as Ireland, Portugal, and Greece were able to garner side payments in the form of structural funds. Thus, the exchange of resources continued, broadening the European allocation of values, albeit under the precondition that national and international alternatives to European integration had been perceived as being less attractive, at least by the ones who called the shots.

8.5   The Enlargements with EFTA Members and Central and Eastern European Countries

In part in exchange for German participation in the EMU, Kohl also acquired support from Mitterrand to launch talks on a European Political Union (EPU), which comprised a mixed bag of proposals related to the power of the European Parliament, social rights, the fight against organised crime, and foreign policy cooperation. In France, there was widespread support for foreign policy cooperation as well. Given the expected American disengagement from Europe, foreign policy cooperation was seen as being a means of locking Germany more firmly into European institutions and strengthening the influence of EC member states in international politics. Therefore, at the French's behest, the Maastricht Treaty included the intergovernmental Common Foreign and Security Policy (CFSP) as part of a new European Union. The CFSP had also been agreed upon in the face of the unfolding crises in the Balkans. Despite various measures to strengthen its capacities for policy coordination and military intervention, the EU had to rely on NATO and the USA several times for effective intervention along its south-eastern boundaries. The Russian Federation maintained its capacity to interfere (militarily) in its neighbourhood, maintaining its presence with forces in Transnistria and Kosovo, for instance. Conversely, the EU largely lacked the capacity to lock in resources and actors by force.

However, the EU was still able to exert influence across its boundaries by offering the prospect of enlargement based on its considerable attractiveness among its neighbours. After these neighbours had been liberated from the competing power centre in Moscow, they looked to the Western alliance, which included the EU, for wealth and security. Thus, rather quickly, the EC's solid eastern boundary disappeared. The external de-consolidation by the prospective entry of a variety of new member states had a profound impact on existing coalitions and alignments in the EU. Immediate pressure for enlargement came from EFTA members. In the 1970s, neutralist EFTA members such as Austria, Sweden, and Finland had concluded free trade agreements with the EC, both bilaterally and multilaterally through the EFTA, despite objections from the Soviet Union. Their neutrality had been a key reason not to apply for full EC membership. However, just before the end of the Cold War, the Austrian government had already submitted a request for EC membership, as it no longer perceived EC membership as a constraint on its neutrality. Additionally, it perceived membership as being beneficial to its trading opportunities. In response to economic decline, experienced in part due to the Cold War, other EFTA members also made steps towards membership. However, European Commission president, Jacques Delors, pushed for talks on a European Economic Area (EEA) consisting of the EC and EFTA to ward off immediate enlargement by EFTA members, which were expected to be more reluctant to engage in monetary cooperation and foreign policy cooperation (Dinan, 2010, p. 104ff; Van der Veen, 2014). To secure the exchanges made in the Maastricht Treaty, in 1992, the European Council agreed that no accession negotiations could start until the treaty was ratified.

Even though EC and EFTA agreed upon the EEA, various EFTA members had already filed membership requests because they wanted to be directly involved in the making of rules in the most important market in Europe. In a series of referenda, entry in the EU also received popular support in most applicant countries. In large part for economic reasons, Austrian voters supported EU membership in a referendum held in 1994. A large share of Finnish elites perceived membership in the EU as being necessary to maintaining the interests of their small state (Raunio, 2016). Despite concerns about the position of small Finland in the EU and also the impact of EU membership on Finnish socio-economic policies and neutrality, a majority of voters supported this choice and expressed this in a referendum held in 1994. In the same year, a small majority of the Swedish voters also perceived the EU as being the better option as compared to national sovereignty, despite concerns about maintaining social and democratic standards and pursuing its neutral and activist foreign policy within the EU. In keeping with its Nordic neighbours, the Norwegian government had also requested EU membership once more, but the Norwegian voters rejected it in 1994. They did not want Norway to be too closely linked to the EU, not only to protect democratic sovereignty and the welfare system of their homeland from the allegedly capitalist impact of the EU, but also to maintain its distinct international voice (Lawler, 1997). The wealth of the Norwegian oil industry also had an impact on generating the majority position against EU membership. The referenda showed that alternatives to European integration were available, that actors were aware of them, and, in the case of Norway, that they were also chosen. Austria, Finland, and Sweden joined the EU in 1995, after tough negotiations between the governments of the EU-nine about the size of the minority in the Council that would be necessary to block a proposal (Dinan, 2010, p. 107).

The rhetoric of an undivided Europe created a certain measure of loyalty among the EC governments and made them somewhat amenable to the idea of the accession of new member states in Central and Eastern Europe (Nugent, 2004, p. 9; Schimmelfennig, 2001). However, much more so than the enlargement with EFTA members, the possibility of accession of Central and Eastern European countries (CEECs) increased concerns about the viability of the EU. Delors, therefore, suggested an associated partnership as an alternative for the time being. Additionally, French governments feared that enlargement would undermine existing coalitions and alignments in the EU to their disadvantage. In their eyes, enlargement with EFTA members had already strengthened the relative power of Germany's governments because of similarities in preferences regarding the economy and foreign policy and that this would only be reinforced by the accession of CEECs (Krotz & Schild, 2012, pp. 146–148). Conversely, German governments *favoured* EU enlargement with the neighbouring countries as was seen as stabilising Germany's neighbourhood and enhancing export opportunities. According to German governments, EU-led engagement with Central and Eastern Europe would also assuage concerns about German (partial) exit tendencies and would create an opportunity to share the costs of reforming the EU neighbourhood. Thus, the issue of enlargement had put the key Franco-German alignment under pressure.

At a summit in Copenhagen in 1993, EU member states agreed on a set of conditions for accepting membership applications, ranging from abidance with values, such as the rule of law and democracy, and economic compatibility with the internal market, to the administrative capacity to adopt EU law. The European Commission closely examined the EU-compatibility of the domestic legislation of candidate member states and offered them assistance to limit the burden of scrutinising their non-compliance (in other words, non-integration) in light of the increasing diversity of systems post accession. Additionally, the EU member states raised the bar for CEECs' entry by deepening European integration. In the Maastricht Treaty, the governments had already agreed to launch intergovernmental cooperation on justice and home affairs in addition to the existing Schengen provisions on common border control among some member states. The idea that organised crime might take advantage of free mobility within the internal market was an important impetus for this. Furthermore, as a result of the fall of the Iron Curtain and the EU's attractiveness as beacon of security and prosperity, the EU was faced with increased entry of a growing number of migrants from the Balkans and elsewhere. In 1997, the EU governments agreed to adopt the Schengen agreements into the EU treaties and to eventually expand supranational decision-making on matters ranging from visas, asylum, and immigration to organised crime. This was partly motivated by the ineffectiveness of intergovernmental decision-making, but the decision was also made with an eye to enlargement (Dinan, 2010, p. 539). The Amsterdam Treaty required the adoption of EU legislation on justice and home affairs by candidate member states, which were often perceived as problem cases in terms of organised crime and boundary control. Furthermore, EU member states agreed on a procedure to sanction (new) member states that violated fundamental values such as the rule of law and democracy, which had been laid down in the Maastricht Treaty (Dinan, 2010, p. 126).

In anticipation of enlargement, existing member states not only sought to secure policy-related benefits but also to preserve their institutional weight and their share of European funds. In particular, French governments linked the decision on enlargement to institutional and funding dossiers (Krotz & Schild, 2012, p. 151). It made for difficult treaty negotiations at the summits in Amsterdam (1997) and Nice (2000) on the distribution of power between and within the Council, European Parliament, and the European Commission. A scramble for power unfolded between governments of small and larger member states in particular. The treaty revisions also included the extension of qualified majority voting in the Council and increasing possibilities for integrative initiatives that did not include all member states, so-called flexible or differentiated integration, in order to circumvent the voice of obstinate governments. The political exchanges made to prepare the EU for enlargement were enshrined in treaties, which could only be changed in agreement of all member states. Inflexibility also marked the budgetary deals made in advance of enlargement, which were laid down in multi-annual financial frameworks. To the disappointment of the candidate member states, their share of structural and agricultural funds was only to be phased in over a period of ten years.

The accession of ten new member states by 2004 thus entailed complicated revisions of voice institutions and exchanges of resources. Their entry exerted less pressure on the existing coalitions and alignments within the EU. Certainly, the new member states have strengthened the liberal, Atlanticist, less pro-integrationist, less environmentalist, anti-refugee, and eastern orientations in the EU. Additionally, they compete for cohesion and agricultural funding with other net EU budget recipients in Southern Europe. Nevertheless, the coalitions in the Council remained relatively fluid running across east and west, and enlargement did not have much of an effect on production and duration of legislation (Toshkov, 2017). Its impact on the substance of decision-making also remained limited, as long as the partisan preferences of new member states did not deviate much from the preferences of existing member states (cf. Schneider, 2014; Toshkov, 2017). In addition, a certain loyalty in the Council apparatus as expressed by the continued consensual culture (in particular in COREPER) kept EU decision-making going (Bickerton, Hodson, & Puetter, 2014). The key alignment between French and German governments underpinning European integration has also kept the EU moving, as it did during the Euro crisis, for example (Krotz & Schild, 2012). Accession also resulted in modifications in voice structuring in the European Parliament. Even if they had to change their internal organisation somewhat to maintain their cohesion, parliamentary groups and European parties managed to absorb most national delegations from the accessory countries (Bressanelli, 2014; Hix & Noury, 2009; Pridham, 2014; Toshkov, 2017). The absorption of the new parties in the EP was facilitated by the resemblance of electorates in east and west to each other, at least with respect to the fundamental dividing line between socio-economic left and right (Van der Brug, Franklin, Popescu, & Tóka, 2009). The voice structuring of European interest groups required even less adaptation in response to the big bang enlargement of 2004. Unsurprisingly, due to their communist past, interest groups from the new member states were rather weakly organised. They did not upset the existing umbrella organisations of interest groups in the EU, but rather functioned as vehicles of Europeanisation in their home countries (Pleines, 2012). In sum, the (prospect of) enlargement entailed modifications of existing voice structures and the exchange of resources, but the presence of existing coalitions such as the Franco-German axis and the parliamentary groupings was strong enough to absorb the entry of new actors.

The political exchanges made in response to external de-consolidation due to the fear of a possible exit by Germany and the enlargements included more supranational decision-making and expansion of the EU centre as a result of the allocation of values on issues of monetary policy, justice and home affairs, and foreign and security policy. Enlargement (widening) was thus accompanied by integration (deepening and broadening of scope), albeit under the condition of there being no better alternative in the eyes of the dominant actors. Despite this continuation of European integration in terms of territory, policy areas, and decision-making, enlargement did serve to undermine European loyalty. There are no longitudinal data on European loyalty among political elites. Concerns have been expressed, however, that elite support for European integration has been lower in the new member states than the old ones (Ross, 2011, p. 52ff). Half of the economic and political elites in a variety of member states also considered the significant social and economic differences among member states to be a threat to social cohesion in the EU (Cotta & Russo, 2012, p. 24). The temporary limitations on free movement of persons from Central and Eastern Europe in various member states could also be interpreted as a sign of limited loyalty, as it shows the reluctance of member states to share work with one another.

The enlarged EU has not become a clear geographical entity with which people identify (Risse, 2010, p. 50). Its values are also more western than exclusively "EU-ish". In terms of identity, solidarity, and culture, citizens do not feel that the EU is particularly distinctive from the rest of the world (Delhey, Deutschmann, Graf, & Richter, 2014). Yet, at first glance, the 2004 and 2007 enlargements did not undermine European loyalty at the mass level. European attachment is an important indicator of support of EU enlargement and deepening (Hobolt, 2014), and, in line with Hirschman's thinking, a buffer against dissatisfaction with the EU. Attachment to Europe among citizens in Central and Eastern European countries has been of a similar or even somewhat higher level than in Western Europe, although the latter had already decreased with the accession of the north-western and the EFTA states (Ceka & Sojka, 2016; Risse, 2010). Enlargement did not affect EU attachment very much. However, the aggregated level of mutual trust among EU citizens dropped significantly after the 2004 and 2007 enlargements because of the low trust of citizens from Central and Eastern European countries across the entire, enlarged EU (Delhey, 2007; Thomassen & Bäck, 2009). In particular, people from

Bulgaria and Romania (as well as candidate member state Turkey) scored low in this respect. Thus, the desire to "return to Europe" has not been met with enthusiasm everywhere. The level of perceived modernisation of a nation, lingual-cultural affinity, and perceived threat (with larger nations distrusted more) appeared to be the most important explanations of (the lack of) mutual trust (Delhey, 2007). Enlargement has thus put European loyalty under considerable pressure. In 2005, the rejection of the European Constitutional Treaty by referendum in France and the Netherlands was partly motivated by the unwillingness to share money, work and power with new and candidate member states like Poland and Turkey.

8.6   The EU's Limited Locking-in Capacity: Loyalty and Boundary Maintenance

The external de-consolidation of the EU and its predecessors had an unsettling impact on their internal construction, as reflected by painful exchanges (on the British budget, for instance), arduous negotiations on voice infrastructure (e.g., the power distribution in the Council), and declining mutual loyalty at the mass level. However, the latter does not corroborate Proposition 2 entirely. Declining loyalty was the result of the particular set of member states that was added rather than a disintegrative spiral. Moreover, the EC/EU developed a voice infrastructure (Council, Commission, Court, and Parliament) and a certain measure of stabilisation in its mutual alignments (the French-German axis, the Council's consensus politics, and parliamentary groups) before the various rounds of enlargement, which allowed it to counter the subsequent unsettling effects. In other words, internal construction also had an impact upon external consolidation. Importantly, in line with Proposition 1, the lack of better alternatives kept non-entry into or (partial) exits from the EC/EU at bay. Thus, being stuck in the EC/EU, member states continued to engage in exchanges with an eye to obtaining the best deal possible given their situation, involving major steps such as expanding the internal market, introducing a common currency, enlargement, enhancing justice and home affairs policies, and strengthening the coordination of external policies. As a result, the congruence of policy areas increased. Also, the permeability of EC/EU boundaries has been decreased by the imposition of external tariffs by the customs union and the "filters" of the Schengen area. This strengthening of external consolidation has increased the cost of exit for actors within the EC/EU, in particular with respect to national governments that had invested more and more politically in the integration process. As such, the EU and its predecessors have remained in an integrative spiral.

Though the EC/EU has made major steps, the EU's locking-in capacity has remained somewhat limited. This holds, first of all, for loyalty at the mass level, which can be measured by the presence of a European sense of community. Almost half of the public does not view themselves as European (Polyakova & Fligstein, 2016) and even the ones who do most often find their national identity to be more important (Risse, 2010). In particular, in Scandinavia and the UK, people identify themselves exclusively as nationals of their respective countries. The "psychological existence" of a European identity (Risse, 2010, p. 61) is also rather restricted, as it is often met with a certain measure of indifference or ignorance (Duchesne & Van Ingelgom, 2013). In addition to limited cognitive identification with the EU, feelings of national attachment have remained stronger and more widespread than European attachment, even though the latter has increased in the 15 older EU member states from 48% fairly to very attached in 1991 to 67% in 2007 (Antonisch & Holland, 2014). Attachment to other European countries is much stronger than to non-European countries, but only 54% feel attached to a country other than their own (Delhey, Richter, & Deutschmann, 2014). As mentioned above, mutual trust among EU peoples is comparatively low with respect to Central and Eastern European member states (Thomassen & Bäck, 2009).

Loyalty can also be expressed in terms of a shared destiny, discussed and created in a common European public sphere (Bartolini, 2005). At the elite level, two distinct destinies for Europe can be discerned: a predominantly secular identity based on values such as peace, human rights, and democracy (to be distinguished from a xenophobic, racist, anti-democratic past) and a thicker, cultural one, depicting Europe as a Christian civilisation (Checkel & Katzenstein, 2009; Risse, 2010). For a long time, however, European integration did not feature prominently in public debates, accession periods being the notable exception. Many people did not have a comprehensive idea of Europe at all, although a clear distinction could be made among those who did: European integration as an instrument of peace and prosperity versus European integration as a threat to national identity and sovereignty (Díez Medrano, 2003). Representations, conceptions, and images of Europe have been shaped heavily by frames originating predominantly from national histories, cultures, and experiences (Díez Medrano, 2003; Harmsen & Schild, 2009). Nevertheless, these public debates can and do reflect increasing commonalities across the EU area in terms of persons, actors, themes, variety of frames, interpretations, and perspectives, as well as timing and issue salience (Risse, 2010; Van der Steeg, 2007). This holds for quality newspapers rather than TV, and the UK remains "the odd one out" in this respect. As a result, a large part of the public does not even experience, let alone participate in, Europeanised public debates.

In sum, national loyalties have remained much stronger than European loyalty in terms of attachment, identification, and public debate. It does not mean that European identification competes with national identification. Rather, the real distinction is between those with an exclusive national identification on the one hand and those with an inclusive national identification on the other (Risse, 2010). The relative stability in terms of European identification both at the mass and the elite levels also reflects the "stickiness of national identity constructions" (Risse, 2010, p. 100). Nevertheless, certain facets of loyalty can and do change. For instance, mutual trust at the mass level increased considerably between the French and German people in the 1950s and 1960s and in people from Southern European countries that acceded to the EC in the 1980s (Klingemann & Weldon, 2013). Over the years, the EU and its predecessors have taken measures that could have fostered loyalty towards the European political system and its members. These measures include the establishment of a set of rights, such as equal treatment of men and women, the right to live and work elsewhere in the EC/EU, the right to participate in European Parliament and municipal elections elsewhere in the EU, the right to petition the European Parliament, the right to refer cases of maladministration to the European Ombudsman, the citizen initiative, and the right to diplomatic consular services from other EU embassies. These rights have also been laid down in the Charter of Fundamental Rights, which became legally binding in the Lisbon Treaty (in force since 2009). In addition to these rights, the EC/EU introduced symbols of European identity including the 12-star flag, a wordless anthem, a motto (unity in diversity), a logo, a common currency, a European passport, and a European health insurance card. Furthermore, among other things, the declaration of European identity adopted by the European Council (1973), the Maastricht Treaty (1993), the Copenhagen accession criteria (1993), and the Sakharov Prize for Freedom of Thought awarded by the European Parliament also reflect the values that are considered central to the EU's identity, such as democracy and the rule of law. In addition, the Erasmus exchange programme for students and the annual European capitals of culture allow people to experience Europe. Through agricultural and social funds, the EC/EU has also redistributed financial resources among its residents and, during the Eurozone crises, the EU and its member states supported heavily indebted countries by offering guarantees and loans.

Have these measures had any impact on European loyalty? Most Europeans are aware of the European flag (Risse, 2010, p. 58). Exposure to European symbols also seems to have an effect on European identification (Bruter, 2005). As the Eurobarometers indicate, many also associate the EU with freedom of movement and peace. The use of rights is somewhat limited though. About 3% of the EU citizens live in a member state other than their own and about 0.3% cross borders yearly (Barslund & Busse, 2016). Electoral turnout for European parliamentary elections is also lower than for national elections, and electoral participation in European elections does not generate a stronger sense of European citizenship (Sanders, Bellucci, & Tóka, 2012, p. 211). Nevertheless, people accept the use of rights by their fellow citizens across the EU to some extent. There is a widespread willingness to give other EU citizens the right to vote in local and even also in national elections (European Commission, 2014; Thomassen & Bäck, 2009). Access to social benefits also has substantial support at the mass level, but access to labour markets is much less so (Thomassen & Bäck, 2009). There are still indications that, at least in Spain, Germany, and Poland, a majority of the public would be willing to accept a Europeanised social policy, with uniform social standards, a harmonised minimum wage, and unemployment subsidies in the poorest member states (Gerhards, Lenfeld, & Häuberer, 2016). Furthermore, a narrow majority in the EU seems to be inclined to support indebted member states (Daniele & Geys, 2012; Lengfeld, Schmidt, & Häuberer, 2015), even in Germany, albeit subject to conditions like enacting solid budgetary policies (Bechtel, Hainmüller, & Margalit, 2014). Rather than being based on utilitarian calculations alone, this solidarity seems to stem from altruism and cosmopolitan affiliation with other countries and citizens beyond one's own nation (Bechtel et al., 2014). Be that as it may, in the most crisis-ridden member states in particular, European identification decreased during the debt crises (Polyakova & Fligstein, 2016). The question therefore remains as to whether or not European loyalty-generating measures have had much of an impact at all. With a budget of roughly 1% of the GNP of the entire EU area, the EU has a few largely legal and regulatory means at its disposal to strengthen loyalty. In contrast, member states still dominate loyalty-generating instruments such as educational, media, and cultural and welfare programmes. Further integration is not necessarily dependent upon a limited sense of community within the EU (Klingemann & Weldon, 2013; Thomassen & Bäck, 2009). In European history, many states were created before nations. However, European loyalty in terms of a European sense of community can function as a buffer against specific dissatisfaction with the EU, while generating support for the EU (cf. Risse, 2014). More importantly, the EU does not have other means (like force) with which to contain or counter actor-level disintegration. The EU's locking-in capacity is therefore highly reliant on the willingness of its member states and citizens to stay, to stick to the rules, and to show solidarity.

Given the voluntary nature of European integration and the alternatives available, member states have adopted several measures to prevent (partial) exit by other actors including non-compliance. First, they comply with the mutual agreements to such an extent that fellow member states are not given reason to engage in non-compliance or other forms of (partial) exit. Mutual credible commitment has also been guaranteed by anchoring agreements (on the free movements and the monetary union, for example) in rigorous treaties and by giving supranational and non-electoral bodies like the European Commission, the Court of Justice of the European Union and the European Central Bank autonomous powers to uphold these agreements. The EU has thus been given regulatory and legal powers that allow it to lock in resources and actors. The EU is still heavily dependent on member states for the actual implementation of, compliance with and enforcement of EU law. Its relative attractiveness vis-à-vis national and international alternatives is instrumental to conformity. This works most effectively when a state is in the process of accession (conditionality), but after their accession it becomes harder to achieve, whether it concerns the rule of law (Poland), the reallocation of refugees (Hungary; Slovakia), or the Stability and Growth Pact (France, Germany, Greece, Italy). This indicates how reliant the EU is on the willingness of its member states to prevent partial exits.

The specific construction of the EU to prevent partial exits also highlights a limitation of its locking-in capacity. This construction has been laid down in treaties. As a result, the EU cannot easily appease voices that are against the content of these treaties because it would require the consent of all the member states. In other words, the EU has been made in such a way that it is largely unresponsive to anti-treaty voices. The aforementioned construction was developed in large part at a time when national executives dominated European integration. The limited say of the greater public in the EC/EU was felt more acutely when European integration expanded and manifested itself more prominently in peoples' daily lives. Accompanying concerns about the democratic legitimacy of the EC grew when the Single European Act (in force since 1987) extended qualified majority voting in the Council. National ministers could thus be overruled, which meant that national parliaments could no longer exert a veto indirectly through them. And with limited alternative locking-in instruments available, the EC/EU has thus become increasingly dependent on acceptance at the mass level.

To sustain the legitimacy of the European integration process at the mass level, the power of the European Parliament has been gradually expanded in terms of the budget, legislation, and scrutiny of the European Commission. However, European parliamentary elections have remained a rather national and lacklustre affair, as reflected by low turnout (Marsh & Mikhaylov, 2010). Additionally, European parties remain by and large powerless in terms of key functions such as mobilisation and recruitment, and eliciting change of leadership in European institutions directly via elections has remained rather difficult. With European groups and parties barely known by the public, let alone rooted at the mass level, EP-centred arrangements also proved to be problematic in terms of propping up the EU's legitimacy (Day, 2014; Lord, 2010). In particular, it remains difficult for Eurosceptic parties to change the course of the EU through the European Parliament. As the accountability of the Council and the European Central Bank to the European Parliament is rather limited, the large, pro-European groups work together, often closely, and treaty revision is the purview of national governments and parliaments.

Functional representation through civil society organisations (CSOs) has also proven to be problematic in terms of providing channels for voice. The confederal umbrella organisations at the EU level are quite removed from their members. The CSOs present at the EU level only represent a select part of the civil societies in the EU, with anti-EU and Eurosceptic organisations much less present (Della Porta & Caiani, 2007; Dolezal, Hutter, & Brecker, 2016; Fitzgibbon, 2013; Kröger & Friedrich, 2013; Saurugger, 2008). Also, because of the introduction of qualified majority voting, since the 1990s, attention has also been increasingly focused on national parliaments to provide the necessary legitimacy to the EC/

EU. They are not only involved in steering their own ministers whose job it is to decide on EU legislation in the Council, but even more so in the approval of treaties negotiated and concluded by their governments. National parliaments have still struggled to put a mark on EU legislation, in spite of the fact that they put more effort into it now than before. Governments do not always provide the necessary information on time, it is difficult to obtain sufficient support from fellow national parliaments to ask the European Commission to reconsider legislative proposals that might encroach upon the principle of subsidiarity, communication is limited on EU issues on the part of national parliamentarians vis-à-vis their citizens, and parliamentarians themselves are not always interested in paying attention to EU issues, as these are not necessarily attractive from an electoral or career perspective (Auel & Raunio, 2014). Leaving a fundamental mark on treaties is also challenging for national parliamentarians, as treaty changes require the approval of all other member states. For those parties representing voters against the current treaties, in particular, it remains difficult to change the EU's course.

In an effort to make treaty revision more democratic, governments of EU member states launched a European Convention in 2003, in which representatives from governments and national parliaments, even those from candidate member states, as well as European institutions drafted a new constitutional treaty. It remained a rather elitist affair that drew little attention from anyone beyond those involved. A more important measure taken to democratise treaty revision has been ratification referendum, which has been put to increasing use. From the standpoint of voters from small countries, it appeared difficult, if not impossible, to change the course of the EU. However, after the rejection of the Maastricht Treaty in Denmark in 1992, the country was offered non-entry (opt-outs) on certain policy areas as an alternative. This indicates that voice structuring in the EU makes it difficult to deal with anti-system voices against market-making and sovereignty-sharing from within the system. Without many opportunities to effectively voice opposition *within* the EU, opposition *against* the EU in its entirety is more likely (Mair, 2007, p. 7).

Last but not least, the EU centre not only has a weak capacity to lock in actors and resources by loyalty-building measures, it has also been limited in terms of the means it has at its disposal to reinforce its boundaries. It lacks, by and large, the coercive instruments required to prevent external powers (like Russia, China, USA, or private investors) from attracting away actors or resources. Its voluntary nature has made it highly dependent on its member states to control goods, capital, services, and persons crossing the borders and to pursue foreign policies in the economic and geopolitical domain.

8.7   Conclusion: Counterforce to Contain Actor-Level Disintegration Limited

As expressed in Hypothesis 2, the external de-consolidation of the EU and its predecessors has put its internal construction under pressure. The permeability of boundaries, reflected by enlargements, concerns about a German *Sonderweg* and flows of capital, unsettled voice structures, alignments, exchanges of resources, and mutual loyalties. Nevertheless, enlargement and other forms of external de-consolidation did not produce a disintegrative spiral. Instead, widening did not prevent the EU and its predecessors from engaging in broader and deeper integration primarily because they had obtained a certain measure of internal construction before they had to process new member states. More importantly, key decision-makers perceived EU membership to be the best (or least bad) option among national and international alternatives and were also able to circumvent voices calling for these alternatives. Thus, exit was kept at bay and the integrative spiral was allowed to continue, although not all member states joined every integrative step.

The lack of better alternatives, at least in the eyes of those in charge, allowed for the European integration process to move on. With member states looking for the best deal available given the circumstances, mutual exchanges resulted in an increasing scope of policy areas and depth of decision-making. External consolidation was strengthened somewhat because of the ensuing congruence of various policy areas, from agriculture and trade to environment and monetary policies. Nevertheless, the EU and its predecessors had to rely foremost on the voluntary cooperation of member states. They had only been given a few means of regulatory and legal nature of enforcing implementation and maintaining boundaries (in other words, curtailing partial exits), with the member states keeping their hold on most of the redistributive, communicative, and coercive power sources. In sum, the EU has only developed a fairly weak locking-in capacity. Its relative attractiveness, rather than its power, has been crucial to preventing exit.

In addition to a lack of better national or international alternatives, limited voice was fundamental to the initiation of European integration and its maintenance. However, slowly but surely, the voice of the masses became more significant. Given the lower support for European integration among the greater public (Best, 2012; Hooghe, 2003), greater involvement of the masses has the potential to increase the electoral costs of European integration. Moreover, the very fact that the agreements among the member states had been laid down in treaties that were rather difficult to change also limited opportunities for Eurosceptic and anti-EU voices. As a result, (partial) exits may have become more attractive than was the case previously in calculations about how to effectively express dissatisfaction. Chapter 10 analyses how, over the past two decades, these calculations regarding voice and exit have played out in the EU with its weak locking-in capacity to counter disintegration among a variety of actors. First though, Chap. 9 will show that European integration has been a source of dissatisfaction due to its disintegrative impact on its member states.

REFERENCES

Antonisch, M., & Holland, E. C. (2014). Territorial attachment in the age of globalization: The case of Western Europe. *European Urban and Regional Studies, 21*(2), 206–221.

Auel, K., & Raunio, T. (2014). Introduction: Connecting with the electorate? Parliamentary Communication in EU affairs. *Journal of Legislative Studies, 20*(1), 1–12.

Barslund, M., & Busse, M. (2016). *Labour mobility in the EU: Addressing challenges and ensuring 'fair mobility'.* Special Report No. 139. Brussels: CEPS.

Bartolini, S. (2005). *Restructuring Europe: Centre formation, system building and political structuring between the nation-state and the European Union.* Oxford: Oxford University Press.

Bechtel, M., Hainmüller, J., & Margalit, Y. (2014). Preferences for international redistribution: The divide over the Eurozone bailout. *American Journal of Political Science, 58*(4), 835–856.

Best, H. (2012). Elite foundations of European integration: A causal analysis. In H. Best, G. Lengyel, & L. Verzichelli (Eds.), *The Europe of elites: A study into the Europeanness of Europe's political and economic elites* (pp. 208–233). Oxford: Oxford University Press.

Bickerton, C. J., Hodson, D., & Puetter, U. (2014). The new intergovernmentalism: European integration in the post-Maastricht era. *Journal of Common Market Studies, 53*(4), 703–722.

Bressanelli, E. (2014). Necessary deepening? How political groups in the European Parliament adapt to enlargement. *Journal of European Public Policy, 21*(5), 776–792.

Bruter, M. (2005). *Citizens of Europe? The emergence of a mass European identity.* Basingstoke: Palgrave Macmillan.

Ceka, B., & Sojka, A. (2016). Loving it but not feeling it yet? The state of European identity after the eastern enlargement. *European Union Politics, 17*(3), 482–503.

Checkel, J., & Katzenstein, P. (Eds.). (2009). *European identity.* Cambridge: Cambridge University Press.

Cotta, M., & Russo, F. (2012). Europe à la Carte? European citizenship and its dimensions from the perspective of national elites. In H. Best, L. Lengyel, & L. Verzichelli (Eds.), *The Europe of elites: A study into the Europeanness of Europe's political and economic elites* (pp. 14–42). Oxford: Oxford University Press.

Daniele, G., & Geys, B. (2012). *Public support for institutionalised solidarity: Europeans' reaction to the establishment of eurobonds.* WZB Discussion Paper, No. SP II 2012-112. Berlin: WZB.

Day, S. (2014). Between "containment" and "transnationalization": Where next for the Europarties? *Acta Politica, 49*(1), 5–29.

De Vries, C. (2007). *European integration and national elections: The impact of EU issue voting on national electoral politics* (dissertation), University of Amsterdam.

Delhey, J. (2007). Do enlargements make the European Union less cohesive? An analysis of trust between EU nationalities. *Journal of Common Market Studies, 45*(2), 253–279.

Delhey, J., Deutschmann, E., Graf, T., & Richter, K. (2014). Measuring the Europeanization of everyday life: Three new indices and an empirical application. *European Societies, 16*(3), 355–377.

Delhey, J., Richter, K., & Deutschmann, E. (2014). *Transnational sense of community in Europe: An exploration with Eurobarometer data.* Oldenburg: DFG Research Unit "Horizontal Europeanization".

Della Porta, D., & Caiani, M. (2007). Europeanization from below? Social movements and Europe. *Mobilization, 12*(1), 1–20.

Díez Medrano, J. (2003). *Framing Europe.* Princeton: Princeton University Press.

Dinan, D. (1994). *Ever closer union? An introduction to the European community.* Boulder, CO: Lynne Rienner Publisher.

Dinan, D. (2005). *Ever closer union? An introduction to European integration* (3rd ed.). Basingstoke: Palgrave Macmillan.

Dinan, D. (2010). *Ever closer union? An introduction to European integration* (4th ed.). Basingstoke: Palgrave Macmillan.

194   H. VOLLAARD

Dolezal, M., Hutter, S., & Brecker, S. (2016). Protesting European integration: Politicization from below? In S. Hutter, E. Grande, & H. P. Kriesi (Eds.), *Politicising Europe: Integration and mass politics* (pp. 112–134). Cambridge: Cambrige University Press.

Duchesne, S., & Van Ingelgom, V. (Eds.). (2013). *Citizens' reactions to European Integration compared: Overlooking Europe*. Basingstoke: Palgrave Macmillan.

European Commission. (2014). *Flash Eurobarometer 364: Electoral rights*. Luxemburg: European Commission.

FitzGibbon, J. (2013). Citizens against Europe? Civil society and Eurosceptic protest in Ireland, the United Kingdom and Denmark. *Journal of Common Market Studies, 51*(1), 105–121.

Franklin, M., Van der Eijk, C., & Marsh, M. (1996). Conclusions: The electoral connection and the democratic deficit. In C. van der Eijk & M. Franklin (Eds.), *Choosing Europe? The European electorate and national politics in the face of union* (pp. 366–390). Ann Arbor: The University of Michigan Press.

George, S. (1998). *An awkward partner: Britain in the European Community* (3rd ed.). Oxford: Oxford University Press.

Gerhards, J., Lenfeld, H., & Häuberer, J. (2016). Do European citizens support the idea of a European welfare state? Evidence from a comparative survey conducted in three EU member states. *International Sociology, 31*(6), 677–700.

Harmsen, R., & Schild, J. (Eds.). (2009). *Debating Europe: The 2011 European Parliament elections and beyond*. Baden-Baden: Nomos.

Hix, S., & Noury, A. (2009). After enlargement: Voting patterns in the sixth European Parliament. *Legislative Studies Quarterly, 34*(2), 159–174.

Hobolt, S. (2014). Ever closer or ever wider? Public attitudes towards further enlargement and integration in the European Union. *Journal of European Public Policy, 21*(5), 664–680.

Hooghe, L. (2003). Europe divided? Elites vs. public opinion on European integration. *European Union Politics, 4*(3), 281–305.

Kelemen, R. D., Menon, A., & Slapin, J. (2014). Wider and deeper? Enlargement and integration in the European Union. *Journal of European Public Policy, 21*(5), 647–663.

Klingemann, H.-D., & Weldon, S. (2013). A crisis of integration? The development of transnational dyadic trust in the European Union, 1954–2004. *European Journal of Political Research, 52*(4), 457–482.

Kölliker, A. (2006). *Flexibility and European unification: The logic of differentiated integration*. Lanham: Rowman & Littlefield.

Kröger, S., & Friedrich, D. (2013). Democratic representation in the EU: Two kinds of subjectivity. *Journal of European Public Policy, 20*(2), 171–189.

Krotz, U., & Schild, J. (2012). *Shaping Europe: France, Germany and embedded bilateralism from the Elysée Treaty to twenty-first century politics*. Oxford: Oxford University Press.

Lawler, P. (1997). Scandinavian exceptionalism and European Union. *Journal of Common Market Studies, 35*(4), 565–594.

Lengfeld, H., Schmidt, S., & Häuberer, J. (2015). *Is there European solidarity? Attitudes towards fiscal assistance for debt-ridden European Union member states.* Arbeitsbericht des Instituts für Soziologie 67. Leipzig: Institut für Soziologie.

Lord, C. (2010). The aggregating function of political parties in EU decision-making. *Living Reviews in European Governance, 5*(3). Retrieved from www.livingreviews.org/lreg-2010-3

Mair, P. (2007). Political opposition and the European Union. *Government and Opposition, 42*(1), 1–17.

Marsh, M. & Mikhaylov, S. (2010). European Parliament elections and EU governance. *Living Reviews in European Governance, 5*(4). Retrieved from www.livingreviews.org/lreg-2010-4

Nicholson, F., & East, R. (1987). *From the six to the twelve: The enlargement of the European Communities.* Harlow: Longman.

Nugent, N. (Ed.). (2004). *European Union enlargement.* Basingstoke: Palgrave Macmillan.

Parsons, C. (2003). *A certain idea of Europe.* Ithaca, NJ: Cornell University Press.

Petersen, N., & Elklit, J. (1973). Denmark enters the European Communities. *Scandinavian Political Studies, 8*, 197–213.

Piers Ludlow, N. (2006). *The European Community and the crises of the 1960s: Negotiating the Gaullist challenge.* London: Routledge.

Pleines, H. (2012). Weakness as precondition of smooth integration? Representation Strategies of Functional Interest Groups from New Member States at the EU Level. In M. Knodt, C. Quittkat, & J. Greenwood (Eds.), *Functional and territorial interest representation in the EU* (pp. 159–174). London: Routledge.

Polyakova, A., & Fligstein, N. (2016). Is European integration causing Europe to become more nationalist? Evidence from the 2007–9 financial crisis. *Journal of European Public Policy, 23*(1), 60–83.

Pridham, G. (2014). Comparative perspectives on trans-national party building in new democracies: The case of Central and Eastern Europe. *Acta Politica, 49*(1), 30–50.

Raunio, T. (2016). Finland. In D. M. Viola (Ed.), *Routledge handbook of European elections* (pp. 396–413). Abingdon: Routledge.

Risse, Th. (2010). *A community of Europeans? Transnational identities and public spheres.* Ithaca, NJ: Cornell University Press.

Risse, Th. (2014). No demos? Identities and public spheres in the Euro crisis. *Journal of Common Market Studies, 52*(6), 1207–1215.

Rittberger, B. (2005). *Building Europe's parliament: Democratic representation beyond the nation-state.* Oxford: Oxford University Press.

Ross, G. (2011). *The European Union and its crises: Through the eyes of the Brussels elite*. Basingstoke: Palgrave Macmillan.

Sanders, D., Bellucci, P., & Tóka, G. (2012). Towards and integrated model of EU citizenship and support. In D. Sanders, D. Bellucci, G. Tóka, & M. Torcal (Eds.), *The Europeanization of national polities? Citizenship and support in a post-enlargement union* (pp. 187–216). Oxford: Oxford University Press.

Saurugger, S. (2008). Interest groups and democracy in the European Union. *West European Politics, 31*(6), 1274–1291.

Schimmelfennig, F. (2001). The community trap: Liberal, rhetorical action, and the Eastern enlargement of the European Union. *International Organisation, 55*(1), 47–80.

Schneider, C. (2014). Domestic politics and the widening-deepening trade-off in the European Union. *Journal of European Public Policy, 21*(5), 699–712.

Segers, M. (2010). De Gaulle's race to the bottom: The Netherlands, France and the interwoven problems of British EEC membership and European political union. *Contemporary European History, 19*(2), 111–132.

Smith, J. (1999). The 1975 referendum. *Journal of European Integration History, 5*(1), 41–56.

Thomassen, J., & Bäck, H. (2009). European citizenship and identity after European enlargement. In J. Thomassen (Ed.), *The legitimacy of the European Union after enlargement* (pp. 184–207). Oxford: Oxford University Press.

Toshkov, D. (2017). The impact of the Eastern enlargement on the decision-making capacity of the European Union. *Journal of European Public Policy, 24*(2), 177–196.

Valen, H. (1973). Norway: "No" to EEC. *Scandinavian Political Studies, 8*, 214–226.

Van der Brug, W., Franklin, M., Popescu, M., & Tóka, G. (2009). Towards a European electorate: One electorate or many? In J. Thomassen (Ed.), *The legitimacy of the European Union after enlargement* (pp. 65–92). Oxford: Oxford University Press.

Van der Eijk, C., & Franklin, M. (2004). Potential for contestation on European Matters at National Elections in Europe. In G. Marks & M. Steenbergen (Eds.), *European integration and political conflict* (pp. 32–50). Cambridge: Cambridge University Press.

Van der Steeg, M. (2007). Gezamenlijkheid ondanks diversiteit: Publiek debat in de Europese Unie. In H. Vollaard & J. Penders (Eds.), *De spankracht van de Europese Unie* (pp. 41–66). Utrecht: Lemma.

Van der Veen, M. A. (2014). Enlargement and the anticipatory deepening of European integration. *Journal of European Public Policy, 21*(5), 761–775.

CHAPTER 9

The External De-consolidation of Member States Increases Dissatisfaction with the EU

9.1 Introduction

The previous chapters have shown how European integration was able to start and how it continued. The relative unattractiveness of national and international alternatives to addressing various sources of dissatisfaction was a crucial factor. Additionally, there were fewer opportunities for actors to give an effective voice to these alternatives. However, destabilising rounds of enlargement and other forms of external de-consolidation have constrained the integrative spiral at the European level. The internal construction of the European Union (EU) and its predecessors has resulted in a limited capacity to lock in actors and resources. As such, the EU has had to rely on its relative attractiveness as compared to other alternatives, rather than loyalty building, enforcement of compliance, and boundary control to prevent member states and other actors from engaging in (partial) exits.

In this chapter, the focus shifts to the level of the member states, which have played a significant role as political organisations in the EU and its predecessors, not least in terms of their being conduits for the expression of dissatisfaction. The third proposition is the central theme here: *the external de-consolidation of the EU's member states has weakened their internal construction*. Globalisation, new means of transportation and communication, and also European integration have led to a decline in the locking-in capacity of member states' systems of allocating values. Section 9.2 provides an explanation of how member states have become externally

© The Author(s) 2018
H. Vollaard, *European Disintegration*, Palgrave Studies in European Union Politics, https://doi.org/10.1057/978-1-137-41465-6_9

de-consolidated by an increasing number of exit and entry opportunities. Section 9.3 shows the varied and often limited use of these opportunities, for which Sect. 9.4 provides an explanation based on the mechanism of exit, voice, and loyalty. Section 9.5 reflects upon how both exit and entry continue to destabilise the internal construction of member states with respect to exchanges made, voice structures, alignments, and mutual loyalty. Subsequently, Sect. 9.6 provides an analysis of how the increasing number of opportunities for member states to leave and enter has been the reason for mounting dissatisfaction with the EU. Whether this dissatisfaction results in exit from the EU (disintegration at the actor level) and the emergence of a disintegrative spiral in the EU (disintegration at the systemic level) will be analysed in the next chapter.

9.2   More Opportunities for Exit and Entry Available to EU Member States

As was discussed in Chap. 6, the histories of states have been characterised by closure. Boundary control, including law enforcement, as well as loyalty building through the creation of nations and welfare systems (in other words, decreasing permeability) have constrained actors and their resources in terms of their ability to withdraw from states. Facing increasing costs of exit, these actors addressed their dissatisfaction *within* states, instead. In addressing this dissatisfaction, the scope of the states' centres' involvement in policy expanded. This led to increasing congruence of economic, cultural, coercive, legal, political, and administrative boundaries within the territorial confines of these states. With the option of mobility becoming increasingly costly, actors looked to mobilisation for voice within states, fostering states' voice infrastructure in the realms of electoral, corporate, and territorial representation. Being permanently locked in, patterns of political exchange stabilised across states' territories. This was reflected in the emergence of more permanent alignments and cleavages, such as labour and capital, left and right, secularism and religion, and/or peripheries and core. The subsequent exchange of resources within states provided states' leadership with a means to strengthen external consolidation. After the Second World War, regional integration heralded a new phase in Europe's political history that followed the formation of states, nations, democracies, and welfare regimes and challenged the process of internal construction described above. In addition to globalisation and new transportation and communication technologies, the creation of a European market and the pooling of sovereignty contributed to the external de-consolidation of the member states. Fundamentally, decreasing congruence and increasing permeability have lowered the costs associated with full or partial exit of the member states.

9.2.1   Decreasing Congruence

To be fair, boundaries had never been fully congruent in most of Europe's political systems before the Second World War. Multilayered, imperial structures such as the Habsburg, Ottoman, and Russian/Soviet ones were prime instances of incongruent systems. Also, multinational states were subject to cultural incongruence, whereas federative states had to deal with political, administrative, or legal incongruence. Furthermore, the existence of international organisations such as the International Labour Organization, the League of Nations, and the *Internationale Kriminalpolizeikommission* (Interpol's predecessor) indicated that allocation of values had not been fully concentrated in the "container" of the territorial state even prior to the Second World War (Taylor, 1994). Nevertheless, the degree of international cooperation increased considerably in Western Europe after the Second World War, which resulted in a decrease in overlapping boundaries. In terms of security, the US-led North Atlantic Treaty Organization (NATO), in particular, has provided a significant, additional layer to state-level organisation of security since the late 1940s. Other international organisations, such as the Western European Union, the United Nations, Interpol, and the Council of Europe, have also generated more incongruence in the realm of security. This also holds for the EU, in that it adds yet another layer of security governance above states with its Common Foreign and Security Policy, including a Common Defence and Security Policy, and its Area of Freedom, Security, and Justice. Even though national governments have remained dominant actors in enacting these policies, they have not stuck to the organisational template of the territorial state. Instead, incongruence has increased above and beyond the territorial state, not only within the security field, but also between the boundaries of security governance and of other policy areas (Herschinger, Jachtenfuchs, & Kraft-Kasak, 2011).

With regard to economic and monetary issues, the International Monetary Fund, the World Bank, and the World Trade Organization (and its predecessor, the General Agreement on Tariffs and Trade) constitute another international layer of governance added to the territorial state; the EU's Common Agricultural Policy, internal and external trade policies, competition authority, and common currency do as well. Incongruence has also increased through the emergence of distinct legal spheres beyond the territorial state based on the European Convention on Human Rights and EU treaties, including the European Charter of Fundamental Rights, in which the European Court of Human Rights (ECHR) and the Court of Justice of the European Union (CJEU) have played a key role, respectively. Also, distinct administrative and political spheres have emerged in the EU concentrated around the European Commission, the Council, and the European Parliament. Even if the bulk of the decision-making still takes place within EU member states, the boundaries of systems of allocating values have become less aligned.

Increasing incongruence can also be seen in the politico-cultural realm, with the rise of political identities such as Western liberalism, cosmopolitanism, and European federalism. These loyalties are not necessarily perceived and experienced as antagonistic to national identities, as they can be part of national identities. Nevertheless, the presence of political identities that extend beyond the territorial state decreases the (cultural) costs of exit and entry. Leavers are less likely to be castigated as disloyal traitors when they move within the area specific to a political identity (the West; the EU), and new entrants are likely to be welcomed in light of their shared political identity, decreasing the price of exit. Similarly, commonalities that exist as a result of European and international cooperation can facilitate exit and entry in other policy areas. The costs of (partial) exit also decrease because actors are no longer fully tied to member states in all policy areas. Whereas dissatisfied regions within states used to be limited to turning to their state centre, it is now easier to imagine becoming an autonomous entity within the larger European framework that provides wealth and security beyond national borders (cf. Colomer, 2007).

9.2.2   Increasing Permeability

It is not just the increasing incongruence of boundaries due to the allocation of values at other levels that has led to a decrease in the cost associated with an actor (partially) withdrawing from an EU member state. The external consolidation of states has also been weakened by the growing permeability of boundaries that has made (partial) exit from territorial states easier. As indicated in Chap. 6, lowering barriers to leaving and entry involves the removal of physical and other obstacles, as well as the removal of coercive and socialising mechanisms that serve to maintain boundaries. Imagining the world as one and a whole (facilitated by seeing pictures of Earth from space) and the development of new transportation and communication technologies (such as air freight, containers, and digitalisation) since the Second World War have contributed to a huge increase in interconnectedness across the world, independent of distance and time and unconfined by state boundaries (Scholte, 2000). This process of globalisation undermines the filtering and selective functioning of state boundaries, for which trans-world connections are not just simply a matter of exit from and entry to states, but a distinct global phenomenon, transcending political divisions at every level. Globalisation, therefore, not only involves the increasing permeability of state boundaries, but also precludes the impermeability of the boundaries of the EU or other regional cooperation schemes.

In addition to globalisation, European integration has weakened the external consolidation of states. To be fair, the impermeability of European states is a rather new concept. In the nineteenth century, innovative transport and communication technologies (such as steam power, railways, and the telegraph), the gold standard, and trade agreements by the major colonial powers, France and the UK, facilitated the flow of goods and capital across state borders, although state governments often took protectionist measures to shield their domestic markets from international competition. But only in the late nineteenth century, and in particular after the First World War, European states also adopted tighter boundary control, requiring identification documents from would-be exiters and entrants, in order to keep sufficient cannon fodder in and potential subversives out (Torpey, 2000). During the economic crisis of the 1930s, immigrants and aliens were increasingly considered to be a threat to labour and wealth (Ferrera, 2005). For reasons of spiritual and biological purity of the nation, as well as public health, the sustainability of compulsory, universal welfare arrangements, and public order, rulers strengthened state boundary control. Despite several attempts to restore the relatively liberal international economic order of the nineteenth century, economic protectionism in the interwar period severely limited the free flow of trade and capital. This ongoing state closure led to considerable economic decline in many countries. In response, various Western states' governments sought the means to advance trade once again after the Second World War, with cross-border flows of capital initially being tightly restricted. Monetary and trade arrangements were launched at the global level (such as IMF and GATT), as well as at the European one. For instance, governments of Western European states agreed upon the Paris treaty on the European Economic Community (1957), which laid down the groundwork for the free movement of persons, services, goods, and capital as the fundamental principle of European integration. Under this principle, a variety of barriers to leaving and entering member states were once again removed.

The free movement of persons began with the establishment of rights for employees to reside and move freely across the area of the EEC member states (Brücker & Eger, 2012). It involved the prohibition of direct or indirect discrimination of citizens of EEC member states, the mutual recognition of diplomas and other professional qualifications and a coordinative arrangement to prevent workers from losing social security rights when they move abroad. According to the latter arrangement, member states lost exclusive territorial control of the access and entry of social security beneficiaries and providers (Leibfried & Pierson, 1995, p. 50ff). Partly the result of CJEU case law and the view of EU citizenship enshrined in the Maastricht Treaty, legal opportunities to reside and move freely in the EU area have been gradually expanded to include all citizens of the EU member states and their family members (also of non-EU nationality), at least in principle. Economically inactive citizens are still required to have sufficient resources and health insurance in order to remain for longer than three months to prevent them from becoming a burden on social security systems. After five consecutive years of legal residence in a member state other than their own, EU citizens obtain the right of permanent residence in another member state, as well as voting rights in local and European elections. Legally residing, third-country nationals have also obtained more and more rights related to movement and residence over the years. In addition, permanent border control has been abolished among a growing number of member states in accordance with the Schengen Agreement. There are, however, still some exceptions to right of free movement of persons. It can be restricted for reasons of public health, public security, or public policy. In addition, member states were allowed to restrict free movement of labour following the enlargement rounds that included Central and Eastern European countries in 2004, 2007, and 2013 to a maximum of seven years. Be that as it may, individuals can more easily enter and leave their member state in the EU as a result of the principle of free movement of persons.

Furthermore, the free movement of services implies a weakening of the impermeability of state boundaries (Brücker & Eger, 2012). It offers individuals the right to provide and receive services in another EU member state. Among other things, this involves workers who are temporarily posted in another member state, but whose employment remains largely subject to the conditions specified in the employers' country of origin. Freedom of services has been developed upon in the last decades, in particular, and faces more obstacles than the freedom of goods (see below). Restrictions are allowed for the exercise of public authority *sensu stricto*, and for reasons of public health, public security, and public policy. Both based on the free movement of services and the coordinative arrangement concerning social security rights, all publicly insured persons now have, albeit under certain conditions, the right to receive reimbursement for publicly insured healthcare obtained elsewhere in the EU (Vollaard, 2017). This exemplifies an opportunity for partial exit from member states without changing residence in the EU.

It is not only natural persons that have obtained more opportunities to leave and enter member states. The rights of free movement and establishment also apply to *legal* persons. Interest and pressure groups can, therefore, enter other member states more easily to advocate public or private interests of whatever nature. Also, business has obtained more unrestrained access to member states elsewhere in the EU. This includes previously state-owned companies involved in areas such as telecommunication and energy, as a result of privatisation programmes in various member states that have been enacted in part due to EU pressure. Companies are also considered legal persons, and, as such, they are allowed to move and establish themselves freely across the EU. Furthermore, business can use the free movement of services to employ posted workers and trade other services. In addition, EU legislation has aimed to eliminate obstacles to the free movement of goods between member states. In this way, the cost of partly or entirely relocating a company to another member state becomes lower, as companies maintain full market access across the EU. Free movement of goods began with the removal of customs duties and quotas between member states in the 1960s and continued with the reduction of all kinds of other non-tariff barriers, in particular, as a result of the Single European Act (1987). By the time of the Schengen Agreement, a number of member states abolished permanent physical border control between them. The harmonisation of legislation on the production of goods, indirect taxation and taking over companies at the EU level, and the mutual recognition of member states' legislation on standards pertaining to goods have enhanced opportunities for the free movement of goods. The stability of exchange rates brought about by monetary cooperation and, subsequently, the establishment of a single, common currency has further facilitated intra-EU trade. The free movement of goods can also still be restricted for reasons of public morality, public health, or public security, if applied non-arbitrarily and transparently.

Whereas opportunities for the free movement of persons, services, and, to a lesser extent, goods have been created first and foremost between EU member states, opportunities for the free movement of capital have been created that also extend past EU boundaries. In other words, in principle, non-EU capital can also freely leave and enter EU member states. The free movement of capital involves financial transactions such as cross-border loans and credits, the purchase of or investment in real estate elsewhere in the EU, greenfield investments abroad, Foreign Direct Investment (FDI; by which the investor obtains effective control of the assets or company), and portfolio investments, such as bonds, stocks, or other financial assets (by which investors do not have control) (European Commission, n.d.). It also facilitates cross-border payments, for instance, by allowing actors to open a bank account elsewhere in the EU. Removing obstacles to the free movement of capital has been pursued in the EU in particular since the 1980s. Certain limitations can be applied for reasons of public policy and public security, among other things. The introduction of a single currency, the Euro, and ongoing harmonisation of legislation on financial products and services have also provided greater opportunities for the free movement of capital across state boundaries. These opportunities have been enhanced by the development of information and communication technologies in the global financial markets.

Exit opportunities have not only been created by the free movement of goods, services, persons, and capital. Individuals, business, political parties, NGOs, and interest groups can also seek to influence EU policies via their member state governments, which, in turn, can shape EU policies in the Council and the European Council. However, the EU decision-making process also allows individuals, political parties, business, and interest groups to circumvent member state governments and address EU institutions directly to voice their preferences. As such, they use their political capital at the EU level to promote their interests. They can do so in the context of the European parliamentary elections, the citizen initiative, the European Commission's expert committees, the Economic and Social Committee, and/or lobbying of EU institutions, among others. Furthermore, actors can seek adjudication outside states' boundaries through the CJEU and the ECHR on a range of issues.

In addition to individuals, businesses, and interest groups, sub-state authorities, such as regions, have also seen an increasing number of (partial) exit opportunities from EU member states. The EU budget and the international financial market (through the free movement of capital) offer potential opportunities for sub-state authorities to obtain funding separate from and in addition to that of state authorities (Bartolini, 2005, p. 273). Border regions can obtain (financial) support for establishing arrangements to foster cross-border cooperation, which allows them to pursue international contacts autonomous from state authorities in their area. Expanding EU legislation has had a constraining effect on sub-state authorities in addition to national legislation. Nevertheless, EU legislation, which is, in part, specifically targeted at regions, can also incentivise sub-state authorities to become involved in EU decision-making to *shape* as opposed to simply *take* EU policies (Fleurke & Willemse, 2007). The Committee of the Regions offers them a formal channel through which to express their opinions. Sub-state authorities might also be invited to take part in EU decision-making at the request of EU institutions in order to provide legitimacy and expertise for various EU initiatives. Thus, sub-state authorities are offered the opportunity of para-diplomacy, without the consent of their member states' governments (Tatham, 2010), rendering the latter no longer the exclusive gatekeeper between domestic and foreign politics.

Exit opportunities for regions have also increased as a result of other forms of external de-consolidation. The free movement of capital and business has undermined policies of state-wide, integrative egalitarianism as a result of large-scale, centralised, and redistributive investment programmes designed to redevelop backward regions (Brenner, 2003; Keating, 1998, 2013). Contrary to this "spatial Keynesianism", member state governments have tended to pursue policies (such as lower corporate taxes, a better-educated workforce, or more efficient infrastructure) that increase the state's attractiveness to business in order to keep up sufficient access to domestic and foreign capital and maintain employment. This has provided an impetus to give priority to economically competitive regions, entrepreneurial cities, and innovative sectors that will draw (foreign) investment, new technologies, and business in the de-industrialising economies of Western Europe. As such, competitive regions have often been prioritised by state governments in an effort to seek economic development outside states' boundaries in global markets. As a result, multinational companies have emerged as significant actors due to the increasing opportunities available to them to expand across state borders (cf. Bartolini, 2005, p. 271ff).

Meanwhile, development programmes for backward regions have not only been constrained by the shift in priority in relation to states' economic policies, but also by ongoing European integration in the form of the prohibition of state aid and the introduction of a common, single currency, for which devaluation aimed at making products internationally more attractive is no longer the sole purview of the state. In addition, state governments have reallocated responsibilities in an effort to make states as a whole more effective and efficient in the hopes that this would lower the financial and regulatory burdens on business. This reallocation also involved devolution, decentralisation, and federalisation. The growing responsibilities of sub-state authorities have given them more reason and greater means to pursue para-diplomacy. Nevertheless, the reluctance of the EU to automatically accept sub-state entities that have seceded from existing member states as new member states, as evidenced in discussions on the independence of Scotland and Catalonia, limits the attractiveness of full exit options from the standpoint of these entities.

In sum, a combination of European integration, globalisation, and new transport and communication technologies has led to increasing (partial) exit opportunities from EU member states. The costs of leaving and entering member states have become lower because of the removal of obstacles between member states, but also by the increasing resemblance of member states (cf. Hirschman, 1970, p. 81). The next section will discuss to what extent actors such as individuals, business, interest groups, and regions have actually used these exit and entry opportunities.

9.3   The Varied and Often Limited Use of Exit and Entry Options

A variety of actors have more opportunities available to them to (partially) leave or enter EU member states due to the growing incongruence of governance boundaries at the level of member states and the increasing permeability of their boundaries. What have the consequences been of this external de-consolidation for the internal construction of member states? The key question is, first, whether or not, and if so, which actors have made use of the exit opportunities available to them. As defined above, exit refers to the partial or full withdrawal of an actor and its resources from a political system, which is related to the allocation of values.

Exploitation of the option of exit by individuals has remained limited within the EU and its predecessors. Initially, it involved low-skilled, Italian workers who sought better labour opportunities elsewhere. Later on, Greek, Spanish, and Portuguese workers did the same. By the turn of the century, however, on average a meagre 1% of the labour force of the EU member states came from another member state. Workers of foreign origin most often originated from *outside* the EU, from countries like Turkey, Morocco, and Algeria (CPB/SCP, 2007). However, intra-EU labour migration increased considerably with the EU's big bang enlargement to include countries in Central and Eastern Europe in 2004 and 2007, which brought with it what was often temporary and circular labour mobility. In absolute numbers, most workers from the east came from Poland and Romania. Though smaller than east-west flows, south-north flows of labour also intensified during the Great Recession. Today, it is not only low-skilled labourers, (who were already mobile in the earlier stages of European integration) who work outside of their home countries; increased intra-EU labour mobility is now also seen in middle-class and highly quali-fied workers (European Commission, 2017a; Favell, 2009; Fligstein, 2008, pp. 170–171). Yet, mobile labour has remained below 5% of the total labour force of EU member states, even if the numbers of workers living in another member state (11.3 million in 2015) are combined with those of cross-border commuters (1.3 million in 2015) and posted work-ers (2 million in 2015) (European Commission, 2017a). On an annual basis, just over 0.3% of the EU population moves to another member state. In absolute numbers, Germany and the UK have received the most workers, and Germans, Italians, Polish, Portuguese, and Romanians have been the most important movers (European Commission, 2017a).

Exit and entry at the individual level not only relates to employment. According to a 2009 survey, 13% of the EU population travelled abroad for their education (European Commission, 2010). Others moved abroad for family reasons or in search of better living conditions. One-third of the 1.4 million retirees in the EU who live outside their country of citizenship seemed to have moved abroad specifically for their retirement (European Commission, 2017a). In total, 10% of the EU population has worked or lived abroad, according to the above-mentioned survey. However, less than 4% of the EU population was born in a member state other than the one they reside in (Eurostat, 2015). Individual exits have simply remained limited, with 84% of EU citizens *not* living or working abroad, be it inside or outside the EU (European Commission, 2010). In addition, just about

1% of public expenditures on healthcare is spent on healthcare obtained abroad, which includes emergency care during holidays (Vollaard, 2017). In sum, despite considerable variation, individuals' use of exit and entry opportunities has remained limited.

In contrast to individuals, the cross-border flows of goods, capital, and, to a lesser degree, services have increased much more significantly within the EU, as well as between the EU and the rest of the world (CPB/SCP, 2007). In particular, it is the involvement of the increasing number of multinational enterprises (MNEs) that have come into being since the 1970s, as well as financial businesses in these cross-border activities that is worthy of note. When it comes to small and medium-sized enterprises, 88.5% are still primarily active in (much) less export-oriented industries (European Commission, 2016). As said, exit concerns the withdrawal of actors and their resources from a system of allocation of values. Therefore, trade does not necessarily represent exit. The issue here is whether or not enterprises and their resources fully or partially withdraw from member states, either legally or illicitly. This includes international sourcing, cross-border flows of capital, as well as international tax avoidance and evasion. International sourcing refers to enterprises that move certain business activities, such as ICT services, R&D, and administration, abroad. The key motives of enterprises from variety of EU member states to engage in this activity are reducing costs (labour costs in particular) and, to a lesser extent, accessing new markets (Eurostat, 2013). Multinational enterprises are, by far, the most prominent actors in international sourcing, as evidenced by the moving business activities to another country, in particular. India and China are important destinations for international sourcing from the standpoint of a variety of member states, but the largest share of international sourcing is conducted *within* the EU. Many manufacturing enterprises in the old member states relocated activities to the Central and Eastern European member states that acceded to the EU in 2004 and 2007. In relative terms, the degree of unemployment caused by international sourcing remains relatively minor (Eurostat, 2013). Moreover, in the period between 2009 and 2011, domestic sourcing became much more common than international sourcing in many member states (Eurostat, 2013).

Just after the Second World War, cross-border flows of capital had been largely limited to trade financing and were restricted by the requirement to obtain permits for transactions involving foreign currency. By the 1950s, these restrictions had been mostly abolished. Cross-border capital flight became more common as a result. However, flows of capital within the EU, as well as those to non-EU destinations across the world, started to grow more strongly in the 1980s, peaking twice, once around the turn of the century and, for the second time, just before the Great Recession (CPB/ SCP, 2007; European Commission, 2017b). When the Great Recession began in Europe in 2008, these flows dropped quite dramatically, only to more or less recover in the decade that followed. The share of EU member states engaged in the global inflow and outflow of capital declined simultaneously. Southern and Eastern European countries faced a shift from inflows to outflows of capital, showing how much and how quickly capital can be withdrawn from member states without capital controls.

In 2015, investors in the USA, Switzerland, and Bermuda held the largest share of FDI stock from the EU, whereas investors from these countries also happened to be the most important sources of FDI flown into the EU (Eurostat, 2017). Much of the outflowing FDI (e.g., from the Netherlands, Belgium, Luxembourg, Austria, and Hungary) involves so-called "special purpose entities", which direct capital through these countries without producing any real economic activity or employment in that location. This says something about the attractiveness of tax environments in these countries—or the extent to which the countries facilitate the (legal) avoidance of taxation. Furthermore, the free movement of capital also facilitates taking advantage of differences between member states' taxation regimes. Arrangements such as "Double Irish" and "Dutch Sandwich" have garnered a certain degree of fame in this respect. The degree of international tax avoidance is difficult to estimate, but within the EU, it certainly amounts to at least 50 to 70 billion Euros in corporate income tax lost annually (Dover, Ferrett, Gravino, Jones, & Merler, 2015). The degree of illegal practices of tax evasion and money laundering taking place via cross-border capital arrangements is even more difficult to calculate, but has become a salient issue due to recent revelations about these practices (LuxLeaks; Panama Papers) and initiatives by the OECD, G20, and EU to combat them.

More so than individuals, businesses have made use of exit options from member states; in particular, in relation to capital and large enterprises. What about interest groups? Have they withdrawn their political capital from member states' centres? Indeed, many European interest groups have been established since the integration project began, with those representing business interests being the most prevalent (Beyers, Eising, & Mahoney, 2008). In more recent years, the number of pressure groups representing diffuse interests has grown as well. Interest groups have also been invited by the European Commission and the European Parliament to participate in EU politics to provide resources such as legitimacy and expertise. However, it is not simply a matter of the replacement of representation at the level of member states with EU-level lobbying. Interest groups with access to domestic policy-makers also seek to influence policy in various venues at the EU level (Beyers & Kerremans, 2012). Whereas business interest groups, often with well-informed members, are more active in influencing EU legislation at both the domestic and the EU level, *public* interest groups, with members who are less informed about the EU, concentrate their lobbying efforts on the more publicly visible, member state level (Dür & Mateo, 2014). Business interest groups with more resources expend more effort lobbying for particular EU legislation at the EU level than their poorer counterparts (Dür & Mateo, 2014). EU activities also depend on the degree of European integration. Broad interest associations are different in that they face the challenge of the fragmented, sector-specific pattern of integration across a variety of sectors, for which highly specialised expertise is also requested by EU institutions. Fragmentation not only challenges interest groups at the EU level; certain business groups also reorient their activities to focus on the regional level, given the greater regional competences in various member states and the relevance of regions as competitive entities in the global economy (Keating, 2013).

For their part, sub-state governments have set up associations, interest groups, networks, and offices to represent their interests at the EU level (Tatham, 2010). More powerful sub-state governments are more active at the EU level (Callanan & Tatham, 2014). This also seems to hold for sub-state governments with access to more resources, although the literature is not unequivocal on this issue. Stronger sub-state authorities cooperate more with member state governments because the former are more able to influence the latter's position in terms of EU decision-making through the national channel (Tatham, 2010). Sub-state governments are more inclined to adopt a strategy of bypassing when the sub-state governing party is in opposition at the member state level. Still, the overall preference seems to be to cooperate with member state governments as opposed to bypassing, let alone seeking conflict with them (Callanan & Tatham, 2014). This is not necessarily a surprise, as member state governments are still more decisive in the area of EU decision-making, in part due to their participation in the Council. In contrast, the Committee of the Regions is purely advisory and internally divided by the wide variety of sub-state authorities represented. Member state governments also play a prominent role in EU funding for sub-state territories because they decide on the EU budget, are required to match EU funding, and are responsible for reporting proper use of EU funding. Furthermore, the EU does not appear to be willing to readily accept seceded regions as new member states. The real exit opportunities have, therefore, remained somewhat limited by sub-state authorities. This also holds for border regions, which have established international contacts, just across the border, without involvement of member state governments. However, border regions remain dependent, by and large, on member state governments for cross-border cooperation and coordination. This is, in part, because many policies that constitute barriers to establishing cross-border contacts are still determined by the member states' political centres. Moreover, opportunities for sub-state authorities to obtain funding outside the member state have also been curtailed by stricter supervision of regional banks' lending schemes and restrictions on the debts of sub-state authorities within the framework of the Fiscal Compact's rule of balanced budgets.

Even though EU-induced exits of sub-state authorities have been limited in practice, the external de-consolidation of member states as a result of EU market-making and globalisation has induced globally competing regions to limit state-wide welfare arrangements for the benefit of poorer regions. Shedding the burden of state-wide solidarity allows competitive regions to lower taxation, which is intended to make them more competitive in exporting goods and services (due to lower labour costs) and more attractive to (international) business and capital in terms of investment. Italy, Belgium, and Germany have been home to this "revolt of the rich" against state-wide solidarity (Beyers & Bursens, 2013; Keating, 2013). Even without making explicit reference to European integration, these regions are seeking partial exit from their member states. In contrast, regions such as Catalonia and Scotland specifically refer to Europe in their movements to withdraw from their respective member states. Whereas the left-leaning Scottish independent movement used to be more sceptical of the market-oriented nature of European integration, it changed its strategy in the late 1980s when it began campaigning with the slogan "Independent in Europe". In this way, it signalled that the existence of the EU has limited the costs of leaving the UK and that the EU is not simply another outside, political centre imposing its will on a small nation. On a similar note, the Catalonian independence movement presented EU membership as its destiny after leaving Spain (Colomer, 2007). However, these strategies may largely be in vain, as the EU has indicated its unwillingness to automatically adopt seceded regions as new member states. Other regional independence movements, such as that of Northern Italy, are more critical of EU membership. They dislike the external de-consolidation of boundaries EU membership brings with it, which makes it easier for migrants to cross boundaries within the EU. Thus, when (partial) exits are used by regions at all, the nature of their use varies from member state to member state and from region to region. This also holds for the other actors discussed above. The next section provides an explanation of the varied and often limited use of exit and entry options.

9.4   Why Exit and Entry Options Within EU Are Used Differently and Why Their Use Is Often Limited

European integration, globalisation, and new transportation and communication technologies have de-consolidated EU member states. Over the last two to three decades in particular, it has become easier and easier to leave and enter them. Nevertheless, the use of exit and entry options is varied and often also limited among actors such as individuals, businesses, and interest groups. The mechanism of exit, voice, and loyalty offers an explanation as to why this is so. The decision to make use of full or partial exit from member states depends on a number of considerations related to the degree of dissatisfaction, the degree of loyalty, the availability and costs of all exit options, and the voice options available to effectively address dissatisfaction.

First of all, whether or not exit options are used is dependent on the degree of dissatisfaction. Without dissatisfaction, no exit is expected at all. The level of dissatisfaction about job perspectives among the unemployed and workers was much higher in Southern Europe and, later, in Central and Eastern Europe than in the economically prosperous parts of the EU. In contrast, businesses were more often dissatisfied by higher labour costs in these prosperous parts, which prompted them to move business activities to areas with lower wages. Moreover, thanks to advanced information technologies and the introduction of the Euro, it is easier for affluent individuals and businesses to find out where more satisfactory tax environments exist.

Another consideration relates to the level of loyalty of a dissatisfied actor, which can prevent it from seeking exit abroad at all. This loyalty may be linked to family ties, friends, or community, as well as the member state itself. Given the level of control of member state governments on socialising agencies, like education and media, loyalty still plays a significant role (see also Chap. 8), with the regions with autonomous cultural powers being the exception to this. Foreign investors and multinational enterprises, with their home bases elsewhere, are presumably less constrained by feelings of attachment to an EU member state than place-bound companies that are focused on their domestic market.

A subsequent consideration relates to all exit options that are available and their respective costs. Dissatisfied actors can opt to withdraw from contributing to the member state by moving into the shadow economy to avoid paying taxes (individuals; business) or to partially exit the member state by no longer complying with the law (regions). Whether these exit options are perceived as costly also depends on the actor's ethics and the member state's capacity to enforce compliance effectively, and these factors vary widely among actors and member states, respectively. As explained above, European integration and globalisation also offer exit options. However, these options can be rather expensive. The range of actions available to many actors is often limited by geographical constraints. The intra-state mobility of individuals, in particular, is often limited, whether in relations to job seeking or receiving planned healthcare (European Commission, 2010, 2017; Vollaard, 2017). In addition, small and medium-sized enterprises tend to focus on local or regional markets rather than on export. Geographical distance, therefore, prevents actors from moving to another EU member state. Moreover, exit from a member state also involves entry into another system. It involves costs associated with the acquisition of information to determine whether or not the new system will satisfy the needs of the individual in question. Other costs are related to overcoming linguistic and cultural differences; the administrative burden of de- and re-registration; becoming acquainted with new regulations, taxation, and the overall quality of governance; and, in the event of full exit, the need to find new housing and establish new contacts. MNEs also tend to be reluctant to leave when market share is the most important consideration when choosing a location (Walter & Sen, 2009, p. 212ff). In sum, (partial) exit from a member state within the EU can be quite expensive, which makes it relatively unattractive for many actors in comparison to other exit options or to using voice.

Last but not least, the use of exit options depends on the relative cost of using voice. When the use of voice can effectively deal with dissatisfaction in the context of the member state, exit (including bypassing) will be seen as being less advantageous and will be used less often.

In this respect, it is no surprise that interest groups and sub-state authorities seek cooperation with member state governments to influence EU legislation, given their central position in EU decision-making. As a result of having been closed off, member states feature well-developed structures for electoral, territorial, and corporate representation. Making use of these existing voice institutions lowers the costs of voice. Yet, the skills and resources required for effective voice differ from actor to actor. Dissatisfied, unemployed, or low-paid workers often have fewer resources and skills to rely on, although they do enjoy the resource of legitimacy derived from political participation. Individuals that perceive themselves as having a high degree of political efficacy will presumably be less inclined to leave.

Effective voice also depends on the capability of authorities in member states to effectively meet the demands of dissatisfied actors. As the governments of Central and Eastern European member states are perceived by their own citizens as delivering *less* than their Western European counterparts, voice is seen by these same citizens as being less effective in their countries. Furthermore, the effectiveness of voice also depends on the willingness of member state governments to listen to actors' dissatisfaction. Affluent citizens, regions, interest groups and enterprises control significant resources upon which state governments can be highly dependent for income and economic growth. As such, these actors enjoy a high degree of access to member state governments and a high degree of responsiveness. This is particularly true when these actors can credibly threaten to withdraw crucial resources or leave fully in light of the exit options available. In such a scenario, exit options are still not exercised, not because actors cannot do so or do not want to, but because the very threat of using them yields effective influence without the costs of exit. Moreover, MNEs can sometimes strengthen their voice by involving the government of their home country (Walter & Sen, 2009, p. 212ff). If effective, this provides yet another incentive to stay.

Given the considerations above, it is unsurprising that the use of exit is varied and largely limited. In spite of this, it is not necessarily the case that internal construction will be left intact. The growing incongruence and decreased permeability of state boundaries can also increase principled resistance, resulting in a political realignment on the issue at hand. Also, the threat of using exit can modify existing political exchange and alignments in a member state, as will be discussed in the next section.

9.5   HOW THE EXTERNAL DE-CONSOLIDATION OF MEMBER STATES UNSETTLES THEIR INTERNAL CONSTRUCTION

External de-consolidation weakens the internal construction of any polity, as stipulated in Chap. 6. This also holds for EU member states; however, it is not just the actual use of exit (and entry) options within the EU that puts internal construction under pressure. The threat of their use by dissatisfied actors is sufficient in and of itself. The (possible) exit and entry of actors destabilise the existing exchange of resources, voice structures, political alignments, and mutual trust.

In particular, multinational and financial enterprises can and do move taxable profits, investments, and/or their business activities from member states to elsewhere. Although the number of foreign-owned enterprises is still quite marginal in EU member states, on average, 14% of all employed individuals worked for such an enterprise in 2013 (Eurostat, 2014). That means that the threat of leaving can have a major impact on employment. That threat is an incentive for member states to offer better tax treatment to exit-prone businesses. Indeed, corporate tax rates have been declining in OECD member states (Genschel & Seelkopf, 2015). Similarly, governments are more willing to acquiesce with business preferences to improve the investment climate, for instance, with respect to administrative efficiency, infrastructure, and housing and education for (future) employees. Exit-prone businesses have more leverage in bilateral or trilateral negotiating arrangements with organised labour and governments on socio-economic issues. They do not necessarily abandon these arrangements. When trade unions accept lower wages in exchange for employment, businesses have an effective voice without the cost of exit (Walter & Sen, 2009, p. 212ff). Given the relative immobility of labour in contrast to capital and business, trade unions are dependent on existing voice structures to address their dissatisfaction. As such, both exit-prone businesses and labour have an incentive to continue to use corporatist arrangements or to conclude national pacts to sustain the attractiveness of a firm or location (such as a member state or region) in global or European competition. Voice structures may thus remain unmodified, while the exchanges within them do not necessarily. Alignments within the business community can also change under the pressure of states' growing external de-consolidation with antagonising firms from domestically sheltered industries, on the one hand, and exit-prone businesses on the other (Grande, 2012, p. 294).

The external de-consolidation of states also unsettles alignments, voice structures, and trust because of changing regional politics. Referred to before as the "revolt of the rich", competitive regions demand more allowances in terms of competences and to make fewer contributions to state-wide welfare arrangements to increase their global competitiveness further. These partial exits from member states put existing exchange, multi-level voice structures, and state-wide solidarity (as expression of mutual trust) under pressure (Keating, 2013). An emerging dividing line between competitive and needy regions subsequently undermines existing cross-regional alignments. It results in less stabilised mutual expectations, as there is uncertainty not just in terms of substantive issues but also constitutive ones.

The option to bypass member state governments in an effort to shape EU policies also has a fragmenting effect on interest groups and pressure groups. Some continue to focus on the domestic arena, whereas others shift their lobbying efforts to the EU institutions. The sector-based set-up of the EU produces a further break-up of broad state-wide interest groups, such as business federations. Last but not least, individuals' exits often involve a loss of brains, skills, or resources, an example being the migration of engineers, doctors, and construction workers from East to West Europe. The departure of highly educated citizens to other member states means that the citizens that are left behind lose eloquent defenders of their shared interests, as a result of migrants being less involved in civil society and voting less often from abroad (see, e.g., in Italy: Anelli & Peri, 2016). They might, thus, contribute less to their member state of origin. On the other hand, temporary migrant workers can learn a great deal while abroad, which they can then put into practice back home and their remittances also constitute an important source of income. However, the exits of affluent citizens' profits limit the tax intake of member states. Whether or not (potential) exits are profitable for the home member state, they have an impact on exchanges made, as well as use of their voice structures.

External de-consolidation not only unsettles the internal construction of member states by way of (potential) exits of MNEs, financial businesses, competitive regions, EU-focused members of interest groups, tax-avoiding citizens, or migrating workers. The internal construction of a member state is also disrupted by a variety of non-state voices that enter their participatory and sharing arrangements. Foreign-owned enterprises can voice their priorities with or without the support of the government of their home country, which can raise suspicion as to whether their loyalty is to their home country or company or the member state. Foreign interest and pressure groups can also raise their voices in support of causes that have received limited or no attention thus far. Non-state authorities, such as the European Central Bank, the European Commission, and the Court of Justice of the European Union, have influential voices on issues like inflation, exchange rate, member states' budgets, competition, state aid, and socio-economic rights, based on non-state sources like EU treaties and EU soft law. Last but not least, the arrival of non-state individuals may mean that there are new (potential) users of welfare arrangements, new participants in the job market, and new citizens with voting and legal rights based on the principle of non-discrimination codified in EU law. This raises the question of with whom member states' citizens want to share their work, money, and power. This issue of identity directly challenges the mutual loyalty that underpins the sharing and participation within member states and brings with it the potential for realignments of those in support of and those against sharing and participation with non-state voices.

To conclude thus far, external de-consolidation clearly disrupts existing voice structures, exchange, alignments, and trust in the corporate, regional, and individual levels. The claim that European integration and globalisation have brought about a new phase in the history of states (Bartolini, 2005) is, therefore, justified. These forces have exerted pressure on all aspects of state life that appears to unravel everything from national democracy (who participates), national solidarity (who shares), and national sovereignty (who has the final say), to national identity (who belongs). As will be explained in the next section, the external de-consolidation of member states has also increased dissatisfaction more and more, unsettling the political arena and sowing growing divisions on issues such as immigration, European integration, and globalisation across the entire EU (Kriesi et al., 2008, 2012; Teney, Lacewell, & de Wilde, 2014).

9.6   EU-Directed Dissatisfaction
with the External De-consolidation of Member States

As has been described in the chapters on the EU's history, shifting responsibilities vis-à-vis the EU (incongruence) and growing opportunities to cross state borders (permeability) have often been seen as the best, or at least the least unattractive option in an effort to achieve a variety of goals like economic growth and security. Similar pragmatic considerations are reflected in the reasons provided for the support of the continuation of the EU by actors such as individuals and political parties. Thus, the EU has been evaluated positively as a means of obtaining economic benefits for individuals and/or entire member states, including economic growth, additional funding or better labour perspectives (see for an overview of public opinion surveys on EU: Hobolt & De Vries, 2016). Other pragmatic reasons of an economic nature include protection against globalisation offered by the EU and increasing business opportunities brought about by economic liberalisation within member states (through privatisation), between member states (by creating the internal market), and beyond (through trade agreements). Beyond economic considerations, the EU has also been recognised as being instrumental to securing peace and stability within the EU, as well as throughout its neighbourhood. Furthermore, the EU has been endorsed as being better able to address policy issues like terrorism, immigration, organised crime, environmental pollution, climate change, and preserving fish stocks than individual states or other forms of international cooperation. The EU has also received pragmatic support as a means of circumventing domestic opposition or garnering support from non-national voices including foreign NGOs and the European Commission to achieve certain goals.

In addition to these pragmatic reasons, the values implicit in the making of a European polity that extends above and beyond traditional states have also received principled support. The exclusionary nature of an impermeable state with fully congruent boundaries has been rejected as a recipe for nationalistic hatred, if not war. Instead, cooperation and mutual understanding are pursued in a federative polity built on shared values such as peace, freedom, solidarity, democracy, and the rule of law. The growing incongruence of state boundaries in the federative entity has been subsequently endorsed out of principle. According to this view, individuals from other member states should be welcomed as fellow citizens on the basis of the existence of a *European* demos. According to a more cosmopolitan understanding, the increased permeability of state boundaries as evidenced by migrating EU citizens, as well as human beings from anywhere else, is desirable in and of itself.

This principled support of European federalism was initially seen in Christian-Democratic parties in particular. Today, it is present predominantly in cosmopolitan parties, such as social-liberal and green ones. Pragmatic support for European integration has been even more widespread among mainstream parties. It has fluctuated, however, depending on what the EU was expected to deliver at any given moment, be it economic liberalisation, protection against global market forces, or a cleaner environment. Both principled and pragmatic support have also been present at the mass level. Individuals that identify themselves as (also) European are more in favour of European integration than those who identify themselves exclusively with their member state (Hooghe & Marks, 2005). Catholics and those with a more cosmopolitan, culturally liberal attitude tend to be more supportive of the EU (Nelsen & Guth, 2015; Teney et al., 2014). In addition, EU support is stronger among those who perceive the EU as being economically beneficial to their country, which are often the highly educated people, more highly skilled workers and managers.

European integration has also generated principled resistance among parties and individuals. This resistance is referred to here as Euroscepticism. The key principles of European integration of sharing sovereignty and creating a European market encountered resistance from nationalist and communist parties from the very beginning. Euroscepticism has always been based upon two underlying substantive logics (cf. Kriesi et al., 2012). The first logic relates to politico-cultural resistance to the external de-consolidation of states. The Maastricht Treaty (1993) was an important catalyst for politico-cultural Euroscepticism, as it endowed the EU with state-like features, exemplified by the introduction of a common currency, common citizenship, common foreign and security policy, common boundary control, and a decisive say for the European Parliament. The failed European Constitutional Treaty (2005) symbolised a further decline of state sovereignty and identity in its enshrining of a Charter of Fundamental Rights, a flag, and an anthem in a document that brought to mind a constitution of a common polity, positioned above the traditional state. Meanwhile, deepening integration, laid down in a series of treaties starting with the Single European Act (1987), opened the door to non-national voices, such as the Court of Justice of the European Union, the European Commission, and the European Central Bank, in an increasing range of policy areas within the member states with increasing sway. In addition, EU enlargement meant the addition of new member states and EU citizens with whom money, work, and power had to be shared. Resistance to this was expressed by means of protest against so-called welfare tourism. However different various conceptions of the nation can be, from ethnic to civic, politico-cultural Euroscepticism seeks to restore the self-determination of sovereign nations and resist the increasing dissolution and permeability of state boundaries (cf. Halikiopoulou, Nanou, & Vasilopoulou, 2012). Thus, Rokkanian thinking shows how external de-consolidation of states as a result of European integration can lead to a "revivification of national thinking and acting" (Flora, 2000). This thinking is present predominantly among extreme-right and radical-right parties or nationalist factions within conservative parties. At the mass level, it is reflected by much lower EU support among people who identify exclusively with their nation (Hooghe & Marks, 2005).

The second substantive logic underpinning Euroscepticism is of a socio-economic nature. It concerns the economic liberalisation policies pursued by the EU that involve the creation of a common market and non-interventionist governments without expansionary budgets. In particular, radical-left parties perceive liberalisation as undercutting social and environmental protection and national solidarity among all workers and regions for the benefit of business, and MNEs and capital in particular. After the launch of the Single European Market and its expansive application by the Court of Justice of the European Union, the austerity programmes implemented in response to debt crises in Southern Europe formed an important impetus for this socio-economic resistance. However, socio-economic Euroscepticism does not reject European integration *per se*; it seeks an alternative to the economic liberalisation that has been characteristic of the EU.

Some member states simply harbour more actors that have an exclusive understanding of the national state or more opponents of economic liberalisation than others. As a result, levels of dissatisfaction stemming from politico-cultural or socio-economic Euroscepticism vary across member states. Dissatisfaction also stems from pragmatic supporters of European integration. The (economic) costs and benefits of European integration are not evenly spread among actors and member states, and, as such, dissatisfaction about the EU varies in accordance with this too. Lower-educated individuals and less-skilled workers tend to be less supportive of European integration (see among others Dolezal & Hutter, 2012). Levels of dissatisfaction also fluctuate in accordance with a pragmatic calculation of whether or not the EU is able to meet specific policy goals. For instance, green parties have become increasingly supportive of the EU since the 1990s as it is seen as being a good venue in which to forward their environmentalist agendas. In contrast, an aversion to (growing) market regulation and budgetary burden-sharing in the monetary union have led to dissatisfaction with the EU among free-market liberals. Social-democratic parties have shifted between hope and dissatisfaction in relation to opportunities to strengthen social protection within the EU. These pragmatic sources of dissatisfaction are more of an evaluation of the current functioning of the EU, rather than the principled objection to key principles of European integration that is characteristic of Euroscepticism (cf. Kopecký & Mudde, 2002; van Elsas, Hakhverdian, & van der Brug, 2016).

Actors evaluate the merits of European Union differently, based on principled or pragmatic reasons. Over the past 30 years or so, these differences have grown in breadth and depth and affect more actors more actively—to use three common indicators of politicisation (De Wilde & Zürn, 2012; Hutter & Grande, 2014). In the 1990s, the general public was already more divided on the issue of the EU than on left-right issues (Van der Eijk & Franklin, 2004). As a consequence, parties on the left and right have had to deal with divided constituencies, often prompting them to divert attention away from the issue altogether. However, the salience of the EU issue has grown in various member states, although not to the same level as other issues like the domestic welfare state (Höglinger, 2016; Kriesi et al., 2012). Moreover, there has tended to be greater support for European integration at the level of elites than among the broader public (Schmitt & Thomassen, 1999, pp. 202–203). Euroscepticism and dissatisfaction with the EU have been expressed by mainstream parties including the Gaullists, Labour, PASOK, and the Conservatives before. However, the above-mentioned factors have provided political entrepreneurs with the opportunity to distinguish themselves from mainstream ones. It explains why Eurosceptic parties often adopt an anti-establishment and populist streak by positioning themselves as "the people's voice" against the elites who squander national solidarity, national democracy, and national identity (Taggart, 1998).

Politicisation of the external de-consolidation of states not only stems from European integration. Global liberalisation of trade in goods, capital, and services has garnered protest from radical-left social movements and political parties (Kriesi et al., 2012). In terms of the politicisation of the external de-consolidation of states, a more long-standing and polarising issue than European integration and globalisation, however, has been the issue of migration. It continues to be a divisive and salient issue among the electorates across Europe. The share of Eurosceptic, often radical-right parties, in parliament has thus expanded in large part due to electoral support for their position on migration, rather than support for their position on European integration. However, dissatisfaction with external de-consolidation has also been focused specifically on the EU. EU institutions constitute a visible target at which dissatisfaction can be directed. Moreover, the EU and its predecessors have clearly played a significant role in pooling sovereignty (in other words, in increasing incongruence) and in the international and global liberalisation of markets (in other words, increasing permeability). Referenda on EU issues and elections for the European Parliament and national parliaments also provide the infrastructure to do this. Events such as the establishment of treaties, an EU referendum, enlargement, the extension of loans to debt-stricken Euro members, the imposition of austerity measures, and EU migration from Central and Eastern Europe have been specific reasons for the politicisation of the unbinding and growing permeability of state boundaries within the EU (cf. Hutter & Grande, 2014). As such, a cleavage has emerged among voters and parties between those in favour of open state boundaries for socioeconomic or politico-cultural reasons and those against them, for reasons that are principled or pragmatic (Kriesi et al., 2012; Teney et al., 2014). This dividing line cuts across the existing left-right dividing line, though the latter remains more important. This underlines the destabilising impact of states' external de-consolidation on their internal construction.

9.7   Conclusion

Dissatisfaction in the corporate, regional, and electoral arenas can exist for many reasons. This chapter explained how the external de-consolidation of member states, and subsequent destabilising of their internal construction, has generated dissatisfaction with the EU for both principled and pragmatic reasons. The divisions that exist over European integration have become deeper and more salient and involve a broader range of actors than was the case in the earlier decades of European integration. Electoral arenas have been increasingly marked by a cleavage between supporters and opponents of open state boundaries (Kriesi et al., 2012; Teney et al., 2014). After having explained the sources of this dissatisfaction, the next question is how dissatisfaction will be processed in the EU. The external de-consolidation of states prevents new cleavages from developing in the way that previous ones based on class or religion did. As of now, the issue is more complex than a conflict over a substantive issue that needs to be settled within relatively closed state boundaries. The incongruence and permeability of member state boundaries have undermined territorial, corporate, and electoral representation (Bartolini, 2005). It is now easier for competitive regions, capital, multinational enterprises, and individuals to withdraw partially or fully from their member states, instead of simply being bound to use their existing resources in political exchanges with their opponents. Adherents of political-cultural Euroscepticism would see the restoration of traditional state boundaries. This gives the new political cleavage a constitutive edge and has an impact on the way dissatisfaction is processed. How this will be done and whether nor not it will lead to European disintegration is the subject of the next chapter.

REFERENCES

Anelli, M., & Peri, G. (2016). *Does emigration delay political change? Evidence from Italy during the Great Recession.* NBER Working Paper No. 22350. Retrieved August 2, 2017, from http://www.nber.org/papers/w22350

Bartolini, S. (2005). *Restructuring Europe: Centre formation, system building and political structuring between the nation-state and the European Union.* Oxford: Oxford University Press.

Beyers, J., & Bursens, P. (2013). How Europe shapes the nature of the Belgian federation: Differentiated EU impact triggers both co-operation and decentralization. *Regional & Federal Studies, 23*(3), 271–291.

Beyers, J., Eising, R., & Mahoney, W. (2008). Researching interest group politics in Europe and elsewhere: Much we study, little we know? *West European Politics, 31*(6), 1103–1128.

Beyers, J., & Kerremans, B. (2012). Domestic embeddedness and the dynamics of multilevel venue shopping in four EU member states. *Governance, 25*(2), 263–290.

Brenner, N. (2003). Metropolitan institutional reform and the rescaling of state space in contemporary Western Europe. *European Urban and Regional Studies, 10*(4), 297–324.

Brücker, H., & Eger, Th. (2012). The law and economics of the free movement of persons in the European Union. In Th. Eger, & H.-B. Schäfer (Eds.), *Research handbook on the economics of European Union law* (pp. 146–179). Cheltenham: Edward Elgar.

Callanan, M., & Tatham, M. (2014). Territorial interest representation in the European Union: Actors, objectives, and Strategies. *Journal of European Public Policy, 21*(2), 188–210.

Colomer, J. M. (2007). *Great empires, small nations: The uncertain future of the sovereign state.* London: Routledge.

CPB/SCP. (2007). *Europese verkenningen: Marktplaats Europa.* Den Haag: Centraal Planbureau/Sociaal en Cultureel Planbureau.

Dolezal, M., & Hutter, S. (2012). Participation and party choice: Comparing the demand side of the new cleavage across arenas. In H. Kriesi, E. Grande, M. Dolezal, M. Helbling, D. Höglinger, S. Hutter, et al. (Eds.), *Political conflict in western Europe* (pp. 67–95). Cambridge: Cambridge University Press.

Dover, R., Ferrett, B., Gravino, D., Jones, E., & Merler, S. (2015). *Bringing transparency, coordination and convergence to corporate tax policies in the European Union (Part I: Assessment of the magnitude of aggressive corporate tax planning)*. Luxembourg: European Parliamentary Research Service.

Dür, A., & Mateo, G. (2014). The europeanization of interest groups: Group type, resources, and policy area. *European Union Politics, 15*(4), 572–594.

van Elsas, E., Hakhverdian, A., & van der Brug, W. (2016). United against a common foe? The nature and origins of Euroscepticism among left-wing and right-wing citizens. *West European Politics, 39*(6), 1181–1204.

European Commission. (2010). *Geographical and labour market mobility* (Special Eurobarometer 337). Luxembourg: European Commission.

European Commission. (2016). *Annual report on SMEs 2015/2016*. Brussels: European Commission.

European Commission. (2017a). *2016 annual report on intra-EU labour mobility*. Luxembourg: European Commission.

European Commission. (2017b). *Commission staff working document on the movement of capital and the freedom of payments* (SWD(2017) 94 final). Brussels: European Commission.

European Commission. (n.d.). Capital movements. Retrieved July 18, 2017, from https://ec.europa.eu/info/business-economy-euro/banking-and-finance/financial-markets/capital-movements_en

Eurostat. (2013). International sourcing of business functions'. Retrieved July 18, 2017, from http://ec.europa.eu/eurostat/statistics-explained/index.php/International_sourcing_of_business_functions#Further_Eurostat_information

Eurostat. (2014). Foreign affiliates statistics. Retrieved July 18, 2017, from http://ec.europa.eu/eurostat/statistics-explained/index.php/Foreign_affiliates_statistics_-_FATS

Eurostat. (2015). *People in the EU: Who are we and how do we live?* Luxembourg: Eurostat.

Eurostat. (2017). Foreign direct investment statistics. Retrieved July 18, 2017, from http://ec.europa.eu/eurostat/statistics-explained/index.php/Foreign_direct_investment_statistics

Favell, A. (2009). Immigration, migration, and free movement in the making of Europe. In J. Checkel & P. Katzenstein (Eds.), *European identity* (pp. 167–192). Cambridge: Cambridge University Press.

Ferrera, M. (2005). *The boundaries of welfare: European integration and the new spatial politics of social protection*. Oxford: Oxford University Press.

Fleurke, F., & Willemse, R. (2007). Effects of the European Union on subnational decision-making: Enhancement or constriction? *Journal of European Integration, 29*(1), 69–88.

Fligstein, N. (2008). *Euroclash: The EU, European identity and the future of Europe*. Oxford: Oxford University Press.

Flora, P. (2000). Externe Grenzbildung und Interne Strukturierung: Europa und seinen Nationen: Eine Rokkanische Forschungperspektive. *Berliner Journal für Soziologie, 10*, 157–166.

Genschel, Ph., & Seelkopf, L. (2015). The competition state: The modern state in the global economy. In S. Leibfried, E. Huber, M. Lange, J. D. Levy, & J. D. Stephens (Eds.), *The Oxford handbook of the transformations of the state* (pp. 237–252). Oxford: Oxford University Press.

Grande, E. (2012). Conclusion. In H. Kriesi, E. Grande, M. Dolezal, M. Helbling, D. Höglinger, S. Hutter, et al. (Eds.), *Political conflict in western Europe* (pp. 277–301). Cambridge: Cambridge University Press.

Halikiopoulou, D., Nanou, K., & Vasilopoulou, S. (2012). The paradox of nationalism: The common denominator of radical right and radical left Euroscepticism. *European Journal of Political Research, 51*, 504–539.

Herschinger, E., Jachtenfuchs, M., & Kraft-Kasak, C. (2011). Scratching the Heart of the Artichoke? How International Institutions and the European Union constrain the State Monopoly of Force. *European Political Science Review, 3*(3), 445–468.

Hirschman, A. O. (1970). *Exit, voice, and loyalty: Responses to decline in firms, organizations and states.* Cambridge: Harvard University Press.

Hobolt, S., & de Vries, C. (2016). Public support for European integration. *Annual Review of Political Science, 19*, 413–432.

Höglinger, D. (2016). The politicisation of European Integration in domestic election campaigns. *West European Politics, 39*(1), 44–63.

Hooghe, L., & Marks, G. (2005). Calculation, community, and cues: Public opinion on European integration. *European Union Politics, 6*(4), 419–443.

Hutter, S., & Grande, E. (2014). Politicizing Europe in the national electoral arena: A comparative analysis of five western European countries, 1970–2010. *Journal of Common Market Studies, 52*(2), 1002–1018.

Keating, M. (1998). *The new regionalism in western Europe: Territorial restructuring and political change.* Cheltenham: Edward Elgar.

Keating, M. (2013). *Rescaling the European state: The making of territory and the rise of the meso.* Oxford: Oxford University Press.

Kopecký, P., & Mudde, C. (2002). The two sides of Euroscepticism: Party positions on European integration in East Central Europe. *European Union Politics, 3*(2), 297–326.

Kriesi, H.-P., Grande, E., Dolezal, M., Helbling, M., Höglinger, D., Hutter, S., et al. (Eds.). (2012). *Political conflict in western Europe.* Cambridge and New York: Cambridge University Press.

Kriesi, H.-P., Grande, E., Lachat, R., Dolezal, M., Bornschier, S., & Frey, T. (2008). *West European politics in the age of globalization.* Cambridge: Cambridge University Press.

Leibfried, S., & Pierson, P. (1995). Semisovereign welfare states: Social policy in a multitiered Europe. In S. Leibfried & P. Pierson (Eds.), *European social policy: Between fragmentation and integration* (pp. 43–77). Washington, DC: Brookings.

Nelsen, B., & Guth, J. (2015). *Religion and the struggle for European Union*. Washington, DC: Georgetown University Press.

Schmitt, H., & Thomassen, J. (1999). *Political representation and legitimacy in the European Union*. Oxford: Oxford University Press.

Scholte, J. A. (2000). *Globalization: A critical introduction*. Basingstoke: Macmillan.

Taggart, P. (1998). A touchstone of dissent: Euroscepticism in contemporary western European party systems. *European Journal of Political Research, 33*, 363–388.

Tatham, M. (2010). "With or without you?" Revisiting territorial state-bypassing in EU interest representation. *Journal of European Public Policy, 17*(1), 76–99.

Taylor, P. (1994). The state as container: Territoriality in the modern world-system. *Progress in Human Geography, 18*(2), 151–162.

Teney, C., Lacewell, O. P., & de Wilde, P. (2014). Winners and losers of globalization in Europe: Attitudes and ideologies. *European Political Science Review, 6*(4), 575–595.

Torpey, J. C. (2000). *The invention of the passport: Surveillance, citizenship and the state*. Cambridge: Cambridge University Press.

Van der Eijk, C., & Franklin, M. (2004). Potential for contestation on European matters at national elections in Europe. In G. Marks & M. Steenbergen (Eds.), *European integration and political conflict* (pp. 32–50). Cambridge: Cambridge University Press.

Vollaard, H. (2017). Patient mobility, changing territoriality and scale in the EU's internal market. *Comparative European Politics, 15*(3), 435–458.

Walter, A., & Sen, G. (2009). *Analyzing the global political economy*. Princeton: Princeton University Press.

de Wilde, P., & Zürn, M. (2012). Can the politicization of European integration be reversed? *Journal of Common Market Studies, 50*(S1), 137–153.

CHAPTER 10

Disintegration or Not?

10.1 Introduction

The previous chapter provided an explanation of the origins of dissatisfaction with the EU. The key question of *this* chapter is whether or not this dissatisfaction will lead to European disintegration. This depends on the way dissatisfaction is processed within the EU. Throughout the history of the EU and its predecessors, voicing support of alternatives to European integration was often effectively avoided (see Chaps. 7 and 8). This has become increasingly difficult as a result of the increase in salience of dissatisfaction with the EU in the electoral arenas of member states. The growing relevance of dissatisfaction with the EU among electorates has the capacity to increase the cost of staying as perceived by political parties and governments. Meanwhile, the world around the EU has changed as a result of factors like ongoing globalisation and the rising power of China, to mention only a few such global developments. These developments could make national or international alternatives to the EU more attractive, or at least less unattractive, than before, making exit more likely. This chapter focuses on whether or not and how, on the basis of the mechanism of exit, voice, and loyalty, EU-directed dissatisfaction will lead to actor-based disintegration. Proposition 4a specifies the conditions under which full exit is expected: *the stronger the EU-directed dissatisfaction, the lower the EU loyalty, the fewer (perceived) options to effectively use voice at the EU level, the lower the compensation for EU-directed dissatisfaction, the lower the perceived costs of leaving*

© The Author(s) 2018   227
H. Vollaard, *European Disintegration*, Palgrave Studies in European
Union Politics, https://doi.org/10.1057/978-1-137-41465-6_10

the EU, and the better the perceived provision of values and goods by national or international alternatives to the EU, the more likely full exit will be. In situations in which dissatisfied actors do not see a viable exit option outside of the context of the EU, these actors will seek partial exits within the EU and take other cost-diminishing measures instead. As Proposition 4b states: *given high costs associated with leaving fully, and in the absence of high EU loyalty, effective voice in the EU, compensation for EU-directed dissatisfaction, and attractive full exit options, EU-directed dissatisfaction will induce partial exits within the EU and prompt the use of voice for the purpose of encouraging the exit and non-entry of expensive others.* Section 10.2 deals with the various considerations that might lead to full and partial exit on the part a variety of actors. In Sect. 10.3, these considerations are subsequently applied to a number of member states. Finally, Sect. 10.4 provides an analysis of whether or not and how the exits that are unfolding and expected might send the EU into a disintegrative spiral.

10.2   No, Partial, or Full Exits

Various actors and resources can fully or partially leave the EU's allocation of values. For instance, a few tens of thousands of often highly skilled and well-educated individuals leave the EU for the USA every year (Choi & Veugelers, 2015). Also, capital and firms have partially or fully left the EU partially in search of better business or investment opportunities elsewhere (see Chap. 9). Nevertheless, it is generally the case that more Foreign Direct Investment flows inward than outward in the EU, indicating that EU member states are still able to attract financial resources. In addition, the sourcing of business activities is still concentrated *within* member states and the EU (see Chap. 9). Northwestern European member states, in particular, perform quite well in terms of global competitiveness and the ease of doing business (World Bank, 2017; World Economic Forum, 2016). The EU also appeals to economic migrants trying to access an area of relative peace and prosperity, either legally or illicitly, over the past few decades. In sum, the EU may lose some actors and resources, but it also attracts a great deal of (potential) labour and capital. To explain the behaviour of individuals and companies that fully or partially leave the EU, the mechanism of exit, voice, and loyalty can be applied in the same way as was done in Chap. 9 with actors leaving EU member states.

In addition to individuals and companies, member states can fully or partially leave the EU. The EU is highly reliant on its member states for resources like its budget and the administrative capacity to enforce compliance.

Therefore, the focus in this chapter is on actors like political parties, voters, and governments that seek the exit of their member state. Also, here, according to the mechanism of exit, voice, and loyalty, it is the interplay between a variety of factors that explains whether or not and why some actors may be more inclined to select no, partial, or full exit of their member states than others. To start with, exit is a means of expressing dissatisfaction. If an actor is not dissatisfied, there is no reason to consider withdrawal. The higher the level of dissatisfaction, the more likely it is that an actor will consider exit. As was explained in the previous chapter, the level of EU-directed dissatisfaction differs across actors in the EU. For this reason alone, the relative inclination of member states to exit the EU's allocation of values will vary.

EU-directed dissatisfaction can still be stemmed by compensation for those who perceive themselves to be losers in the process of external de-consolidation of their member state; this, in particular, when they have become disappointed in the EU for socio-economic reasons. In this way, the root causes of dissatisfaction (such as immigration or business relocation) are not addressed, but the costs of losing are partially or fully compensated. Compensation in the form of education might also help (potential) losers avoid losses or even gain from their states' external de-consolidation. Dissatisfaction with the (increasing) costs of EU membership can thus be reduced by (re)distributing benefits. In the nineteenth century and after the Second World War, as well, Western European governments provided social protection to workers, regions, and business that experienced loss of income, job perspective, market share, and/or economic development as a result of international economic competition (Swank, 2002). Resistance to opening state boundaries can be lessened once again. Whether or not member state governments provide compensation depends on their willingness and capacity. Certain governments lack the financial means or administrative efficiency to offer effective compensation to immobile workers, needy regions, or domestically oriented business. When governments lack sufficient sources of income to engage in these compensatory arrangements, governments have to attract capital and business to invest in their member states. This, however, requires the very external de-consolidation that was the basis for the emergence of certain strands of Euroscepticism.

Furthermore, the EU shapes the array of possibilities that are available to compensate the losers. On the one hand, the restructuring of public budgets in the context of the Economic and Monetary Union (EMU) and the Open Method of Coordination on social policies may have helped member state governments to adopt financially sustainable and effective measures for compensation. On the other hand, EU rules on state aid and non-discrimination limit the ability of governments to support certain categories of losers. In addition, austerity measures required in exchange for loans and guarantees to support debt-ridden Euro members during the Great Recession resulted in major cuts to welfare arrangements. Compensation at the EU level is only available to a limited extent through the structural funds for economically less-developed member states, regions, and groups. As explained in Chap. 8, the limited locking-in capacity of the EU has constrained opportunities for EU-wide solidarity. Moreover, enhancing existing social-sharing arrangements would elicit opposition from those who resist European integration for politico-cultural reasons rather than socio-economic ones. These individuals are reluctant to share their money with non-nationals. Furthermore, feelings of politico-cultural alienation fuelled by European integration and migration are more difficult to assuage than those feelings based on dissatisfaction with the redistributive consequences of European integration (cf. van Elsas, Hakhverdian, & van der Brug, 2016). As such, an inclination towards exit not only varies with the level of dissatisfaction, but also with the possibility of receiving and availability of compensation. Variation in exit tendencies is strengthened by the variation in the level of loyalty vis-à-vis the EU, as attachment to the EU varies across EU actors. The more attached actors are to the EU, the less inclined they will be to partially or fully leave. However, EU loyalty is much lower than loyalty to member states, and it is also of a voluntary and civic, rather than cultural and thick, nature (Conti, Cotta, & Tavares de Almeida, 2010). Its ability to constrain is therefore limited.

A subsequent consideration concerns the ability to voice EU-directed dissatisfaction effectively. Member states, themselves, feature well-developed voice infrastructure, from electoral systems, party systems, and parliaments to corporatism and federalism. Also, the media landscape is much more developed at the national level than the EU level, which means that social movements, protests, and demonstrations are able to receive attention *outside* the more formal voice infrastructure. Non-electoral voice, including protests, still requires a certain measure of organisational skill and endurance, whereas the costs of using voice in the context of elections are fairly low within member states. It is therefore no surprise that losers' frustration with European integration and other forms of external de-consolidation such as globalisation has been expressed first and foremost in member states' electoral arenas in the form of voting for parties that call for the reconsolidation of state boundaries (cf. Grande, 2012, p. 287).

In addition, member states' parliaments and governments can decide to withdraw the member state from the EU, with or without a referendum on the issue. This might constitute a more effective exit from the EU than simply no longer taking part in the EU's political process or complying less with EU law, particularly for those who resist the EU for principled reasons. Voters hold the important resource of legitimising parties, parliaments, and governments. Existing or new political parties can seek to capitalise on the existing EU-directed dissatisfaction. The question remains, however, whether or not they are able to obtain sufficient voter support to enter parliament and government. Voters that express low or no support for European integration are often less-educated and less-skilled workers (see among others Dolezal & Hutter, 2012). These groups have a rather low self-perception of political efficacy. It may, therefore, be more difficult to motivate them to vote, as they might prefer to opt for less costly, more effective partial withdrawals such as political non-participation, limited compliance, and/or moving into the shadow economy. This diminishes the power of parties that propose to restore state boundaries. However, given this lack of faith in effective voice in member states, populist calls to defend the "pure" people against morally corrupt elites who are spoiling national democracy, solidarity, identity, and sovereignty can also be seen as a rallying cry for EU-directed dissatisfaction.

In addition to the electoral and party systems, the efficacy of the use of voice by parties dissatisfied with the EU also depends on the power of their opponents—the parties that advocate for European integration. These parties can also use the well-developed voice infrastructure of member states to counter attempts to rewind the external de-consolidation of member states either fully or partially. Opponents of state closure can seek support from actors in favour of open boundaries, in the form of funding or publicity, from competitive regions and export-oriented business, or electoral legitimacy from pro-EU voters. The self-perceived political efficacy of the often more highly educated and highly skilled, pro-EU voter is above average, as a result of which they are more likely to seek out the ballot box in parliamentary or presidential elections. The influence of pro-EU actors can be even stronger, as some of them can threaten to withdraw resources such as taxable income and profits from the EU if other actors, parliament, or the government are less willing to support European integration. The varying strength of pro-EU forces in member states contributes further to the differentiated pattern of effective calls for partial or full exit from the EU.

Even when Eurosceptic parties manage to enter government, or win a larger share of seats in the European Parliament, the question remains as to whether they can exert effective voice (see also Chap. 8). Part of EU decision-making is in the hands of non-elected, technocratic institutions like the European Central Bank and the Court of Justice of the European Union. EU decision-making on other issues involves many actors in the European Commission, Council, the European Parliament, and member states. Many decisions related to the politico-cultural and socio-economic set-up of the EU have been laid down in the treaties and the multi-annual financial framework. Changing the EU's course towards a Eurosceptic direction is, therefore, a challenge. With limited opportunities to effectively voice Eurosceptic opposition *within* the EU, Eurosceptic parties are pushed to express opposition *against* the EU (Mair, 2007). This has the capacity to strengthen the tendency towards partial or full exit.

In sum, the more widespread and stronger the EU-directed dissatisfaction, the less compensation available or possible, the lower the EU loyalty, and the less effective the use of voice for EU-related dissatisfaction, the more actors will be inclined to seek exit from the EU (see Fig. 10.1). The question that follows from this is whether or not this exit will be full or partial. First, this depends on the costs associated with the full exit of a member state, including the degree of integration. When a member state is fully part of the Economic and Monetary Union and the Area of Freedom, Security, and Justice (including the Schengen arrangements), exit costs will be higher. These costs include the incidental expenses associated with leaving, but also structural costs associated with the reintroduction of legal and administrative arrangements for monetary and border policies. Cost of a full exit also depends on the degree of geopolitical and economic dependence on other EU member states. The stronger the dependence, the higher is the cost of a full exit in terms of reputation, reintroduction of trade barriers, and lost opportunities to coordinate security measures (although growing dependence can also yield satisfaction as a result of its de-consolidating effect). The cost of full exit also depends on the perception of the costs and benefits of EU membership with respect to the level of economic growth attributed to the EU, EU budget contributions, migration, policy flexibility, security, and, in case of parties, electoral vulnerability, for example. When the costs of a full exit are too high, actors will opt for partial exits instead.

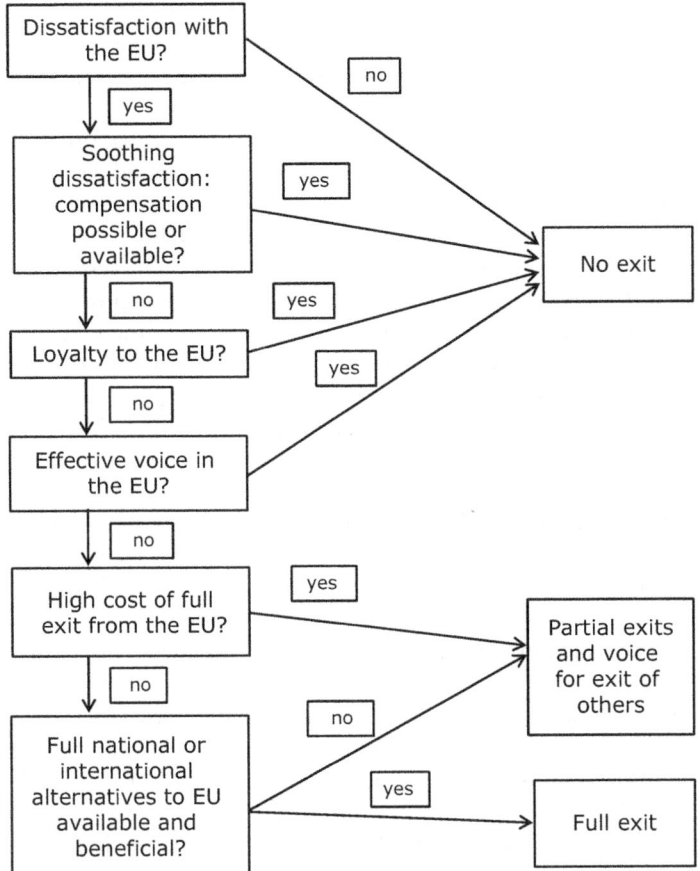

Fig. 10.1 No exit, partial exit or full exit

The next question concerns the availability and the relative costs and benefits of adopting national and international alternatives to the EU. Actors in member states that have a sense of national superiority, greater trust in their state's institutions, and (self-perceived) international weight are expected to be more inclined to believe that their member state can do without EU membership. In addition, a wide variety of international organisations including the United Nations, World Trade Organization, and the International Monetary Fund continue to offer a basis for international cooperation after leaving the EU. International organisations, such as the EFTA or the Russian-led Eurasian

Union, can also provide alternatives to the EU, either independently or in combination with national and other international alternatives. When actors believe that their member state can bear the costs of leaving, and the alternatives to the EU are more attractive, a full exit is expected.

However, the lack of availability of (a combination of) national and international alternatives or the uncertainties that may surround them can easily discourage actors from promoting full exit of their member state. In particular, actors in smaller member states might be more likely to worry that their government might lose its say in international politics if it were to exit from the EU, as they usually lack the former colonial ties or the positions in international bodies such as the UN Security Council to strengthen their negotiating position in other ways. A lack of international alternatives that are more beneficial (or less costly) than the EU would discourage actors from seeking full exit. Nevertheless, their Eurosceptic dissatisfaction is still there. In those cases, it will be expressed in the form of partial exits. Where Euroscepticism is found alongside an actor's positive assessment of a member state's capacity, expressed in terms of trust in political institutions and the perceived superiority of the national politico-economic system, partial exits such as opting-out, declining budgetary solidarity in the Eurozone, and renationalisation of competences will follow. To reduce the costs of EU membership, these partial exits will be accompanied by growing resistance to enlargement with costly or culturally distant countries, and calls for the full or partial exit and non-entry of costly member states. Where Eurosceptic dissatisfaction takes hold in member states where actors have a negative assessment of the member state's capacity, partial exits such as less compliance with both national and EU law will be the strategy employed to limit the costs of EU membership. Costs can also be reduced by increasing the benefits of EU membership. Given limited effective voice, in particular to address politico-cultural dissatisfaction about the EU, this will be pursued less often. Figure 10.1 summarises the considerations that lead to no, partial, or full exit.

10.3   Which Member States Will Opt for No, Partial, or Full Exit from the EU?

The previous section explained in general terms why member states might choose no, partial, or full exit from the EU. As pointed out, there is variation across the member states with respect to the level of EU-directed dissatisfaction, the degree of loyalty to the EU, the presence of effective voice options to express this dissatisfaction in the EU, opportunities to compensate dissatisfaction, costs associated with exiting the EU, and the availability of national or international alternatives that are perceived as being able to deliver more than the EU. This section specifies which member states, in particular, are more and less inclined to seek no, partial, or full withdrawal.

Empirical analyses that trace the way in which the mechanism of exit, voice, and loyalty functions among individuals, political parties, or governments are not yet available. Nevertheless, there is sufficient existing data to provide indirect evidence as to why actors decide to seek no, partial, or full exit of their member states. The focus is first on individuals. If a referendum on EU membership is held, it is up to the individual to decide to be in favour of membership or against it. In addition, individuals can express their EU preferences in national and European elections. The semi-annual Eurobarometer surveys of public opinion in EU member states gives us an indication of whether or not and how exit, voice, and loyalty are connected from the standpoint of individual citizens on the basis of their indication of the salience of various relevant factors. As a first step, this is carried out at the aggregate level on the basis of the Autumn 2016 edition of the Eurobarometer (see Table 10.1).

There is no question in the survey that inquires specifically into the nature of EU-directed dissatisfaction, whether it relates to being a disappointed pragmatic supporter or a politico-cultural or socio-economic Eurosceptic. Here, EU-directed dissatisfaction is measured more generally by the share of respondents that agree with the statement that EU membership is a bad thing. With dissatisfaction below 10%, exit is an unlikely option to be selected from the standpoint of the general public of Germany, Poland, Ireland, Luxemburg, the Netherlands, Lithuania, Malta, Slovakia, and Estonia. Conversely, relatively high dissatisfaction can be discerned in the UK, Austria, Romania, Cyprus, Italy, France, Greece, and the Czech Republic. EU loyalty is relatively low in these countries and, as such, it functions less as a constraint on the propensity to seek exit. Loyalty is indicated here by the share of respondents per member state that feels "fairly" or "very" attached to the EU. Relatively high loyalty towards the EU (greater than 55%) constrains exit-seeking behaviour in Germany, Poland, Ireland, Luxemburg, Latvia, Spain, and Hungary.

The next step deals with effective voice in the EU. As the key issue here is the withdrawal of an entire member state, the question pertaining to the degree to which the interests of respondents' country are taken into account in the context of the EU is selected as an indicator of this. On

Table 10.1 To exit or not

Factor	Dissatisfaction	Loyalty	Effective voice in the EU	Remain	Exit
Member state			EB question		
	Is the EU a bad thing? (% agree)	Please tell me how attached you feel to the EU (% very and fairly attached)	The interests of our country are well taken into account in the EU (% agree)	Our country could better face the future outside the EU (% disagree)	Our country could better face the future outside the EU (% agree)
EU-28	16	51	43	58	32
BE	11	53	52	65	31
BG	13	50	33	51	29
CZ	19	31	26	50	41
DK	12	46	51	75	18
DE	9	58	64	74	17
EE	7	48	43	68	21
IE	9	57	60	67	25
EL	29	32	16	57	38
ES	15	58	44	65	24
FR	17	53	36	58	31
HR	16	42	44	51	41
IT	25	41	28	42	45
CY	20	26	22	44	49
LV	10	68	33	57	31
LT	8	55	58	68	25
LU	4	76	75	76	20
HU	11	58	37	61	28
MT	8	55	55	73	14
NL	8	38	45	79	17
AT	24	41	39	47	44
PL	9	64	50	53	37
PT	10	51	42	61	30
RO	17	54	42	49	42
SI	13	49	28	43	50
SK	9	48	44	62	29
FI	10	44	44	67	25
SE	13	47	53	67	29
UK	26	46	39	42	48

Source: Eurobarometer 86 and 86.1 (Autumn 2016). European Commission (2016), European Parliament (2016)

average, 43% of the respondents agreed that the interests of their country were well taken into account (49% disagreed). Given that 50% or more agreed that their member state has an effective voice in the EU in Germany, Poland, Ireland, Luxemburg, Latvia, Belgium, Denmark, Malta, and Sweden, exit is less likely to be seen there. In contrast, exit-seeking behaviour in the dissatisfied member states of the UK, Austria, Romania, Cyprus, Italy, France, Greece, and the Czech Republic is less constrained by the perception that these countries have an effective voice within the EU. In combination with the relatively low level of EU loyalty revealed in these countries, it is no surprise that a relatively large share of the respondents in these countries agree with the statement that their country would be better off facing the future outside of the context of the EU—an indicator of a preference for full exit. Only in France is the preference for exit somewhat lower than expected, whereas in Slovenia and Croatia it is somewhat higher than the level of EU loyalty and perceived efficacy of voice in these member states would suggest. Interestingly, in no country is the majority of those surveyed in favour of full exit, though a large share is in favour in Cyprus, Slovenia, Italy, and the UK. More respondents prefer the option of remaining compared to leaving the EU in the Czech Republic, Greece, Croatia, Austria, and Romania. The lack of attractive national or international alternatives to EU membership might explain why, in these relatively dissatisfied member states (and also in France), full exit does not receive wholehearted support. Given the low dissatisfaction, relatively high EU loyalty, or perceived efficacy of voice in the EU, the support for full exit in Germany, Luxemburg, Malta, the Netherlands, and Spain is low. In Latvia and Ireland, it is somewhat higher and in Poland the level of support is higher than the EU average of 32%. Denmark and Estonia show rather low support for full exit despite low levels of loyalty. Here too, the lack of a viable alternative to the EU might be the explanation.

With some exceptions, public opinion in the member states fits the pattern as expected according to the data available on dissatisfaction, loyalty, voice, and exit. Nevertheless, this is just a first step in validating the mechanism of exit, voice, and loyalty as an explanation of actor-based disintegration. Other relevant factors such as compensation for EU-directed dissatisfaction, the perceived costs of exit, perceived geopolitical and economic dependence, the perceived capacity and international standing of the member state, and the availability of attractive international alternatives have not been explicitly taken into account. The positioning of cutoff points indicating higher or lower levels of dissatisfaction, loyalty, and effective voice is up for debate in seeking to find out when exactly these factors might diminish or encourage preferences for the full exit of a member state. In addition, (the interplay between) these factors are not examined at the individual level. Still, the Eurobarometer data provide a first impression of which member states might leave or remain if it were up to their citizens.

The decision of whether a member state remains in or leaves (fully or partially) the EU is not the exclusive purview of citizens. In quite a few member states, binding referendums can only be organised at the behest of parliament or government, and, in certain instances, only after constitutional change. Political parties in and also outside parliament, governments, as well as businesses, regions, and pressure and interest groups can play an active role in referendum campaigns. In the member states in which referendums are binding, the parliament and governments would also be actively involved in the formal process of withdrawal from the EU, as well as in calls for the exit of other member states or partial exits such as steps towards lower contributions to the EU, renationalisation of competences, or decreased compliance. Governments and parties in parliament should, therefore, be examined too in trying to determine whether a member state might remain or leave partially or fully.

10.3.1   *The UK: Full Exit*

The withdrawal of the UK from the EU, otherwise known as Brexit, has received the most public and scholarly attention to date. The Brexit referendum held in June 2016 revealed divisions within and between parties and the various nations of the UK, as well as within the electorate about the question of whether the UK should stay or leave. Although the mechanism of exit, voice, and loyalty played in differently for each and every group, it also indicates why the decision to pursue full exit was not unlikely in the UK. Euroscepticism has always been present in the British mainstream parties. A plea to leave the European Economic Community in its 1983 manifesto reflected the Labour Party's resistance to the "capitalist club". Politico-cultural reservations about European integration were also present in the Labour Party, but these became increasingly pronounced in the Conservative Party as of the late 1980s. Beyond the traditional governing parties, the British National Party and, in particular, the UK Independence Party have received considerable support in European parliamentary elections for their politico-cultural

Euroscepticism. Politico-cultural Euroscepticism emphasises the defence of parliamentary sovereignty and British/English identity against the power of non-national voices like the unelected European Commission and the Court of Justice of the European Union. Resistance to supranational authority was a reason not to join the European integration process in the 1950s. In making the EU more political in nature, the Maastricht Treaty was a significant factor in generating this resistance in the Conservative party (Startin, 2015). At the mass level, the enlargement to include Central and Eastern European countries fostered the emergence of a mixture of social-economic and politico-cultural Euroscepticism, alongside increased concerns about MNEs relocating business activities to lower-wage areas, as well as intensified job competition and (ab)use of welfare arrangements by an increasing number of labour migrants (Startin, 2015). The salience of the migration issue was buoyed by migration flows from Syria and elsewhere trying to enter the EU and the UK at Calais. Immigration featured prominently as a drawback of EU membership (Lansons, 2013). The idea that the UK could regain control of immigration by leaving the EU had a significant impact on voting to end EU membership (Goodwin & Milazzo, 2017).

In addition to Eurosceptic dissatisfaction, there was also growing dissatisfaction among pragmatic supporters of EU membership. The Conservative Party had pursued EEC membership foremost for pragmatic economic reasons. A majority of voters shared this economic pragmatism in the previous Brexit referendum in 1975. The continuous discussions about the British contribution to the EEC/EU budget weakened the pragmatic case, however (and strengthened the politico-cultural unwillingness to pay to "foreigners"). And whereas pragmatic EU support increased within Labour with the prospects of social protection against market forces in the 1990s, Conservatives increasingly expressed concerns about the costs of EU bureaucracy and regulation, which tied in with the politico-cultural resistance to non-national rules over which a non-national court has the final say. The effectiveness and direction of the Common Security and Defence Policy was also met with growing disappointment in the UK. The EU's handling of the debt crises further undermined the case for the EU as an effective instrument for encouraging economic growth. At the mass level, there have always been more people that view the EU as a bad thing than those that see it as a good thing, except for in the mid-1990s. In sum, there has thus always been a considerable level of dissatisfaction in the UK.

In contrast to welfare states elsewhere in the EU that are organised differently, the pluralist, majoritarian, and liberal UK saw considerable welfare state retrenchment with cuts to pensions, unemployment and disability insurance, and sick pay (Swank, 2002, pp. 229–238). Compensation for the impact of international economic competition has, therefore, been more limited in the UK, which has done less to assuage concerns about external deconsolidation, in particular among those that depend on the welfare state.

Also, EU loyalty functions as only a rather limited constraint on British exit-seeking behaviour. The UK and England, in particular, are perceived by the British people as being quite distinct from continental Europe, for reasons of geography (the UK being separated by sea), history (the UK having not been on the losing side in the two world wars), politics (having had a parliamentary system for centuries), and religion (its protestant background) (Daddow, 2011). From a comparative perspective, attachment to the EU both at the elite and mass levels was very low in 2007 (Best, 2012). British people also feel more closely connected to non-EU countries such as the USA than to their counterparts in the EU (Lansons, 2013). For its part, the British tabloid press, and the *Daily Express* in particular, has never expressed warm feelings for the EU (Startin, 2015).

Effective voice in the EU may not have been much of a constraint on exit-seeking behaviour either. The UK government could and did play an important role in issues such as economic liberalisation and foreign and security policy, but it was more constrained by its opt-outs on justice and home affairs, as well as the monetary union. Additionally, the governing Conservative Party lost influence in 2014 by leaving the group with the European People's Party in the European Parliament. Still, at the mass level, perception of the efficacy of the country's voice in the EU was only slightly lower than average (see Table 10.1).

With the UK not fully taking part in the Schengen area and the monetary union, exit costs have been much lower than they might have been for other, more entwined countries. In contrast to other EU member states, the British economy is also less integrated with EU economies, which also diminishes potential costs in relative terms. Between 2003 and 2015, the ratio of intra-EU export of goods to extra-EU export of goods dropped by 14.9% (EU average: minus 5.9%). Nevertheless, the EU is on the receiving end of 44% of British exports of goods, and the FDI flows between the UK and the rest of the EU are similar in terms of scale. Given this, remain voters saw the economic cost of Brexit, including a decline in trade and employment, as an important reason to reject withdrawal

(Hobolt, 2016, p. 12). However, much of the British public thought that Brexit would only involve limited costs, if any, in terms of the UK's international standing, economy, and daily life. They saw the Brexit as yielding net benefits, as it would end non-national rule, migration, and contributions to the EU (Lansons, 2013).

In addition, the presence of a combination of national and international alternatives to the EU made full exit a viable option in the eyes of leave campaigners and voters. They referred to the UK's nuclear power and seat in the UN Security Council, the ties with former colonies in the Commonwealth, the special relationship with the USA, and its membership in international organisations such as NATO and the WTO. A sense of high national self-esteem has also been present in the UK (European Commission, 2001). In sum, the choice to pursue a full exit from the EU is, therefore, unsurprising in light of the mechanism of exit, voice, and loyalty (see also Vollaard, 2014).

10.3.2   Greece: No Full Exit

Next to the UK, the possibility of the full or partial withdrawal of Greece, a Grexit, has received the most attention. On one hand, this was the result of non-Greek actors arguing that Greece should leave the Eurozone or the EU. On the other hand, a growing dissatisfaction with the EU in Greece led to speculation as to whether the Greek themselves would decide to pursue Grexit. Dissatisfaction with European integration was not a new phenomenon in Greece. When right-wing and centrist parties sought to incorporate Greece into the Western bloc more strongly through an Association Agreement with the EEC in the early 1960s, left-wing parties rejected it as an imperialist and capitalist ploy (Verney, 2011). The steps towards EEC membership from the mainstream, right-wing ND party in the 1970s encountered resistance again from the socialist PASOK and the communist KKE. They rejected EEC membership as capitalist exploitation of the Greek periphery. The KKE party has maintained its socio-economic Euroscepticism, rejecting all EU treaties to date. When PASOK assumed office in 1981, it abandoned its socio-economic Euroscepticism, however, joining the ND in a pragmatic acceptance of the EU as economically beneficial. Since the 1990s, partisan Euroscepticism has re-emerged, this time of a politico-cultural nature, as well, partly due to the influx of migrants from Africa and Asia. After Greece became embroiled in the debt crisis, Eurosceptic parties with a socio-economic bent (Syriza) and those with a politico-cultural one (LAOS, Independent Greeks, Golden Dawn) blossomed considerably. This reflected the growing dissatisfaction with the EU among the greater public that began in 2009, prior to which the public had appreciated the EU's economic benefits since the late 1980s (Clement, Nanou, & Verney, 2014). The expansion of the Greek welfare state that began in the 1980s came to an abrupt standstill as a result of the austerity measures adopted to reform the Greek budget, resulting in cuts to healthcare and pensions. Compensation to assuage the growing dissatisfaction from the state or the EU became less of an option. Meanwhile, the EU's handling of the migration crisis only served to increase politico-cultural dissatisfaction with the EU.

EC/EU membership was a symbol of incorporation with the Western bloc and also the stabilisation of domestic democracy. This could have provided a basis for strong EU loyalty. From a comparative perspective, however, attachment to the EU both at the elite and mass levels was relatively low in 2007 (Best, 2012; Conti et al., 2010). During the crisis, absence of attachment to the EU reached 72% at the mass level, more or less the same as it was in the UK (Verney, 2015). EU Loyalty could thus only exit-seeking behaviour to a limited extent in Greece.

Also from a comparative perspective, in 2007, 69.4% of Greek elites disagreed (quite strongly) with the statement that the interests of their country were not taken into account in the EU decision-making (Conti et al., 2010). At the time, the Greek public was less convinced, with 38% agreeing that their country's interests were not taken into account, somewhat below the EU average of 45%. After the debt crisis unfolded, as of 2009, this declined even further to very low levels, far below British evaluation of effective voice of their country (Verney, 2015). This is not surprising, as the austerity programmes formulated by EU institutions and the International Monetary Fund had to be followed regardless of the composition of government or rejection by referendum. Nevertheless, the Eurosceptic government and a majority of the public refrained from seeking full exit from the EU (Pew Research Center, 2017; Verney, 2015). Even if Greece were to leave the EU or EMU, it would still face a huge debt burden in Euros. The Greek government would have also had to reintroduce a national currency under severe time pressure with a less than effective administrative apparatus in place (Eichengreen, 2010). The uncertainties associated with and potential costs of leaving also made the Greek public more inclined to keep the Euro (Dinas, Jurado, Konstantinidis, & Walter, 2016). Although its export of goods to non-EU countries (such as Turkey and Israel) has grown faster than to EU countries in the time period between 2003 and 2015, it still exports over half of its goods to the EU. Leaving the internal market and customs union would thus unsettle key trade relations. And despite dislike of the EU, the EU still has the capacity to steer the distrusted national elites. International alternatives, such as closer contact with the Russian government, are not sufficiently attractive in terms of Greece being able to maintain its geopolitical position. A full exit, therefore, remained an unattractive option, however dissatisfied the Greeks were with the EU. Instead, they have opted for partial exits. Mobile citizens, businesses, and capital have moved abroad. Those that remain have sought to renationalise power from the EU to Greece, in particular, on issues of migration and trade agreements (Pew Research Center, 2017). Greece has always struggled with compliance due to problems with its administrative capacity. As a reflection of an inclination towards partial exit, however, Greek authorities only complied with the austerity measures, at least in terms of adopting the requested legislation, under significant external pressure. Thus, the Greek example shows that dissatisfaction can lead to disintegration, just in the form of a partial exit rather than a full one.

10.3.3   *The Netherlands: Partial Exits*

After the Brexit referendum, it was often suggested that the Netherlands would be the next member state to leave. The Netherlands used to be known as a very pro-European member state. Indeed, as early as the late 1940s, the two largest parties in parliament, the Catholics and social-democrats, embraced European federalism, while the main protestant and conservative-liberal parties initially showed more reservation in their endorsement. However, the Dutch government only reluctantly accepted *supranational* European integration, seeing it as economically necessary and politically inevitable for a small trading nation on the European continent. It regarded European supranational decision-making pragmatically, as an instrument to bind larger continental states to trade agreements, though it preferred the intergovernmental and transatlantic NATO for security cooperation over the continental EEC. In the 1960s, pro-federalist rhetoric became more widespread when the Netherlands increasingly began to enjoy the economic benefits of European integration and explicit expressions of loyalty to the Dutch nation-state had become not just outdated, but also increasingly reprehensible. Only extreme-left and orthodox-protestant parties resisted European integration on the basis of social-economic or politico-cultural principles, respectively (Vollaard & Voerman, 2015).

In the 1970s and early 1980s, the social-democrats also resisted the EEC due to its being capitalist and undemocratic, at least on paper, but they remained committed to the ideal of European federalism. In the early 1990s, the conservative-liberal VVD party discarded the federalist ideal, as it was seen as widening the gap between political elites and the still predominantly nationally oriented citizens. It adopted a pragmatic position, accepting European integration when necessary and inevitable to tackle cross-border problems effectively and efficiently. After its ambitious unifying proposal in the run-up to the Maastricht Treaty failed (according to which larger states would also be more constrained, in particular in the realm of foreign policy), the government also adopted a more explicitly pragmatic discourse. This discourse became increasingly widespread among mainstream parties after the rise of both left-wing and right-wing Eurosceptic, populist parties, and the no vote in the referendum on the European Constitution (2005). Traditionally, European integration received widespread support from Dutch citizens, primarily due to the economic benefits it yielded (Van Holsteyn & Den Ridder, 2015). However, the Dutch public began to grow more sceptical of these benefits in response to the Dutch contribution to the EU budget, the entry of poorer member states and labour migrants, the EU institutions it believed to be cost-inefficient and dysfunctional, increasing prices after the introduction of the Euro, violations of monetary agreements by France and Germany, and the loans and guarantees to debt-stricken Euro members. In addition, the big bang enlargement, negotiations with Turkey, and the proposal for a European Constitutional Treaty elicited politico-cultural concerns about the decline of Dutch power and identity disappearing into a "European super state". While the left-wing, populist Socialist Party also expressed social-economic Euroscepticism around the liberalising course of European integration, EU-directed dissatisfaction has been largely politico-cultural and pragmatic in nature. In response to the debt crises, the anti-Islam Freedom Party proposed the reintroduction of the Guilder and leaving the EU altogether, a so-called Nexit, with the aim of restoring Dutch sovereignty and wealth. However, it is very unlikely that Dutch political parties, parliament, government, or the public would accept a full Dutch exit, in spite of the EU-directed dissatisfaction that exists.

The Dutch welfare state was developed, in part, to compensate workers for the losses they sustained in making the Netherlands internationally competitive (Jones, 2008; Katzenstein, 1985). Welfare arrangements in the Netherlands remain extensive, making them able to assuage social-economic dissatisfaction, in particular. However, the use of these extensive arrangements by labour migrants from within the EU also has the potential to breed EU dissatisfaction. Furthermore, many people are pessimistic about the availability of social protections for future generations. In addition, welfare arrangements cannot fully address politico-cultural dissatisfaction with ongoing European integration and enlargement. Feelings of attachment to the EU inhibit a possible Nexit to a limited extent. At the mass level, the emotional sense of belonging to the EU has always been relatively low in the Netherlands (European Commission, 2001). Whereas most political parties used to express their adherence to the federalist ideal in the 1980s, this is now in large part limited to the cosmopolitan parties, the social-liberal D66 party and the green *GroenLinks*. Supporters of the Eurosceptic parties, in particular, who tend to be less-skilled workers and less educated than average, are less convinced of the effectiveness of the Dutch voice in an enlarged EU.

Nevertheless, most people and parties accept EU membership for the Netherlands because they perceive European cooperation as being necessary for a small, trading nation on the continent, even when the perceived benefits are declining and costs are growing. Much more so than is the case with the UK or Greece, Dutch exports of goods are directed to other EU members like Germany (while most services and FDI are directed *outside* the EU). According to the government, and a majority of parties, the Netherlands also has more international sway as member of the EU than as an outsider like Switzerland or Norway. It is, therefore, not possible for full exit to garner majority support, despite a strong sense of national self-esteem. Instead, dissatisfaction has resulted into actors seeking partial exit. Proposals to renationalise competences and limit the EU budget have, therefore, been launched by the government, and by economically and culturally right-wing parties in particular. In addition, these same actors have suggested (in the international media) that a Grexit from the Eurozone may be desirable. They also worked to block the full entry of Romania and Bulgaria to the Schengen area. Also, a closer association between the EU and poor and corrupt Ukraine met considerable resistance. This voice in favour of exit and non-entry is directed towards member states that are perceived as being culturally distant (Thomassen & Bäck, 2009) or being costly additions to the group. These partial exits clearly indicate dissatisfaction, but, however grumpily, the Dutch continue to accept EU membership by a substantial majority.

10.3.4   Partial Exits Elsewhere

EU-related dissatisfaction is rife throughout the EU. In Italy, France, Cyprus, and Slovenia, economic liberalisation and austerity measures pursued by the EU have met considerable criticism from populist and radical-left parties, due to not only their economic implications but also the political limitations imposed against national politicians in terms of preventing the adoption of a different economic policy. Disapproval of the EU's handling of economic issues is widespread at the mass level in Italy and France (Pew Research Center, 2017). Cuts to welfare arrangements will not stem this dissatisfaction. Also, citizens in Italy and France strongly disapprove of the way the EU has dealt with the refugee crisis. This ties in with politico-cultural dissatisfaction with migrants arriving from Africa and Asia. In response, parties like Lega Nord, the Five Star Movement, Front National, and Front de Gauche have pleaded for a reintroduction of permanent state border control, referendums on withdrawal from the Eurozone, or a full exit from the EU to restore national control. Eurosceptic, anti-migration parties and politicians in Sweden, Denmark, the Czech Republic, Hungary, Austria, Germany, and Finland have also called for referendums on full exit. Apart from the constitutional hurdles that must be overcome in order to hold such a referendum, it is doubtful that the respective electorates will choose a full exit, regardless of how dissatisfied they are with the EU, how ineffective their voice is perceived as being in the EU, or how low their attachment to the EU is. Strong economic connections with Germany and membership in the Euro would make leaving a rather expensive affair. The lack of viable international alternatives to the EU would also deter parties and voters from choosing a full exit. The EU will continue to be accepted pragmatically, as the "lesser evil", as a Hungarian respondent once put it (Lengyel, 2011).

A lack of preference for full exit does not mean that there is no preference for every form of disintegration. Governments and parties of the aforementioned member states have sought partial exit and non-entries, for instance, by reintroducing state border control (e.g., Denmark and Austria), calling for a decrease in the EU budget (e.g., Finland), refusing to comply with the Stability and Growth Pact (e.g., France), relocating refugees (e.g., Hungary), or revising migration law (e.g., Italy). At the mass level, full restoration of national competences with regard to migration issues can also count on widespread support (Pew Research Center, 2017). More reservations exist with regard to the way to best address social-economic dissatisfaction; some are willing to accept more European integration, attributing greater powers to the EU, with richer member states showing solidarity with their poorer counterparts (cf. Raines, Goodwin, & Cutts, 2017). However, these calls for European transfers also elicit politico-cultural resistance from others (Pew Research Center, 2017).

As a matter of fact, the EU as political system includes more than its current 28 member states, as the EU's allocation of values also involves candidate member states like Macedonia and Serbia, as well as neighbours like Ukraine. Dissatisfaction with the process of accession is not easily expressed within the EU, given the reservations regarding EU enlargement in public opinion in older member states in particular. The ensuing inclination to engage in partial exit can tie in with Russian and Chinese efforts to strengthen their economic and political influence in the Western Balkans and in the EU's wider neighbourhood in particular in areas in which attachment to the EU is low (in Serbia, for instance). Maintaining closer ties with the EU is still perceived as more advantageous in the long run, but it shows that the EU is engaged in competition with other expansive political entities to remain attractive in its peripheries.

10.4   The EU in a Disintegrative Spiral?

As Chap. 9 outlined, the very process of European integration has engendered dissatisfaction among some of the governments, parties, and voters within the EU. The question is how this dissatisfaction is processed *within* the EU. Eurosceptic resistance to the socio-economic and politico-cultural set-up of the EU is rather difficult to address effectively within the EU. The EU's handling of debt crises and migration also failed to garner much support among pragmatists for the EU as an effective means of pursuing national interests. Given the limited opportunities to employ voice, EU-related dissatisfaction results in exits, full or partial, in situations in which loyalty is low and compensation is lacking. At first sight, one might expect this to bring the EU into a disintegrative spiral. Its external deconsolidation is weakened by increasingly permeable boundaries. This is not only reflected by the British act of leaving but also by the emergence of the idea of a Grexit, Frexit, Nexit, Italexit, Fixit, Auxit, Czexit, and so on and so forth. According to the bounding-bonding mechanism, this should have an unsettling impact on the EU's internal construction. And it does. With the UK leaving, it is harder for member state governments that are in favour of economic liberalisation to form a blocking minority in the Council. Non-Euro members lose an important partner in defending their say on monetary and economic issues. Atlanticist member states will lose an ally, as will anti-Russian member states. Budgetary exchanges will be challenged by the departure of a significant contributor to the EU. This also holds for the member states that seek to partially exit by limiting their contribution to the budget. These countries will face strong demands from recipient member states that seek to cover the costs of the UK's withdrawal, as well as social-economically dissatisfied member states seeking financial solidarity at the EU level. This will intensify their pursuit of partial exit to avoid sharing more money, work, and power at the EU level.

Nevertheless, a disintegrative spiral within the EU will be kept at bay. Relatively satisfied member states, such as Germany, generate substantial political and economic resources that will keep the EU centre to up and running, and the EU as a whole will continue to attract FDI. The EU's internal construction can also limit the destabilising impact of external de-consolidation. The voice infrastructure of the EU has now been fully institutionalised, and the European Parliament, Council, and Court of Justice remain intact in spite of full or partial exits. Key alignments such as the French-German axis and the parliamentary groupings are also able to continue to function in spite of these exits. For instance, 27 member states have been able to produce a common position on the negotiations on the departure of the UK. With the exception of the UK, of course, all other member states are expected to remain in the EU, however dissatisfied they may be. There will be time to settle the issue without completely unravelling the EU's internal infrastructure. It is not so much the strength of the EU's locking-in capacity that will keep them in, but rather the unattractiveness of being on the outside. However bad the EU is in the eyes of some governments, parties, and voters, the situation outside the EU is often perceived as being worse. In response to the debt crises, The EU could thus expand in terms of value allocation in the realm of monetary and budgetary policies in the Eurozone, expecting dissatisfied Euro members to follow (grudgingly). However, in relying on the willingness of member states to cooperate rather than on its organisational power in the area of justice and home affairs, the EU will face partial exits such as reinstated internal border control, non-compliance with refugee relocation, and the rule of law.

Alignments between politico-cultural anti-federalists and social-economic anti-liberalists may still be strengthened in the context of European Parliament and the Council. However, effective anti-system opposition, both of a politico-cultural and social-economic nature, is fairly difficult to wage in the EU. Due to the weak locking-in capacities of both the EU and member states, as opposed to exchange of resources within closed boundaries to settle dissatisfaction, the EU will feature "exchanges of partial exits". These partial exits will continue to constrain the building of the EU centre, limit its capacity to carry out boundary control (to counter cyber interventions or regulate migration, for instance), and effectively engage in rule enforcement. Thus, the EU's external de-consolidation remains constrained. The stifling of Eurosceptic voices could result in an increase in votes for protest parties, or, alternatively, political apathy or withdrawal into alternative self-sustaining communities to avoid state or EU interference. In this way, the locking-in capacity of the EU remains limited. However, it will not enter disintegrative spiral as long as disappointed pragmatic supporters of the EU do not find any more attractive national or international alternatives to the EU, and continue to conduct their political exchanges within the EU, instead.

10.5   CONCLUSION

This chapter provided an analysis of whether or not and how the unmaking of the EU's allocation of values might unfold. It showed how a wide variety of factors and actors play roles in this process. The mechanism of exit, voice, and loyalty, as well as the mutual dependence between internal construction and external consolidation, offered insight into the dynamic interconnections between these factors and actors within and across member states, and within the EU and across the rest of the world. The mechanisms showed how the external de-consolidation of states not only resulted in substantial conflict involving a wide range of actors including electorates, but also in shifting power constellations to the advantage of more mobile and competitive actors. Member states' governments may continue to play a key role in this fluid and multi-level situation, but it will no longer be limited to the template of the territorial state, as much as Eurosceptics might long for it to. The incongruence and permeability of boundaries in the composite EU make disintegration a different process than simply integration in reverse.

Despite growing dissatisfaction with external de-consolidation of states and its substantial and constitutive consequences, the likelihood of an immediate, complete disintegration of the EU is quite small. As has been the case throughout its history, the lack of viable national or international alternatives to the EU allows for its continuation, at least for the time being. However, attempts to assuage social-economic dissatisfaction might be blocked by politico-cultural Eurosceptics, resulting in political grid-lock. Even if all EU governments were Eurosceptic, it would be difficult to agree on a common position on dissolving or completely modifying the EU. In addition to this stalemate, the Eurosceptic combination of declining compliance and reduced means to enforce compliance would result in a concomitant decline in the implementation of the EU's allocation of values. The EU will yet survive also a series of crises due to the remaining resourceful member states, albeit under one important condition: that there are not any viable national or international alternatives to the EU. In this sense, the fate of the EU will not be decided by its own locking-in capacity, but by the evolution of outside powers that are able to attract capital, brains, as well as member states.

REFERENCES

Best, H. (2012). Elite foundations of European integration: A causal analysis. In H. Best, G. Lengyel, & L. Verzichelli (Eds.), *The Europe of elites: A study into the Europeanness of Europe's political and economic elites* (pp. 208–233). Oxford: Oxford University Press.

Choi, G., & Veugelers, R. (2015). *EU immigration to the US: Where is it coming from, and is brain drain real?* Brussel: Bruegel. Retrieved July 31, 2017, from http://bruegel.org/2015/09/eu-immigration-to-the-us-where-is-it-coming-from-and-is-brain-drain-real/

Clement, B., Nanou, K., & Verney, S. (2014). "We no longer love you, but we don't want to leave you": The Eurozone crisis and popular Euroscepticism in Greece. *Journal of European Integration, 36*(3), 247–265.

Conti, N., Cotta, M., & Tavares de Almeida, P. (2010). Southern Europe: A distinctive and more pro-European region in the EU? *South European Society and Politics, 15*(1), 121–142.

Daddow, O. (2011). The UK, 'Europe' and the 2009 European parliament elections. In R. Harmsen & J. Schild (Eds.), *Debating Europe: The 2009 European parliament elections and beyond* (pp. 125–143). Baden: Nomos.

Dinas, E., Jurado, I., Konstantinidis, N., & Walter, S. (2016). Keeping the Euro at any cost? Explaining preference for Euro membership in Greece. Presentation APSA Philadelphia, PA, 1–4 September.

Dolezal, M., & Hutter, S. (2012). Participation and party choice: Comparing the demand side of the new cleavage across arenas. In H. Kriesi, E. Grande, M. Dolezal, M. Helbling, D. Höglinger, S. Hutter, & B. Wüest (Eds.), *Political conflict in western Europe* (pp. 67–95). Cambridge: Cambridge University Press.

Eichengreen, B. (2010). The breakup of the Euro area. In A. Alesina & F. Giavazzi (Eds.), *Europe and the Euro* (pp. 11–55). Chicago, IL: University of Chicago Press.

van Elsas, E., Hakhverdian, A., & van der Brug, W. (2016). United against a common foe? The nature and origins of Euroscepticism among left-wing and right-wing citizens. *West European Politics, 39*(6), 1181–1204.

European Commission. (2001). *Perceptions of the European Union.* Luxembourg: European Commission.

European Commission. (2016). *Standard Eurobarometer 2016.* Luxembourg: European Commission.

European Parliament. (2016). *Parlemeter 2016: Analytical overview.* Brussels: European Parliamentary Research Service.

Goodwin, M., & Milazzo, C. (2017). Taking back control? Investigating the role of immigration in the 2016 vote for Brexit. *British Journal of Politics and International Relations, 19*(3), 450–464.

Grande, E. (2012). Conclusion. In H. Kriesi, E. Grande, M. Dolezal, M. Helbling, D. Höglinger, S. Hutter, et al. (Eds.), *Political conflict in western Europe* (pp. 277–301). Cambridge: Cambridge University Press.

Hobolt, S. (2016). The Brexit vote: A divided nation, a divided continent. *Journal of European Public Policy, 23*(9), 1259–1277.

Jones, E. (2008). *Economic adjustment and political transformation in small states.* Oxford: Oxford University Press.

Katzenstein, P. (1985). *Small states in world markets: Industrial policy in Europe.* Ithaca, NY: Cornell University Press.

Lansons, Opinium Research and Cambre Associates. (2013). In or out? Britain's future in Europe. Retrieved December 8, 2013, from http://opinium.co.uk/sites/default/files/opin-inouteurope.pdf

Lengyel, G. (2011). Supranational attachment of European elites and citizens. *Europe-Asia Studies, 63*(6), 1033–1054.

Mair, P. (2007). Political opposition and the European Union. *Government and Opposition, 42*(1), 1–17.

Pew Research Center. (2017). *Post-Brexit, Europeans more favorable toward EU.* Washington, DC: Pew Research Center.

Raines, T., Goodwin, M., & Cutts, D. (2017). *The future of Europe: Comparing public and elites attitudes.* London: Chatham House.

Startin, N. (2015). Have we reached a tipping point? The mainstreaming of Euroscepticism in the UK. *International Political Science Review, 36*(3), 311–323.

Swank, D. (2002). *Global capital, political institutions, and policy change in developed welfare states.* Cambridge: Cambridge University Press.

Thomassen, J., & Bäck, H. (2009). European citizenship and identity after European enlargement. In J. Thomassen (Ed.), *The legitimacy of the European Union after enlargement* (pp. 84–207). Oxford: Oxford University Press.

Van Holsteyn, J. J. M., & Den Ridder, J. (2015). Europinie: Nederlandse burgers en houdingen ten aanzien van Europa. In H. Vollaard, J. van der Harst, & G. Voerman (Eds.), *Van Aanvallen! naar verdedigen? De opstelling van Nederland ten aanzien van Europese integratie* (pp. 355–384). Den Haag: BoomBestuurskunde.

Verney, S. (2011). An exceptional case? Party and popular Euroscepticism in Greece, 1959–2009. *South European Society and Politics, 16*(1), 51–79.

Verney, S. (2015). Waking the sleeping giant or expressing domestic dissent? Mainstream Euroscepticism in crisis-stricken Greece. *International Political Science Review, 36*(3), 279–295.

Vollaard, H. (2014). Explaining European disintegration. *Journal of Common Market Studies, 52*(5), 1142–1159.

Vollaard, H., & Voerman, G. (2015). De Europese opstelling van Nederlandse Politieke Partijen. In H. Vollaard, J. van der Harst, & G. Voerman (Eds.), *Van Aanvallen! naar verdedigen? De opstelling van Nederland ten aanzien van Europese integratie* (pp. 99–182). Den Haag: BoomBestuurskunde.

World Bank. (2017). *Doing business 2017: Equal opportunity for all (Regional profile European Union).* Washington, DC: World Bank. https://doi.org/10.1596/978-1-4648-0948-4

World Economic Forum. (2016). *Global competitiveness report.* Geneva: World Economic Forum. Retrieved July 31, 2017, from http://www3.weforum.org/docs/GCR2016-2017/05FullReport/TheGlobalCompetitivenessReport2016-2017_FINAL.pdf

Epilogue

The key purpose of this book has been to recognise and explain European disintegration. Theories help us to make sense of political phenomena like the evolution of the European Union. A wide variety of theories have been examined here in an effort to identify the key dynamics of the European (dis)integration process. The application of some of these theories was problematic in that they simply assumed that the EU would fall apart into its constituent states again. While this is a possibility, other outcomes should not be disregarded out of hand. Other theories saw only one particular factor as being fundamental to the EU's sustainability, such as economic interdependence or the balance of power. Yet, European (dis)integration is a process in which a whole variety of factors are at play, as comparative analyses of disintegrating regional organisations, federations, and empires have also pointed out. The most promising starting point for conceptualising and explaining European disintegration is a theory of polity formation developed by political scientist Stefano Bartolini, on the basis of the previous work of political sociologist Stein Rokkan and political economist Albert Hirschman, on the history of states and dissatisfactory organisations, respectively.

On the basis of this theory, unbiased, nuanced definitions of disintegration can be developed, one relating to political systems, such as the EU in its entirety, and one regarding individual actors, such as member states. Drawing a distinction between actor-level and system-level disintegration

© The Author(s) 2018

H. Vollaard, *European Disintegration*, Palgrave Studies in European Union Politics, https://doi.org/10.1057/978-1-137-41465-6

is necessary for the simple reason that a system can continue to function in the face of one or more actors leaving. Actor-level disintegration is withdrawal from a political system, which is a system of allocation of values. This kind of withdrawal can be full, as well as partial. A member state can withdraw from the EU entirely, but it can also do so partially by boycotting decision-making related to the allocation of values (think of the Empty Chair Crisis), no longer participating in the allocation of values in a particular policy area (think of the various French attempts to withdraw from monetary arrangements), complying less with the EU's basic principles (think of the rule of law in Poland and Hungary), reclaiming key competences from the EU (think of Dutch calls to partly renationalise the Common Agricultural Policy), or reducing budget contributions to the EU (think of the various rebates). Thus, the EU and its predecessors have always faced disintegrative forces, not just since the discussions on Grexit and Brexit began. The accompanying advantage of this conceptualisation of actor-level disintegration is that it applies not only to member states, but also to individuals, companies, investment funds, regions, and groups of states. These actors can also withdraw their brains, money, and power from the EU's allocation of values by moving outside the EU, for example, or by no longer complying with EU law.

To avoid generating an unwieldy list of potential factors affecting actor-level disintegration, mechanisms have been identified here as a more manageable analytical tool to explain this process. The Hirschmanian mechanism of exit, voice, and loyalty provides an explanation for why actors opt to withdraw when they are dissatisfied with an organisation. Whether or not an actor engages in full or partial exit from the EU depends on the interplay between the availability of channels through which to express dissatisfaction effectively in the EU, attachment to the EU, and the presence of more attractive national or international alternatives to the EU. The important implication of this mechanism is that (Eurosceptic) dissatisfaction will not necessarily lead to full exit. First, dissatisfaction voiced in the EU can be addressed at the root or assuaged by compensation, such as welfare arrangements to cope with international competition. Loyalty to the EU is another constraint on exit. Throughout the history of the EU and its predecessors, many governments, parties, and voters have, at various times, been rather unhappy with the EU for one reason or another. Yet, the lack of viable national or international alternatives to the EU kept them from opting out. However unsatisfactory the EU is perceived as being, the situation outside is often seen as being worse. Greece, at the time of the debt crisis, is a case in point. As much as the EU response was disliked, a majority wanted to remain. Nevertheless, in situations in which dissatisfaction could not be effectively dealt with by voice or a full exit, governments, parties, and voters have sought partial exit in the form of less compliance with EU law, or lower contributions to the EU.

Disintegration not only concerns the members of a political system, it also relates to the system itself: the allocation of values. Disintegration, like integration, is fundamentally related to the locking-in capacity of a system. Disintegration is the declining capacity to lock members in through the provision of infrastructure to effectively voice dissatisfaction, the maintenance of the external boundaries and internal boundaries (i.e., enforcing compliance), and cultivating loyalty. This locking-in capacity increases the cost of exit for actors and decreases the price of voice. The bounding-bonding mechanism is a concise analytical tool that helps explain system-level (dis)integration. It concerns the mutual dependence of a system's external consolidation and its internal construction. The more strongly a system is able to tie in a stable set of members, the higher the cost of full exit will be, the more members will raise their voice and exchange resources to address dissatisfaction internally, the more mutual coalitions and alignments will stabilise, and the more resources the system's power centre will attract. The resources accrued by the system's centre in this process of internal construction can be used to strengthen boundaries, voice infrastructure, and loyalty. Thus, external consolidation and internal construction reinforce each other in an *integrative spiral*, strengthening the locking-in capacity of the system.

With external *de*consolidation, however, a system's integrative spiral is hampered. As such, French president, Charles de Gaulle, should be regarded as vital to the European integration project because of his first refusal to allow British entry in the 1960s. Keeping the external deconsolidation of the EU's predecessors at bay, he allowed for the build-up of the organisations that would follow in their fragile early years. However, enlargement and other forms of external deconsolidation have constrained the subsequent internal construction of the EU, leaving it with limited means to maintain its boundaries, enforce compliance, and strengthen European loyalty. As opposed to the strength of EU's locking-in capacity, it has been in large part the lack of viable national or international alternatives to the EU that have kept member states in, thereby allowing the integrative spiral to continue. Another way to interpret this is that the EU has remained sufficiently attractive to prompt actors to stay, though some companies, investment funds, and individuals have decided that the USA, Japan, and China offer better prospects.

In political terms, most of the calls to leave the EU fully or partially stem from the national state and not a variety of other constellations such as a group of states or a region. But why is this so? National states do not necessarily have an optimal size in terms of security in the age of air warfare, nuclear weapons, and terrorism, or in terms of the rate of economic growth in the age of globalisation, for that matter. It is because states remain the main object of political loyalty in Europe (with the exception of some subnational regions), and because states still provide the most important voice infrastructure, through which conflicts about opening and closing state borders are fought in elections and referenda. There is also a formal procedure providing for the departure of a member state, laid down in Article 50 of the EU Treaty. This exit clause offers member states a peaceful way out of the EU. After the Brexit referendum in June 2016, the British government drew on this clause to negotiate its departure. And indeed, in contrast to many instances of disintegrating empires or federations, the process has been peaceful, by and large.

Although the mechanism of exit, voice, and loyalty played out differently among the various nations and social strata in the UK, it is no surprise a majority opted for a full exit in the referendum (Vollaard, 2014). Politico-cultural dissatisfaction with the lack of national control on migration is difficult to address, and EU loyalty is quite limited in England, in particular. In March 2017, the European Commission (2017) presented five scenarios for the EU's future, ranging from a single market to a full political union. However, it did not include a disintegration scenario, in spite of the fact that members of the public, the business community, and the German army consider the prospect of other member states leaving or the entire EU collapsing to be likely (Bughin et al., 2017; Der Spiegel, 2017; Raines, Goodwin, & Cutts, 2017). So, what is the likelihood of the EU's disintegration given the explanation presented in this book?

Dissatisfaction with the EU is present in many member states. Some governments, parties, and voters have pragmatic concerns about the extent to which the EU serves national interests. Left-wing Eurosceptics oppose the EU's market liberalisation and austerity policies on principle, whereas their right-wing counterparts resist the EU's encroachment upon national sovereignty and identity. Dissatisfaction is politics as usual. Also, Eurosceptic resistance to the principles underpinning the EU system is not unusual. Many political systems have harboured anti-system forces before, be they of ideological or ethnic nature. The question is how this dissatis-faction is processed within the EU. Dissatisfaction with the EU can be assuaged by providing social-economic security to those who fear eco-nomic competition and budget cuts in the framework of the Economic and Monetary Union. Widespread pessimism about the future, with many expecting retrenchment in the welfare state, limits the impact of this com-pensation. Additionally, politico-cultural dissatisfaction about migration and power sharing in the EU is even harder to address. Providing compen-sation is, therefore, difficult in Southern Europe (given socio-economic concerns) and Northern and Eastern Europe (given politico-cultural concerns).

Loyalty to the EU is more difficult to come by than national loyalty, although this also varies between various groups and countries. Furthermore, providing effective voice to Eurosceptics is rather difficult because market and sovereignty-sharing principles of the EU are enshrined in treaties and enforced by unelected bodies, such as the European Central Bank and the Court of Justice of the European Union. It is also difficult for the collectives of the Council and the European Parliament to be responsive to dissatisfied voices in light of divergent preferences across and within member states and between and within the elite and the masses (Raines et al., 2017). Some governments, parties, and voters see more European integration as a solution to the problem of too little democracy and solidarity in the EU. Others would have the national states regulate migration, share money and work, and organise the people's will. Provided that national states cannot do better than the EU or that other interna-tional organisations such as the World Trade Organization (WTO) and the Eurasian Economic Union (EEU) cannot offer states a better deal, most governments, parties, and voters are expected to prefer to remain in the EU, as has been the case in the EU's past. The UK is the exception here. As an alternative to full exit, dissatisfaction will be expressed by engaging in forms of partial exit or partial non-entry, such as electoral apathy, non-compliance with relocation of refugees, pleas against risk-sharing in the monetary union, calls for lower budget contributions, and demands to returning competences to the state (from the EU level). As the exit, voice, and loyalty mechanism plays out differently across the EU due to of vary-ing degrees of dissatisfaction, compensation, voice options, and exit opportunities, this will enhance the evolution of a differentiated EU, with various degrees of integration and disintegration. In other words, Brexit will most likely *not* be followed by the departure of any other member state.

Partial exits can still undermine the EU in its entirety, decreasing the exchange of resources and reducing compliance with its law. Yet, with no other full exits foreseen, the EU still has the time to reform itself to deal with some of the dissatisfaction that exists. Furthermore, the only full exit that has taken place is that of a peripheral member, the UK. However abundant the resources were that the British state exchanged in the EU, its departure does not strike at the heart of the union; German and French governments are still willing to continue exchanging resources to keep the EU running, based in part on EU loyalty and in part on the calculation that the EU is the "least bad" option in present circumstances in terms of its capacity to address migration, as well as monetary and economic stability. France and Germany can push forward knowing that other member states will (at times grudgingly) follow with no full exit option available. Yet, with only limited means to enforce participation or compliance, the EU will continue to face partial non-entries and partial exits.

Theoretically, creating more conduits to effective voice should constrain disintegration, partially or fully. Calls for the democratisation of the EU are many; increased parliamentary control of the European Stability Mechanism or a greater role for the European Parliament and national parliaments in EU decision-making have been proposed. This introduction of more checks and balances might improve the performance of the EU. It remains doubtful, however, that these measures will strengthen the perceived effectiveness of voice among governments, parties, and voters. The greater the say actors have in decision-making, the harder it is to detect its influence. Without a full-exit option, this is likely to strengthen the tendency to engage in partial exits in the form of electoral apathy, reclaiming competences, and non-compliance.

As said, the EU is limited in its capacity to maintain its boundaries, enforce compliance, keep intruders out, and keep actors in by force. The EU is also limited in its ability to generate loyalty. The key factor to keep member states in has always been its relative attractiveness as compared to national or international alternatives in areas such as trade. However, its handling of debt crises and migration crises has actually lessened the EU's attractiveness in the eyes of companies, investment funds, and existing member states A key challenge for the EU is reinforcing its attractiveness vis-à-vis competing systems, such as national states, Russia, China, and the USA, if it wants to survive.

The EU's weakness in terms of being able to maintain its boundaries may also actually be a strength. Enhancing its security powers might drum up politico-cultural Euroscepticism internally, thereby increasing the likelihood of actors seeking partial or even full exit. Additionally, the EU's soft approach might be a plus from the standpoint of new member states that fear military interference from their powerful neighbour, Russia. Moreover, the use of force is rather expensive tactic in terms of trying to keep members in, as evidenced by empires of the past. At some point, the contributing central members will no longer be willing to keep certain peripheries in by means of costly operations. For now, the EU can also rely on the USA and NATO to counter attacks on most of its members. Exit by NATO's European members has been suggested on occasion, but transatlantic loyalty remains intact, and alternatives are perceived to be worse. It underlines once more that the EU's future is partly determined by the availability of viable, external alternatives.

A theory helps us to recognise and explain political phenomena, as well as to map future developments that are more or less likely to occur and make and assessment of the choices are more or less likely to be made. The full disintegration of the European Union is unlikely, according to the explanation presented here. No other member state is expected to follow in the UK's full-exit footsteps. Dissatisfied governments, parties, and voters will seek partial exit, instead, as long as no better national and international alternatives appear. Thus, the continuation of a differentiated European Union, muddling through, with its evolution highly dependent upon external alternatives, is likely. Having said that, the explanation of European disintegration presented can and should be developed further by testing it at the individual level by quantitative analysis and process tracing. As the two mechanisms identified are, in principle, applicable to any political system, they can also be tried out in the context of the many other instances of disintegrating systems in the past and present, including empires, Spain and the United Kingdom. In this sense, the EU remains quite fascinating in its position as one of the few present-day examples of large-scale integration, as opposed to disintegration.

REFERENCES

Bughin, J., Labaye, E., Mattern, F., Smit, S., Windhagen, E., Mischke, J. & Bragg, K. (2017). *European business: Overcoming uncertainty, strengthening recovery.* Brussels: McKinsey.

Der Spiegel. (2017). *Denken auf Vorrat.* Week 45.

Raines, T., Goodwin, M., & Cutts, D. (2017). *The future of Europe: Comparing public and elite attitudes.* London: Chatham House.

Vollaard, H. (2014). Explaining European disintegration. *Journal of Common Market Studies, 52*(5), 1142–1159.

© The Author(s) 2018
H. Vollaard, *European Disintegration*, Palgrave Studies in European Union Politics, https://doi.org/10.1057/978-1-137-41465-6

261

INDEX

A
Adenauer, Konrad, 155, 158, 166
Austria, 65, 150, 152, 179, 180, 209,
  235, 237, 246

B
Balancing, 33–35, 37, 38, 63, 72,
  101
Bandwagoning, 33, 38
Bartolini, Stefano, 7, 119, 120, 124,
  129–138, 141, 142, 185, 205,
  206, 217, 222
Belgium, 19, 61, 65, 66, 85, 166,
  168, 209, 211, 237
Beyen, Jan-Willem, 157, 158
Brexit, 1, 2, 76, 149, 238–241,
  243

C
Czech Republic, 235, 237, 246

D
De Gaulle, Charles, 14, 31, 149,
  159–161, 166–168
Delors, Jacques, 179, 180
Denmark, 4, 98, 103, 149, 150, 166,
  168, 170, 176, 190, 237, 246
Differentiated integration, 3, 69,
  102–106, 181
Doyle, Michael, 91–94, 109–111, 122

E
European Coal and Steel Community
  (ECSC), 36, 38, 148, 154–160,
  162, 163, 166
European Economic Community
  (EEC), 35, 36, 76, 89, 148–150,
  157–163, 166, 167, 170, 173,
  176, 202, 238, 239, 241, 243,
  244
European Neighbourhood Policy
  (ENP), 89, 96, 97, 100, 101

© The Author(s) 2018
H. Vollaard, *European Disintegration*, Palgrave Studies in European
Union Politics, https://doi.org/10.1057/978-1-137-41465-6

CPI Antony Rowe
Eastbourne, UK
July 10, 2019